Death Threats and Violence

Stephen J. Morewitz

Death Threats and Violence

New Research and Clinical Perspectives

 Springer

Stephen J. Morewitz
San Francisco, California
Tarzana, California
Buffalo Grove, Illinois
USA

ISBN 978-1-4419-2631-9   e-ISBN 978-0-387-76663-8
DOI: 10.1007/978-0-387-76663-8

Printed on acid-free paper

9 8 7 6 5 4 3 2 1

springer.com

Preface

Until recent decades, there was little emphasis on studying death threats as a social or psychological phenomenon. However, since the 1960s, attacks on public officials and celebrities and the ubiquitous nature of homicidal threats in face-to-face relations have spawned research and new organizational responses to death threats and related behaviors, such as stalking. Publicized workplace-related death threats and shootings, such as the 21 separate incidents since 1986 in which U.S. Postal Service employees were shot, and the death threats and attacks directed at schools and universities have helped to transform death threats from a private phenomenon into a social problem. Political leaders have developed new policies, organizational structures, and laws in an attempt to prevent death threats and related violence. Moreover, in the aftermath of 9/11, the U.S. government and other governments around the world have formulated new policies and organizational structures to deal with the threat of terrorist attacks.

At the level of interpersonal relations, the weakening of social control processes allows individuals to make homicidal threats against people and organizations in different settings. This book will address such questions as, Under what conditions are individuals able to evade social control by making death threats? What factors trigger the response of social control mechanisms to death threat makers? How effective are the institutional responses to death threats? At the macrolevel, this book assesses how governments and paramilitary and terrorist groups also employ death threats to achieve their desired social and political objectives.

Data from the Stalking and Violence Project (SVP) and other sources are used to explore the nature of death threats and the process of regulating offenders in different relationships (see Appendix A, "Research Methods," and Appendix B, "Study Results," Tables B.1 to B.14). The SVP data are derived from a random sample of 519 victims of self-reported domestic violence who filed restraining orders in two large metropolitan areas.

Chapter 1 explores the different forms in which death threats are communicated and their impact on the social control process. This chapter emphasizes the different meanings and consequences of death threats in different settings.

Chapter 2 describes the characteristics of death threat makers and focuses on the risk factors that weaken the mechanisms of social control and increase the likelihood that individuals will make death threats. In addition, the duty of health care professionals to report death threats is examined.

Chapter 3 determines the attributes of individuals that increase the likelihood that they will be the victims of homicidal threats. This chapter also analyzes the psychosocial impact of death threats on partners and their families and emphasizes the different forms of emotional trauma that face death threat victims and their families. The uses of medical, counseling, and shelter services by death threat victims are compared with the uses by non–death threat victims.

Chapter 4 examines the possible link between stalking and death threats that result in homicide and other acts of violence. The psychosocial impact of stalking and death threats is presented.

In Chapter 5, the ways in which access to and use of weapons weaken the mechanisms of social control and increase the chances that persons will make death threats are discussed.

Chapter 6 examines the role of substance use and abuse in weakening the social control process and increasing the probability of death threats and related violence.

In Chapter 7, the nature of death threats made against schools and colleges is explored.

The prevalence and risk factors for workplace-related death threats are analyzed in Chapter 8.

Chapter 9 discusses the weakening of social controls due to wars, cultural and personal pressures, and ethnic/political conflicts.

In Chapter 10, the role of homicidal threats in the commission of hate crimes is assessed.

Chapter 11 explores how the weakening of social control allows terrorists to make death threats to achieve their social, cultural, religious, and political objectives.

Chapter 12 discusses the legality of death threats and the responses of the legal system to such threats. The ways in which the police and the courts respond to complaints of death threats are evaluated. It describes the situations that create probable cause for the police to arrest a person for making death threats. The chapter also examines the degree to which police contacts and arrest patterns differ between partner violence offenders who make death threats and those who do not.

San Francisco, California, USA   Stephen J. Morewitz

Acknowledgments

I would like to thank Mrs. Myra Kalkin Morewitz and Dr. Harry A. Morewitz for their advice and support. I would also like to thank Sharon Panulla, Executive Editor, and Anna Tobias, Associate Editor, Behavioral Sciences, at Springer Science + Business Media, LLC, who have been supportive as well as thorough and thoughtful.

San Francisco, California, USA

Stephen J. Morewitz

Contents

Chapter 1
Homicidal Threats

Every day in the media we hear about death threats. Death threats are often made against individuals, i.e., "I am going to kill you," and groups, organizations, industries, and countries, i.e., "Death to America." Often these threats are accompanied by shouts, specific gestures, and other threatening behaviors.

This book proposes that people who make death threats (DTMs—death threat makers) do so in socially patterned ways. Norms and behaviors associated with demographic status (age, gender, etc.), plus socioeconomic factors help to influence the frequency and intensity of death threats and other forms of related violence. Religious and political beliefs, pregnancy, the use of alcohol and other drugs, and access to weapons may alter the ways in which death threats are made.

DTMs make their threats in an attempt to dominate and control another person by instilling terror and subordination. In some cases DTMs will assault strangers on the street having previously terrorizing them with a death threat. At other times, the mere voicing of the threat may be enough to satisfy the DTM.

Death threats also can be used to achieve specific agendas, such as "encouraging" victims to move out of a neighborhood, or paying "protection" in order to stay in business. In cases of domestic violence, the threats can be used in an attempt to prevent the victim from leaving the relationship. False accusations of homicidal threats have been made in order to gain a legal advantage in domestic violence or child custody proceedings.

Paradoxically, however, when death threats prove ineffective, DTMs will frequently escalate the use of other forms of intimidation, including the use of emotional, physical, and/or sexual violence.

Homicidal threats may be made in response to perceived or actual threats. They can reflect the essential social powerlessness and inadequacy of the DTMs. For example, the targets' social characteristics may seem to threaten the DTMs' identity and values and beliefs. In other instances, death threats may be the result of a DTM's inability to function due to mental illness, delusions, or other major dysfunctions.

For DTMs in the context of social interactions, partner, and domestic relations, death threats are about privatizing relationships, dehumanizing the victims, and isolating them from family, friends, the criminal justice system, the mental health system, etc. This can be a cyclical process that mirrors the vicious cycle of domestic

S.J. Morewitz, *Death Threats and Violence*, DOI: 10.1007/978-0-387-76663-8_1,

violence in that DTMs threaten to kill, say they are sorry, reconcile and then repeat the process, thus evading the institutions of social control.

When death threats are socially constructed in face-to-face interactions, some of the recipients may interpret these statements, gestures, and behaviors as threatening while others do not. It is through the social construction of death threats that DTMs are able to dominate and control their victims by repeated threats accompanied by the statement that the police are powerless to intervene.

It is by investigating the varying social and cultural conditions in simple and complex societies that we can begin to determine how and why individuals develop socially constructed meanings about death threats and how they respond to those threats. For example, MacDonald (1968) described how cultural traditions in the Balinese village of Bajoeng Gede, permitted a man to try to slash other people with his machete when they asked to borrow it.

Other societal trends, such as the privacy of the family, the expansion of anonymity in city and suburban life, and the weakening of the socialization process in the family, allow for deviant behaviors, which in simple societies would have been less likely to occur. This breakdown in social control allows DTMs in intimate and non-intimate relations to make death threats in the context of retaliation, conflict, hate, love, frustration, and bitterness.

The breakdown or weakening in social control is also reflected in DTMs who make death threats against work places, schools, universities and other facilities, often because of some real or imagined injustice. In other instances, the DTMs have severe mental disorders and for some irrational reason issue a death threat. Other DTMs threaten organizations as a prank, as an attention getting mechanism, or to exert power and control over an institution.

DTMs who make death threats can evade social control because it is often not against the law to make such a threat unless there are other conditions present, such as a threatening gesture or an otherwise innocent gesture made threatening by accompanying words that create a reasonable apprehension of imminent battery (Merheb v. Illinois State Toll Highway Authority, 2001; Restatement (Second) of Torts, section 29, 1979). Thus, society has a bias in favor of action, e.g., gesture or behavior over mere words.

The inability of victims and their family and friends to effectively respond to the DTMs' death threats is another example of weakened social control processes. The victims may not believe the threat is real. In fact, most death threats are never carried out. Instead, the DTMs use death threats to dominate and control their victims. While death treats in themselves may not serve as a prelude to murder, they do indicate that severe forms of physical, sexual, and emotional abuse are likely to occur in the future.

At times death threats cause such intense fear that the victims are paralyzed into inaction. In other instances, in a reversal of roles, the victims may react by killing their abusers, thus illustrating the tenuous nature of domination and control (Browne, 1984; Walker, 1984).

The social process of making homicidal threats can lead to corrective action whereby victims respond to the threats by seeking the social support of other family members, friends, counselors, and the legal system, thus leading to new or strengthened patterns of social control. Despite the terror experienced by death threat victims, those with effective social support and outside resources may be more likely to attempt to control the DTM than a victim without such support.

Under certain circumstances, the DTMs will be arrested and convicted of making death threats. Formal social control institutions can punish the DTMs and thus restore stability to the victims' social, family, and occupational functioning.

Death threats have been used by both legitimate governments and terrorists as an instrument of social control. After 9/11, the President of the U.S. has publicly stated that Osama ben Laden is "wanted dead or alive." The U.S. and other governments have made death threats against terrorists as well. Similarly, individual terrorists and terrorist organizations and paramilitary groups make death threats against countries, such as the U.S. and the European community.

Governments and organizations, both legitimate and non-legitimate, employ death threats to achieve their political, social, and religious goals. For example, extremist groups may threaten to kill citizens of a country in the name of religion or nationalism.

In recent decades, there has been increased public concern about terrorist death threats, bullying, weapons-related murders, assaults, and violence in workplaces, schools, and universities. Media attention to death threats, especially in the aftermath of 9/11, has helped to transform death threats into an expanding social problem.

In an effort to deal with this expansion, there have been attempts to strengthen existing institutions of social control and/or develop new organizations, laws, policies, and procedures for controlling death threats and related forms of violence. In the United States the terror threat has led to the development of the cabinet-level Department of Homeland Security, and the passage of new laws, such as the Patriot Act and other anti-terrorism laws and regulations.

In a legal response to the threats of school shooting rampages, such as the Columbine massacre, New York State Governor George Pataki in 2000 signed the Safe Schools Against Violence in Education Act (McKay, 2007). Among the various measures of this act (also called Project SAVE) is the requirement that school districts offer a mechanism to enable students to report threats of violence anonymously. Schools are also revising their safety plans to include responses to the threats of attacks.

Public attention also has focused on hate crimes (also known as bias crimes), a term that was coined to describe the use of violence, harassment, and intimidation, including death threats, against victims because of their perceived or actual race, gender, sexual orientation, and/or national origins.

Hate crime-based death threats frequently are carried out by unorganized individuals and groups as well as by organized hate groups and criminal gangs. Hate crimes may increase in prevalence and severity following highly publicized events such as 9/11 and other terrorist attacks. The public awareness of hate crimes as a social problem has led to the passage of new hate crime laws such as Title 18 of the U.S. Code enacted in 1969. This law permits federal prosecution of people

who "by force or threat of force willfully injures, intimidates or interferes with...
any person because of his race, color, religion or national origin and because he is
or has been" attempting to engage in one of six types of federally protected activities, such as voting or going to school. Appellant courts have upheld the constitutionality of the law, and the Supreme Court has declined to review those decisions
(Wikipedia, 2007g).

The media magnifies the public's awareness, knowledge, and fear of terrorist
threats, workplace death threats, and school- and university-related death threats,
and hate crimes-related death threats. As a result, many "copy-cat" threats follow
the publication of incidents, such as school shootings, terrorist attacks, and hate
crimes. Death threats, including bomb threats, were made following the Virginia
Tech massacre. Kostinsky et al. (2001) noted that both bomb threats and threats of
school violence increased after the highly publicized Columbine High School
massacre.

The media increases pubic awareness and knowledge of the nature of workplace-
related homicidal threats, and may even influence the prevalence of job-based death
threats through the process of imitation. In addition, the Internet, through its ease
of use and instant impact, has increased the rate of death threats and other forms of
electronic harassment and intimidation.

In 1968 MacDonald wrote about the use of death threats (MacDonald, 1968). In
random street crime, muggers threaten to kill their victims unless they turn over
their money and valuables, and extortionists threaten to kill those who do not pay
their demands. Conditional death threats often are an essential part of a kidnapper's
modus operandi. They threaten to rape and murder the abducted individual unless
a ransom or other demand is met. Little has changed since 1968.

In other criminal enterprises, women and children are kidnapped, raped, and
forced into prostitution and attacked and threatened with death to secure and maintain their cooperation. According to one report, a girl who tried to escape her
brothel owners reportedly had a nail driven into her skull (Follain, 2005). Others
reportedly are chained and beaten with electric cables. Individuals who help
children and women escape prostitution also can be threatened with death.
A brothel owner who was unhappy with a victims advocate, Somaly Mam, reportedly put a gun to her head and threatened to kill her because she had been talking
to his girls. [In 2006, her 14-year-old daughter was kidnapped and raped as
retaliation for the humanitarian actions of her mother (Wikipedia, 2007k).]

Another form of social control occurs when criminals make death threats to
regulate the conduct of their own members. These leaders apply positive and
negative sanctions, including death threats, to ensure that their members to do not
engage in behaviors that will jeopardize their leader's criminal activities.

Writers and researchers have described how other individuals, groups,
organizations, and governments make homicidal threats, often anonymously, as part
of a larger campaign to assault, harass and intimidate those who oppose their
cultural, ideological, political, and ethnic/racial, and religious goals. Homicidal
threats were made against a pizza chain in Dallas, Texas, which had offered to accept
Mexican pesos (Stoddard, 2007). The pizza chain's action brought it into the larger

controversy over undocumented immigrants in the U.S. and hundreds of emails sent to the company were mostly critical of their decision to accept Mexican pesos.

Before, during, and after wars, genocide, and other armed conflicts, individuals, organizations, and governments make use of homicidal threats as part of a larger campaign to terrorize persons and manipulate their behavior. Conflicts, wars, and totalitarian regimes can trigger animosities toward ethnic, racial, cultural and religious groups resulting in killings, death threats, rape, kidnappings, forced prostitution, hostage-taking, torture, beatings, forced conscription, disappearance, forced relocations, and other forms of violence (Amowitz et al., 2004; Anonymous, 1996a,b). Individuals, groups, and governments make death threats to force people out of their homes and jobs as part of a larger campaign of ethnic cleansing and genocide. In this way, death threats are used as an informal, quasi-legal method of achieving social control in unstable societies.

Death threats are a prevalent form of psychological torture. Based on a study of 69 refugees who were torture survivors, Olsen et al. (2006) discovered that death threats were the most prevalent method of torture (97%).

Terrorists, such as religious and ideological extremists and extremist-backed governments, make death threats and employ other forms of intimidation and terror. For example, "Pro-Life" advocates have reportedly made homicidal threats against abortion clinic staff and providers to dissuade them from performing abortions.

Backlash toward terrorist activities and threats can result in another form of social control in which death threats are made against persons who are thought to be terrorists or those aligned with these terrorist groups because of their ethnic, racial, religious or national background or beliefs.

Other cultural factors influence this informal process of social control. Persons may become targets of homicidal threats and so-called honor killings if they challenge or violate religious, cultural, and gender-based norms. (For instance, in some countries women who are getting married may be threatened with death or the target of an honor killing if the promised dowry is not forthcoming.) According to Nazaneen Rasheed, of the Women's Union of Kurdistan, hundreds of women in northern Iraq, were forced to turn to prostitution in order to survive, were later killed by their male relatives because they had shamed their families (Anonymous, 1996a,b).

Individuals also can be threatened with death if they try to resist cultural norms. In Lesotho, cultural norms permit men to rape and kidnap their prospective brides, and girls and women may be threatened with death if they resist (Everett, 1997). Moreover, in Lesotho, many girls suffer physical and sexual violence within their families, and daughters in poor families are employed in households of more prosperous extended families, where they are further abused. These girls face death threats if they seek to escape.

In addition, investigators have examined the link between homicidal threats and stranger stalking and other violence and have explored the association between several mental disorders and homicidal threats (MacDonald, 1968; Planansky and Johnston, 1977; Renaud, 2004; Valevski et al., 1999; Silva et al., 1994; Leong et al., 1994).

Homicidal threats frequently are made in the context of domestic and partner violence and stalking (Straus, 1979; Browne, 1984; Walker, 1984; Marshall, 1992;

Roberts, 1996a,b; Pakieser et al., 1998; Morewitz, 2003a,b, 2004; see Appendix B—Study Results, Tables B.1–B.14). In Pakieser et al. (1998)'s study of battered women, the researchers discovered that about 54% ($N=90$) of women who had experienced an acute battering incident indicated that the assailant who had injured them had at some time threatened to murder them. MacDonald (1968) found that 80% of the homicidal threats in his study involved family members. The results of the Stalking and Violence Project (SVP) revealed that 33.2% ($N=147$) of the victims of partner abuse were threatened with death.

Individuals may threaten to kill their partners by using weapons, such as a firearm or knife. Yoshihama and Sorenson (1994), in their study of abused female intimate partners in Japan, found that 13.1% ($N=61$) of the physically abused women indicated that they had been threatened with and/or cut with a knife. The authors also showed that 31.7% ($N=166$) of the emotionally abused women reported that their abusive partners had threatened to kill/harm them or threatened to divorce them.

In these incidents, a breakdown in social control enables intimate partners and family members use death threats. For example, in an Illinois 2nd District Appellate Court case, the defendant, Mr. Joseph Cuevas, who dated Ms. Rachel Block between August, 2003 and January, 2004, had been charged with one count of stalking, one count of telephone harassment with the threat to kill, and one count of telephone harassment in violation of an order of protection (*People v. Joseph Cuevas*, 2007). Ms. Block said that the evening after having a violent argument with Mr. Cuevas, she was driving to her parents' home when the defendant jumped out of his automobile and forced her to stop her vehicle. The defendant then pulled Ms. Block out of her vehicle and began yelling at her and threatening to kill her. She also stated that throughout that same evening, Mr. Cuevas had telephoned her several times, threatening to harm her and her family.

DTMs may go to extremes in threatening their current or former partners. For example, David Lee Patrick, who was HIV-positive, was serving a three-year sentence in federal prison for harassing his former girlfriend. However, he apparently did not learn his lesson since he was later convicted for continuing to send threatening letters to her, and his prison sentence was extended by 42 months (Anonymous, 1997a,b).

Prevalence of Death Threats

Little is known about the prevalence and incidence of homicidal threats in the general population, and it has been very difficult to investigate death threats (MacDonald, 1968). The prevalence of death threats varies depending on the context and underlying motivation for the threats. They are prevalent in domestic violence episodes, in time of war, and especially during periods of racial and ethnic conflicts and political instability. Moreover, governments, criminals, paramilitary groups, and terrorists frequently use death threats and/or other types of violence to achieve their goals.

Many victims never report death threats, and DTMs are reluctant to incriminate themselves thus making it impossible to determine the actual prevalence and incidence of death threats. As a consequence, it is not possible to determine how many individuals make homicidal threats and how many make such threats before committing homicide. Knowing the association between death threats and homicide would aid in the apprehending of DTMs and preventing homicide.

MacDonald (1968) noted that determining the prevalence of homicidal threats is also problematic because DTMs are reluctant to incriminate themselves further by admitting to having made previous death threats. Even after being sentenced and incarcerated, inmates are worried about getting negative decisions from parole boards if they admit to previous homicidal threats. Restrictive rules of evidence may preclude persons who know about death threats from testifying in court, especially when they may have criminal records or when they are relatives of the suspect. Since homicide often occurs in the family, family members are often reluctant to testify.

Since MacDonald's time, there has been more research and public attention given to homicidal threats. However, the *Uniform Crime Reports* of the Federal Bureau of Investigation, U.S. Department of Justice (1967) does not report specific data on the prevalence of homicidal threats. According to the *Criminal Statistics England and Wales*, 1986, homicidal threats are on the rise. In 1980, there were 528 death threats reported, and by 1986, the number of reported death threats increased to 1,346 (*Criminal Statistics England and Wales*, 1987; Hough, 1990).

In his analysis of the British Crime Survey findings about reported threats made between 1981 and 1983, Hough (1990) discovered that only 5% of the threats involved threats to kill the respondent. Eighty-five percent of the threats were to "beat up" the respondent. In one third of all of the cases, the victims knew the offenders and in the remaining cases, the DTMs were strangers.

Some threats of violence, including death threats made by strangers, are similar to assaults against strangers (Hough, 1990; Hough and Mayhew, 1983, 1985). Hough (1990) found that these threats often are made in public settings such as clubs and bars. The victims frequently are young men who go out in the evening, e.g., for drinks. It is interesting that the frequency of threats of violence was higher in urban areas than rural areas. In contrast, threats of violence made against non-strangers are more likely to occur at home and in the workplace and are more evenly distributed based on age, gender, and geographical region.

There are various forms of homicidal threats, and threats in general, and they are conveyed in many different ways (MacDonald, 1968; Roberts, 1996a,b). Some of these ways are described below.

Instrumental Versus Expressive Threats

In his study of stalkers, Meloy (1998) described two types of threats: instrumental or expressive. Instrumental threats are those motivated by a purpose or goal of which the DTM may or may not be aware. In this type of threat, the DTM may seek to control the victim, by frightening or otherwise forcing the victim into doing something (Karmen, 2007). Meloy (1998) notes that instrumental threats can be made on the spur of the moment or can be planned carefully to achieve maximum effect. Instrumental threats may also have an emotional component, but emotional expression is secondary to the instrumental effect.

In contrast, expressive threats are based on emotions and help the DTMs control their own affect (Meloy, 1998). Instead of being mainly object-related, like instrumental threats, expressive threats provide a more internal homeostatic function for the DTM. For instance, offenders use expressive threats as a means to express anger or hatred and as a defense against fear, shame or anxiety (Meloy, 1998; Akhtar et al., 1995). DTMs may be anxious because they face a real threat such as a criminal justice intervention or nonexistent threats such as those involved in paranoid delusions.

Threats, whether instrumental or expressive, are often linked to a specific but unconscious psychological defense (Freud, 1966; Vaillant, 1993; Meloy, 1998). Meloy (1998) lists a number of common psychological defenses and articulated threats. For instance, in the idealization defense, the DTM may say: "If I can't have you, no one can." In the devaluation defense, the DTM will say something like: "You ought to die" or "You will die."

Meloy (1998) feels that these psychological defenses and associated threats in stalking incidents are more problematic to assess than direct behavior. Nevertheless, these motivations and defenses offer insight into the mental state, emotional status and personality of the offender.

Detailed Versus General Death Threats

Using a community sample, Roberts (1996a,b) discovered that homicidal threats made against abused women were of a more general nature than those that had been made against women incarcerated for killing their abusive partners. Over 90% of the jailed women had received a death threat from their partner that included a specific method, time, and/or location of their proposed murder. In contrast, only 15% of the abused women in the community sample who had received a death threat reported that the threat had the same specificity, whereas in threats made against the remaining 85% were of a general nature, e.g., "I'll kill you."

SVP case A104 illustrates a detailed homicidal threat. Mr. F, a 40-year-old man who had been spurned by his girlfriend, Ms. G, left a message on her answering machine to "Remember the Saint Valentine's Day massacre" and "When I see you I will put a shank to your head." This message was delivered on February 12th in Chicago, two days before the anniversary of the Saint Valentine's Day massacre.

In some instances, the DTMs may be only partially specific about their proposed methods of murder. In SVP case A101, Mr. B, a 26-year-old man who is married to Mrs. C, threatened to kill her with a knife.

Colorful and Dramatic Homicidal Threats

Death threats can be very colorful and dramatic. In SVP case A102, Ms. E, reported that Mr. D, her ex-husband threatened to "cut me to pieces with a knife." The death threats made in SVP case 159C were more colorful and detailed. In this case, Ms. Y reported that her ex-boyfriend, Mr. X, age 50, threatened to blow up her automobile, and cut her in little pieces and put her in a plastic bag with lye and ammonia. In SVP case 040C, Mr. F reported that Ms. G, his 27-year-old ex-girlfriend, had telephoned him and threatened to shoot him and another person "in the head."

Certain individuals and group may be more likely than others to use colorful and dramatic death threats. Persons who suffer severe mental disorders and are ostracized from society may make colorful and dramatic death threats to help bolster their impaired identity and self-esteem by retaliating against those who they believe have harmed them.

In other instances, individuals who later make death threats and commit violence may first write and mail threatening videos, letters, essays, plays, etc. that contain gratuitous and bizarre violence involving death, stalking, and sexual molestation (Dewan and Santora, 2007). These persons frequently are mentally disturbed.

DTMs who make death threats often either send threatening or explanatory notes or leave those notes at the crime scenes. In the three weeks before Cho Seung-Hui went on his lethal shooting rampage, Virginia Tech received two anonymous bomb threats, and Cho may have been the sender. A note containing a bomb threat was left at one of the scenes of the massacre. After the Virginia Tech massacre, a note was found in Cho's dormitory room in which he railed against "rich kids," "debauchery," and "deceitful charlatans," and concluded with: "You caused me to do this" (Apuzzo, 2007).

Criminals may be more likely to make homicidal threats. In these instances, they make dramatic death threats to emphasize their determination to carry out their acts as well as to gain notoriety. Terrorists make colorful and dramatic death threats to terrorize the population and promote their own ideological goals. Hate crime offenders often use dramatic and colorful death threats against minority groups in an attempt to force them out of their neighborhoods and communities.

Violence that Accompanies Homicidal Threats

Violence against partners and others often occurs at the same time that homicidal threats are made. During the heat of anger, especially during intimate partner and domestic incidents, DTMs often attack their targets while making homicidal threats against them. For instance, in SVP case A103, Mr. A, a 33-year-old man, reportedly hit and slapped his ex-girlfriend. He also scratched her face, pushed her, retrieved his clothes, and left the house, all the while threatening to kill her.

Domestic violence offenders often use handguns, knives, and other weapons to reinforce homicidal threats. Access to and/or use of firearms is associated with making death threat in other settings.

DTMs who make hate crime-based death threats often physically attack their victims. Other criminals, such as extortionists, kidnappers, and terrorists, may use both death threats and physical assaults to achieve their goals. Similarly, during time of war and periods of armed conflicts, both death threats and physical assaults are committed by members of warring groups and governments.

Communication of Threats

DTMs may prepare advance documentation about their intentions and the means they plan on using. Before the Columbine massacre, which took place in Littleton, Colorado, on April 20, 1999, one of the shooters had posted death threats against his school and classmates on his web site. Similarly, in the two-hour interval between his two sets of rampages, the gunman at Virginia Tech mailed vengeful videos to NBC headquarters in New York (Dewan and Santora, 2007). Olutosin Oduwole, a student at Southern Illinois University, Edwardsville, allegedly wrote a note, threatening to go on a murderous rampage similar to the Virginia Tech shootings if his demand for $50,000 was not met (Suhr, 2007).

The DTMs may prepare these communications for a variety of reasons. They give the perpetrators a platform for explaining why they committed violence. The Virginia Tech shooter explained that "his heart had been vandalized, his soul raped, and his conscience torched" (Dewan and Santora, 2007). In cases such as, the DTM may refer to specific persons or categories of individuals or not mention any specific target.

The videotapes also may help reinforce their belief in God, their belief in their cause, and perhaps give some comfort to their surviving family members (Dewan and Santora, 2007).

In the case of the Virginia Tech tragedy, the shooter (Seung-Hui Cho) stated that he was dying like Jesus to inspire weak and defenseless people to continue his struggle (Dewan and Santora, 2007).

Terrorists use videotapes to support their recruitment efforts, to serve as propaganda against their enemies and to pass secret messages to help other terrorists to plan and carry out attacks.

Veiled or Ambiguous Threats

Homicidal threats can be ambiguous or veiled. A man tells his wife: "I'm going to get you." This statement could either constitute a homicidal threat or mean that he is contemplating doing something negative to her in the future. In SVP case 302,

Mr. A, a 32-year-old, single man allegedly threatened his ex-girlfriend by saying that he was going to blow up her house. This could be a veiled or ambiguous homicidal threat, depending on whether or not he was planning to wait until she was in the house before blowing it up.

Michael Carneal, a student at Heath High School in West Paducah, Kentucky, reportedly made a veiled and dramatic threat of violence against the school, days before shooting at a group of praying students, killing three girls and wounding five others. Carneal reportedly had told students that "something big" was going to take place on Friday. However, no one believed him. In fact, he carried out the shootings on a Monday, not on a Friday (Wikipedia, 2007l).

Veiled death threats occur in other contexts. Hate crime-related death threats may also be ambiguous or veiled. In August, 1991, following the automobile accident death of a 7-year-old African-American boy and the injury of his cousin in Crown Heights, Brooklyn, mobs roamed the streets yelling "Get the Jews" (Leadership Conference on Civil Rights, 2002). Two hours later, Yankel Rosenbaum, a Hasidic Jew, was pulled from his car and stabbed to death. Two years later, Lemrick Nelson, Jr., an African-American teenager, pleaded guilty to violating Rosenbaum's civil rights (Wikipedia, 2007j).

Terrorists may also use veiled or ambiguous death threats to frighten their victims or potential victims and achieve their objectives. For instance, Yasin Hayal, an extremist, shouted what seemed to be a threat against the Nobel Prize-winning novelist, Orhan Pamuk, as Hayal was brought to a courtroom in Istanbul, Turkey. Hayal reportedly shouted, "Orhan Pamuk, be smart! Be smart." Hayal, who had been imprisoned for committing a bomb attack in 2004, had also confessed to inciting the murder of the ethnic Armenian journalist, Hrant Dink. Hayal had given a firearm and money to the reported murderer." Thus, a clue to the nature of this type of threat can be gleaned by better understanding the offender's criminal and ideological background and past criminal activities (Harvey, 2007).

How does one determine if this type of statement is actually a homicidal threat? The victim can try to weigh the risks and consequences associated with the threat by considering the DTM's current and former behaviors that accompany the threats, his criminal history, access to and previous use of lethal weapons, use of alcohol and other substances, etc. For example, in SVP case 367C, Mr. F reported that his 30-year-old wife, Mrs. G, one day "threatened to f— (expletive deleted) me up and then shot (at) me many times."

Threats Made Seriously or in Jest

Homicidal threats may be made with the utmost seriousness or they may be uttered in jest (MacDonald, 1968). If the threat is meant as a joke, there may be major negative consequences for the joker. A threat against an intimate partner can result in a restraining order, even though the threat may have been made in jest or without serious intent.

Offenders can be joking when they make homicidal threats and this can produce major effects (MacDonald, 1968). A bomb threat against an airplane, i.e. "I have a bomb in my bag," can lead to a cancellation of the passenger's flight, a thorough search of the aircraft and the arrest of the offending passenger. Since 9/11, this type of airline threat frequently will produce an even more drastic response.

Threats Made Calmly or in the Heat of Anger

Homicidal threats range from those made in a calm casual manner to those screamed out in an angry emotion laden confrontation, such as a heated marital dispute over finances, perceived infidelity, or other emotional issue (MacDonald, 1968). A homicidal threat made in the heat of anger is not necessarily more likely to be carried out than one uttered calmly.

Death threats made in the heat of anger are illustrated in SVP case A101. Mr. B, a 26-year-old man, reportedly yelled at his wife, and complained that she didn't do anything all day long. He finally screamed that he was going to kill her with a knife. Mrs. B stated that her husband had continued his screaming rampage for over an hour and paid no attention to the fact that their young children were frightened and crying.

Individuals who commit hate crimes or terrorist crimes also may make highly emotional death threats. People involved in a mob action or a riot may be so emotionally involved that they will yell out death threats against an individual or group as a way of driving them out of their neighborhood and community.

A calmly spoken homicidal threat may be deceptive since this calm could reflect deadly seriousness of intention. MacDonald (1968) describes how a young soldier calmly told another soldier that he was going to murder a non-commissioned officer and later that same day he carried out his threat.

It is the intensity of conviction that significantly influences the seriousness of the homicidal threat (MacDonald, 1968). A homicidal threat made in a calm, quiet tone, plus a strong level of conviction will invoke intense fear. The key is to evaluate the voice, choice of words, demeanor, body language, and other factors to determine the intensity of the DTM's conviction.

Symbolic Expression

The destruction of a picture of a person by burning it, shooting it, or sticking pins in it is symbolic expressions of death threats against an intended victim (MacDonald, 1968).

The shooter in the Virginia Tech shooting had written morbid plays as part of his writing assignments in the English Department (CNN, 2007a). Cho's writings were full of death, e.g., the stepson in one of his plays tried to choke his stepfather with a half-eaten banana cereal bar.

Creating and sending vengeful videos in which the DTMs strike poses holding lethal weapons is another form of symbolic expression. The 21-year-old gunman in the Virginia Tech tragedy created and sent vengeful videos and writings to NBC (Dewan and Santora, 2007). In other situations, a husband may destroy his wife's clothes or repeatedly stab her pillow. MacDonald (1968) described how a mother once stabbed her favorite childhood doll and then later attempted to murder her infant daughter.

Another form of symbolic expression is sending bouquets of funeral flowers, a casket, or other funeral objects to victims to signify that their death is near. According to a report on the International Federation of Journalists website, three Colombian journalists, Daniel Coronell, Carlos Lozano, and Hollman Morris, received bouquets of flowers as omens of their impending deaths (International Federation of Journalists, 2005).

In SVP case A501, Mr. G, age 29, used flowers in a slightly different way. He had been stalking and threatening his ex-girlfriend, and had told her that "no cop, family, or friend will protect you from me." Mr. G then began to stalk and threaten her at her job. Two days later, he sent her a bouquet of black roses at her workplace.

Hate crimes and death threats made by terrorists often involve the dramatic use of different cultural, ethnic, and religious symbols. Some racially-motivated crimes against African-Americans involve the burnings and bombings of African-American churches and other buildings (Leadership Conference on Civil Rights, 2002). Similarly, anti-Semitic crimes have included the burning, bombing, and desecration of Jewish synagogues and other structures. The Ku Klux Klan and others have burned crosses to terrorize African-Americans and Jews. In 1993, in Fairfax County, Virginia, an African-American woman who was house sitting, heard the doorbell ring and when she looked outside the window saw a cross burning near the front door.

Symbolic expressions of violence may be made in the contexts of partner and domestic violence. In SVP case A102, Mr. D, a 42-year-old man, who reportedly had threatened to cut his ex-wife, to pieces with a knife, had previously damaged her father's automobile and cut their daughter's dress with a knife in an example of symbolic expression.

Threats Expressed with Gestures and Facial Expressions

Gestures and facial expressions may be used to express a homicidal threat (MacDonald, 1968). In fact, no words are necessary in expressing a death threat. Commonly understood gestures include drawing the second index finger across the throat or gesturing with one's hand as if pulling the trigger of a hand-gun.

According to MacDonald (1968), a change in facial expression may convey greater alarm than words themselves. This is illustrated by the expression: "If looks could kill."

Conditional Threats

Certain types of conditional homicidal threats increase the risk of homicide for the victims (MacDonald, 1968). Sexual proprietariness and jealousy often trigger conditional death threats. The threat by a partner, "If I can't have you, then no one will," may indicate that the partner is at the end of his tolerance level. This could have fatal consequences for the wife who "cheats" on her husband.

Mr. Q, in SVP case A110, threatened to shoot the mother of his child, if he ever saw her with another man. Other conditional death threats involve threats to kill a person unless they let the DTM into their residences or offices. In SVP case A108, Mr. K, who was standing outside his estranged wife's apartment, threatened to kill her if she did not open the door.

In other cases, conditional threats involve calling the police. In SVP case A105, Mrs. P called the police after her 32-year-old husband, reportedly had punched her severely all over her body and had smashed her head with the phone that she had used to call the police. One month later, she reported that her husband had shoved her against a wall after she arrived home late from work and said: "if you try to call the police again, you won't wake up tomorrow."

Another type of conditional threat occurs when a DTM makes certain types of hate crime-based death threats, e.g., "If you're not out of town by tomorrow, you n..... (African-American) you'll be dead."

Many conditional death threats are used to achieve criminal objectives. Extortionists use conditional death threats to extort money from their victims. Olutosin Oduwole was arrested for allegedly making this type of conditional death threat against students at Southern Illinois University-Edwardsville (Suhr, 2007). Similarly, kidnappers employ conditional death threats to extort money or achieve other objectives from those who wish the return of the hostage.

Terrorists frequently employ conditional death threats to attain their objectives. They may threaten to murder large groups of people, kill public officials, or blow up buildings if governmental leaders do not submit to their demands.

Homicidal and Suicidal Threats

Individuals can make both homicidal and suicidal threats. Homicidal and suicidal threats are risk factors for homicide-suicides, and may be made against partners, friends, acquaintances, and strangers. Threats may be verbal, written, or nonverbal gestures (Koziol-McLain et al., 2006; Kulbarsh, 2006; Lecomte and Fornes, 1998).

Threats to Kill a Pet or a Person the Victim Cares About

In addition to threatening the victim directly, DTMs often will threaten to kill the victim's pet or a person whom the victim cares about (Rothman et al., 2005). DTMs use these types of threats further harass the victim and increase their domination and control over them.

Threats Made Directly or Outside the Victim's Presence

DTMs can make homicidal threats directly to the intended person or they can make these threats outside their presence (MacDonald, 1968). Death threats motivated by racial hatred or other hate crimes may be made outside the presence of the target. For example, in March 1996, an African-American woman, Bridget Ward, heard a mob of youths marching down her street, chanting, "Burn, mothf___, burn." By making the death threats outside the victims' presence, the DTMs can more easily deny that they ever were involved, but when witnesses or victims are able to identify their tormentors, deniability is less feasible.

Telephoned, Written, Mailed, Electronic, and Videotaped Threats

With improvements in communication technology, a DTM can use a variety of technologies to express a homicidal threat. As described previously, DTMs, such as terrorists, may prepare videotapes describing their plans to carry out death threats. These videotapes offer a visual expression of death threats. With the addition of Internet technology, videotaping of death threats can be made in real time.

Telephone technology can also be effective. An offender who telephones his victim literally "has the ear of his victim" (MacDonald, 1968). Even one telephone death threat can be very disturbing for the victims, but repeated telephone death threats can be traumatizing. Telephone calls require less planning than other forms of communication, however when the victim has voicemail, then he/she can have a recorded history of the threats. Some DTMs are aware of this and may be reluctant to leave a voicemail death threat since it can be used as evidence.

With the development of the Internet, people increasingly have been able to make electronic death threats (Deirmenjian, 2000). These e-mailed threats can be particularly traumatic because they can reach their victims at home, work, and other places where the victim has access to the Internet. It is very easy for DTMs to mount an electronic campaign of death threats and other forms of harassment.

Some DTMs realize that there are permanent records of e-mails on network servers and print outs that can easily be used as evidence by the victims, but other DTMs may be so caught up in their obsession that they ignore that possibility.

DTMs who make electronic homicidal threats may have higher socioeconomic status than those who do not, since the former may have easier access to the Internet. However, with the widespread availability of Internet cafes, libraries, and other public settings, where internet access is available, these differences are becoming less important.

DTMs who make videotaped death threats take advantage of the visual impact of their threats. This can be seen in the gruesome video tapes of the decapitations of first, the American journalist Daniel Pearl in Pakistan on February 1, 2002, and then the decapitation of Nick Berg, an American businessman in Iraq, on May 7, 2004. Both of the videotapes were accompanied by a series of written demands to enhance the effect of their fear-producing messages (Wikipedia, 2007m, n).

DTMs can leave messages or other forms of written death threats at the victim's home or workplace or mail them directly to victim (MacDonald, 1968). These written death threats can be direct, e.g., "I am going to kill you" or they can be disguised in some type of fantasy, e.g., a story about how someone murdered their spouse in a gruesome manner. MacDonald (1968) told the story of a fifteen-year-old boy who wrote an essay in school describing how a boy shot both his parents because they failed to give him a car as they had promised. That night the student shot and wounded both of his parents.

Outsourcing of Death Threats

In order to increase the level of fear, some DTMs not only threaten to kill their victims, but also claim that they have allies waiting to aid and abet them in getting the job done. In SVP case 47C, Mr. E told his daughter that either he or her out-of-state brother would kill her if she didn't follow his orders to come home.

Likewise, in SVP case 302C, Mr. G, age 32, told his ex-girlfriend, that he was going to have his boys "get" her. He previously had threatened to blow up her house.

Copycat Death Threats

High-profile incidents often spawn so-called copycat death threats and related behaviors, which can trigger quick law enforcement responses and other sanctions. For example, following the Virginia Tech massacre, Allen Lee, a high school senior at Cary-Grove High School in Illinois was arrested on two misdemeanor charges of disorderly conduct for writing a violent essay for his English class. He included the following passages: "So I had this dream last night where I went into a building, pulled out two P90s and started shooting everyone, then had sex with the dead bodies. Well not really, but it would be funny if I did" (Starks, 2007). Lee's teacher reportedly had told his class to be creative and that there would be no judgment or censorship. After negotiations with school officials, Lee, an honors student, was readmitted to school. His plan to enlist in the Marines after graduation was terminated because of the misdemeanor charges.

In July, 2007, two male teenagers were arrested and charged with misdemeanor conspiracy in a school plot. They allegedly were planning a bloody assault on students and staff members at Connetquot High School in Bohemia, New York, on the ninth anniversary of the Columbine school tragedy. According to the police, one of the teens is a 15-year-old boy who was suspended recently from Connetquot High School for making violent threats, and the other teenage boy is described by acquaintances as a 17-year-old who seeks attention (Dobnik, 2007).

The case of Olutosin Oduwole, who threatened to go on a murderous rampage similar to the Virginia Tech rampage, also is an example of this copycat death threat (Suhr, 2007).

Denial of Homicidal Threats

Often individuals deny that they made a death threat or claim they have no memory of making a threat, although at times, when confronted with the accusation, the DTM will accept responsibility for it. MacDonald (1968) tells the story of one man who when confronted, stated that if his wife said that he had made a death threat, then he must have done so. In these cases, the DTMs may be distancing themselves from the act of making a homicidal threat, possibly because they recognize the negative and potential illegal nature of their actions. Chronic alcoholics or those who are intoxicated at the time they make homicidal threats may really not remember making the threats. In addition, the passage of time may influence both the DTM's and the victim's perception of the seriousness of the threat, and both may deny the importance of the threat. This is especially true when the threats are made by family members (MacDonald, 1968).

False Confessions

People who falsely confess to making a homicidal threat may do so because of the following factors:

1. They may be suffering from serious mental disorders (MacDonald, 1968).
2. They may be betraying their actual proclivity to commit a murder. Allen (1962) described the case of a young man who falsely confessed that he had murdered someone. His false confession was ignored and a few days later, he murdered a girl.
3. They may wish to ensure their admission to a psychiatric facility. In order to prevent homicides, psychiatric examinations should be required for persons who make false murder confessions (Allen, 1962).

False Accusations

Since individuals may falsely accuse others of making homicidal threats, it is necessary to be cautious when assessing the veracity of a reported threat. A family member may falsely accuse a relative of making homicidal threats in order to have them involuntarily committed to a psychiatric facility. MacDonald (1968) described how a mother accused her son of threatening to kill her with a baseball bat. Upon investigation, it turned out that the baseball bat was in actuality a small, light plastic child's toy.

Russo (2001) reported the case of Edward Drago, a gay student at The College of New Jersey, who falsely claimed that he had received death threats and anti-gay messages. Mr. Drago subsequently confessed to making these false accusations and was charged with a felony for filing false police reports. He was also charged with harassment because he had sent threatening communications to the gay student organization. Mr. Drago indicated that his false accusations and threatening behaviors were due to his mental instability and mixed feelings about his sexual orientation.

Chapter 2
Death Threat Makers

This chapter focuses on the risk factors of death threat makers (DTMs) who threaten to kill their partners, friends, acquaintances, and strangers and how physicians can conduct an emergency evaluation of DTMs.

MacDonald (1968) sampled a group of 100 patients admitted to the Colorado Psychiatric Hospital for making death threats. His sample is unique since it represents a set of individuals who were hospitalized in a psychiatric facility because they were thought to pose a threat to themselves or others. The DTM characteristics and risk factors identified by MacDonald may differ from those of other investigators who studied homicidal threats using nonpsychotic subjects.

Research on the demographic and socioeconomic characteristics of persons who make death threats is limited, and may under certain circumstances reflect the characteristics of the DTMs' community and may not necessarily be associated with an increased risk of making death threats. Below is a description of the demographic and socioeconomic status characteristics of DTMs who have made homicidal threats.

DTMs' Gender

MacDonald (1968) reported that 55% of his psychiatric in-patient sample consisted of males.

The Stalking and Violence Project (SVP) investigated a random sample of 519 people accused of domestic violence (DV) in two large metropolitan areas. About eighty-six percent of DV offenders who reportedly made death threats were males (see Appendix B—Study Results, Table B.4). There were no significant gender differences between DV offenders who made death threats and those who did not.

DTMs' Race/Ethnicity

In MacDonald (1968)'s sample, 95% of the DTMs were white and the remaining 5% were from different racial and ethnic backgrounds.

S.J. Morewitz, *Death Threats and Violence*, DOI: 10.1007/978-0-387-76663-8_2,
© Springer Science+Business Media, LLC, 2008

In the SVP, 51.4% of the DV offenders were African-American, 20.6% white, 24.7% Hispanic, and 3.4% Asian (see Appendix B—Study Results, Table B.4).

For the sample as a whole, there were no significant racial or ethnic differences between people who made death threats and those who did not. However, racial and ethnic backgrounds predicted certain types of abuses committed against both death threat (DT) and non-DT victims (see Appendix B—Study Results, Table B.14). White DV offenders were more likely to threaten to kidnap their DT victims or their children (9.7%) than those victims who had not been threatened with death (6.8%). White DV offenders were about 21 times more likely to threaten victims with a weapon (21.1% vs. 0%) and more than 13 times more likely to actually use a weapon against DT victims than non-DT victims (22.6% vs. 1.7%).

African-American DV offenders were more than 4 times likely to threaten DT victims with a weapon (18.7%) than non-DT victims (4.3%) (see Appendix B—Study Results, Table B.14). Similarly, they were three times as likely to threaten to kidnap DT victims or their children (14.7%) as non-DT victims (4.9%). African-American DV offenders were more likely to come to the DT victims' home (52.0%) than the homes of non-DT victims (38.0%). However, African-American DV offenders were less likely to threaten DT victims with physical harm (44.8%) than non-DT victims (55.2%).

Hispanic DV offenders were more than 3 times likely to threaten DT victims with a weapon (19.4% vs. 5.2%) and more than 3 times likely to rape the DT victims than non-DT victims (25.0% vs. 6.9%) (see Appendix B—Study Results, Table B.14). Hispanic DV offenders also were more likely to push DT victims than non-DT victims (52.8% vs. 29.3%).

These results suggest that differences in social and cultural styles may influence the degree to which DV offenders from different ethnic and racial backgrounds commit different types of offenses against DT and non-DT victims.

DTMs' Age

The ages of DTMs in MacDonald (1968)'s sample ranged from 11 to 83 years of age. Fifty-two percent were between 20 and 40 years old, and the mean age was 43.5 years old.

The SVP results showed that the prevalence of DTMs was 14.0% in the 18–25 year-old age group, 56.6% in the 26–40 year-old age group, 26.5% in the 41–60 year-old age group and 2.9% in the 61-year-old and older age group (see Appendix B—Study Results, Table B.4). These results indicated that the prevalence of DTMs peaked in the 26–40 year-old age group and it went down to a negligible percentage in the 61-year-old age group.

In the sample as a whole, there were no significant age differences between DTMs and those who did not. However, the age group of the DV offender did predict certain different types of abuses committed against the DT victims and non-DT victims (see Appendix B—Study Results, Table B.11). DV offenders in the 18–25 year-old age group were more than twice as likely to threaten DT victims with physical harm (79.0%) than non-DT victims (30.6%). DV offenders in this age group were also much more likely to threaten a DT victim with a weapon (21.1%) than non-DT victims (0%).

DV offenders in the 26–40-year-old age group were much more likely to threaten DT victims with a weapon (20.5% vs. 4.9%), rape the DT victims (14.3% than 5.5%) and threaten to kidnap them or their children than non-DT victims (28.2% vs. 9.8%). They were also more likely to use a weapon against DT victims (28.2% vs. 16.0%) and vandalize their property than non-DT victims (39.7% vs. 23.3%).

In contrast, among DV offenders in the 41–60 year-old age group, there were no differences in the types of abuse committed against DT victims and non-DT victims.

These results support the notion that age-based norms and values may affect the extent to which DV offenders will engage in different types of abuses against DT victims versus non-DT victims.

DTMs' Socioeconomic Status

Little is known about the socioeconomic status of DTMs. Data from the SVP revealed that a majority of DV offenders who made death threats (57.5%) lived in census tracts with median annual household incomes between $20,000 and $39,999, and 34.2% lived in census tracts with median annual household incomes under $20,000 (see Appendix B—Study Results, Table B.4). There were no differences in socioeconomic status between DV offenders who made death threats and those who did not.

Weapons

Firearm ownership and access to and use of firearms, knives, and other lethal weapons increase DTMs' risk of making homicidal threats (MacDonald, 1968; Rothman et al., 2005). There has been an increased rate of homicides by juveniles and the availability of firearms has been associated with this increase (infoplease.com, 2007b).

Studies of pregnant women show that access to a lethal weapon, a threat to kill or harm the pregnant woman, isolation of the pregnant woman, and a history of child abuse in the home predict increased violence and homicidal behaviors (McFarlane et al., 1995; Morewitz, 2004). Campbell et al. (1993) also showed that partner physical abuse during pregnancy reflects the increasing intensity and frequency of abuse and the risk of homicide.

In the SVP, DV offenders who made death threats were more than three times likely to threaten their victims with a weapon than those who did not make death

threats (19.1% vs. 5.1%) (see Appendix B—Study Results, Table B.5). DV offenders who made death threats also were more likely to use a weapon against their
victims than those who did not (25.9% vs. 14.9%).

DV offenders who make death threats also use methods other than weapons to
threaten and harass their victims. Findings from the SVP revealed that being
threatened with death was associated with two non-weapons-related abuses (see
Appendix B—Study Results, Table B.5). DT victims (60.5%) were more likely
than non-DT victims (42.2%) to be threatened with physical harm. DT victims were
also more than twice as likely as non-DT victims to be threatened with parental-
child kidnapping (19.7% vs. 8.5%).

The above results indicate that DTMs are more violent than those who do not
make death threats. These findings demonstrate a link between death threats and
violence. These results also show how death threat offenders can engage in an array
of violent acts while evading social control processes.

Mental Disorders and Dysfunctional Coping Behaviors

Persons who suffer from severe mental problems, including sociopathic personality, psychopathic personality, schizophrenia, borderline personality disorder,
dangerous delusional misidentification syndromes, and Othello syndrome or delusional jealousy, have a greater tendency to commit homicide and may be more
likely to make homicidal threats than persons suffering from other types of mental
disorders (MacDonald, 1968; Planansky and Johnston, 1977; Renaud, 2004;
Valevski et al., 1999; Silva et al., 1994; Leong et al., 1994; Asnis et al., 1997).

Valevski et al. (1999), compared schizophrenic inpatients who had been
found not guilty of homicide by reason of insanity with schizophrenic patients
who had not committed any crime and found that the homicide offenders had a
higher rate of threats and aggressive behaviors, alcohol abuse, and previous
police contact.

Persons suffering from depression, suicidal tendencies, and other severe mental
disturbances frequently are unable to cope with stress and conflict, e.g., have
difficulty expressing hostility, have repressed homicidal impulses and have an
increased probability of making homicidal threats (MacDonald, 1968).

Suicidal ideation may be a risk factor for spousal homicide. In a case-control
study of spousal homicide in Sweden between 1990 and 1999, Belfrage and Rying
(2004) showed that offenders who committed spousal homicides had a suicide rate
four times higher than those in the control group (those who committed homicides
that were unrelated to spousal violence).

Asnis et al. (1997) note that people with mental disorders who have psychotic
symptoms are at greater risk for violence and homicidal behaviors than others with
mental disorders without psychotic symptoms.

Planansky and Johnston (1977) reported that 59 men in a sample of 205
in-patient schizophrenics had made verbal threats to murder or physically assault

individuals during the active phases of their psychoses. Men with paranoid diagnoses were overrepresented among those who had made homicidal threats.

Dangerous patients suffering from the Othello syndrome or delusional jealousy may exhibit hostility, which ranges from verbal threats to acts of homicide (Leong et al., 1994).

Certain types of drugs also have been linked to severe irritability which can result in homicidal impulses and threats. For example, Golomb et al. (2004), using a 6-patient case series design, found that all of the patients suffered severe irritability which manifested itself in homicidal impulses, threats to others, road rage, and damage to property.

MacDonald (1968) reported that of the 100 psychiatric patients who were DTMs, 23 were psychotic and all but two were schizophrenic. In the non-psychotic sample of 77 psychiatric patients, character disorder, such as sociopathic personality, was the primary diagnosis in most of the cases. Patients frequently had features of more than one type of character disorder. Some of these patients suffered from acute neurosis or alcoholism.

Those who have come to the attention of mental health system, whether or not they are diagnosed with a mental disorder, are at risk for making death threats and engaging in other violent acts. For example, Cho Seung-Hui, the gunman in the Virginia Tech rampage, had been declared mentally ill by a Virginia special justice in 2005. The judge declared that Cho was "an imminent danger to himself" due to his mental illness (CNN, 2007b). Cho had exhibited suicidal tendencies. In addition, he reportedly had an imaginary girlfriend named Jelly whom he described as a "supermodel that lived in space" (CNN, 2007e). In addition, Cho used to use a question mark as his screen name to contact girls on instant messaging and in his conversations and other messages (CNN, 2007c).

In SVP case 108B, Mr. A, age 28, had become homeless and told his estranged wife, that her family had turned their back on him and he felt depressed and miserable. He felt like grabbing a gun, knocking on her parents' door, and shooting everyone in the family.

People with mental disorders may threaten to kill strangers as well as those whom they know, such as a spouse, family member, friend or acquaintance. In SVP case A100, Mr. A, a 30-year-old man, had been admitted to a psychiatric hospital for observation after forcing his way into Ms. B's apartment, attempting to abduct their child, and brandishing a knife as he threatened to kill her.

DTMs with mental disorders may also threaten to kill themselves. They may also threaten to kidnap their partners' children or other family members. For example, Mr. A, in the case mentioned above, had made repeated death threats against Ms. B and had frequently threatened to kidnap their child during a 4-month period before being admitted for psychiatric observation.

It is not surprising, that many of the persons who stalk and make homicidal threats against U.S. presidents and other officials and celebrities are suffering from severe mental problems.

MacDonald (1968) suggests that the nature of the threat made by a mentally disturbed person may offer clues to the clinical diagnosis. He describes how a young male paranoid schizophrenic, while being restrained for making an unprovoked assault on his brother-in-law, threatened him by saying "I need to kiss you, Jesus. If I can get up, I'll kill you." The death threats made by the Virginia Tech shooter also offers cues to his clinical diagnosis. Cho Seung-Hui said in one part of his videotaped messages: "Thanks to you, I die like Jesus Christ to inspire generations of the weak and the defenseless people" (Dewan and Santora, 2007).

Criminal History

Criminals, especially those who had committed a prior homicide, assault, or other violent crimes, and those in criminal gangs and crime organizations are more likely to make homicidal threats than others (Karmen, 2007). In MacDonald (1968)'s investigation, 56 of the 100 psychiatric DTMs had been arrested for assault previously. Twenty-three patients had assaulted their victims at the time they made their death threats and another 13 patients had previously assaulted persons whom they had threatened to kill.

In SVP case A105, Mr. O had been sentenced to a federal penitentiary for 22 months. Mr. O had threatened to kill his wife on a number of occasions and had assaulted her repeatedly. In addition, Mr. O had been physically and verbally abusive toward their children for four years.

In SVP case A502, Mr. J, age 30, threatened to kill his ex-fiancee and her children. She later reported that Mr. J was a gang member.

DTMs who are current or former gang members are an added threat to their victims since they can involve other gang members in threatening the victims. For example, in SVP case A107, Mr. S, a former gang member, threatened to kill his ex-girlfriend if she tried to get him arrested and put in prison. He told her that he "knows other gang members who would hurt her if he asked them."

In addition, those who have had prior contacts with the police because of their threatening behaviors are at risk for making death threats. These persons may not have acquired a criminal record, but may still pose a serious threat. Two years before the Virginia Tech massacre, Cho Seung-Hui, the shooter, came to the attention of the police, including campus police, because of his threatening behaviors (Dewan and Santora, 2007). Cho reportedly had written very disturbing class assignments and had stalked two female students in 2005.

In SVP case A105, Mr. O, a 33-year-old man, had been sent to the federal penitentiary for 22 months. While he was incarcerated, he repeatedly made veiled death threats against his wife. Before he was imprisoned, Mr. O had made explicit death threats against her.

Child Abusers

Individuals who abuse children, sexually, physically, or emotionally may be at risk of making death threats, especially in the context of domestic violence. In SVP case 12C, Mrs. O reported that when her children were younger, her husband, Mr. N, would kick and shake them and throw them out of the house. Mr. N also reportedly sexually abused Mrs. O's daughters when they were younger. He had admitted to her and her pastor that he had tried to kill her several times while she was sleeping but stopped when he thought of the children's welfare.

Marital Rape

It is common for men who rape their spouses to threaten them with death. In the above case, SVP 12C, Mr. N reportedly raped his wife, Mrs. O, several times a week. Each time Mrs. O said "no" when he wanted to have sex, he forced himself on her anyway.

Aggressive and Hostile Individuals

Aggressive and hostile persons are likely to make death threats or commit other violent acts.

Individuals Who Have Been Bullied and Teased

Persons who have been previously bullied and teased, especially during childhood and adolescence, may be especially at risk of making death threats and carrying out these threats or committing other forms of violence. School bullying and teasing are wide spread in schools, and may result in serious social problems (Kim et al., 2006; Nansel et al., 2003). Cho Seung-Hui, the 21-year-old gunman in the Virginia Tech shooting rampage on April 16, 2007, reportedly was bullied and teased by his school classmates because he had a Korean accent and may have had some difficulty in speaking English (CNN, 2007d).

Antisocial and Isolated DTMs

Antisocial and isolated persons may be particularly likely to make death threats and engage in violent activities. As noted previously, a large percentage of the DTMs in MacDonald (1968)'s study were diagnosed as having sociopathic personalities. The university student who committed the Virginia Tech massacre was character- ized as a quiet person who rarely spoke and refused to make eye contact with others (CNN, 2007d).

Sadism and Cruelty to Animals

Individuals with a history of sadism and exhibiting cruelty to animals have a greater risk of making homicidal threats than those who are not sadistic or cruel to animals.

MacDonald (1968) found that some patients in his sample exhibited sadistic tendencies for years and their homicidal threats were part of their overall clinical presentation.

In SVP case 157C, Mr. C, a 44-year-old married man, reportedly punched and otherwise abused his wife's dog and cats. In addition, his wife reported that he came home intoxicated almost every night, cursed her, made death threats, and broke household items. This case illustrates that alcohol (and/or drug abuse) can be a risk factor in individuals who are cruel and sadistic toward pets.

Passive-Aggressive and Passive-Dependent Personalities

Thirty percent of the psychiatric DTMs in MacDonald (1968)'s study were diagnosed with passive-aggressive personality.

Prior Suicidal Behaviors

Suicidal ideation may be a risk factor for spousal homicide (Belfrage and Rying, 2004) and maternal filicide (Rouge-Maillart et al., 2005). Prior suicidal behavior also may indicate an increased risk for making death threats. MacDonald (1968) found that 46 of his 100 DTMs had a history of attempted suicide. Eight patients had attempted suicide at the time of the death threats. Five patients had taken drugs, one cut his wrist, one walked in front of an automobile, and one shot himself in the face. A ninth patient had shot himself in the abdomen four days after making the death threat. This patient had threatened to kill his brother if the brother informed his parents that he had contemplated suicide following an argument with his girlfriend.

Cho Seung-Hui, the shooter in the Virginia Tech, massacre reportedly had been suicidal in 2005, two years before he made death threats and went on a shooting rampage (Dewan and Santora, 2007).

In SVP case A100, Mr. A had made repeated threats to commit suicide, in addition to repeatedly threatening to murder his wife and kidnap their child.

Substance Use

Substance use by DTMs and victims often triggers violent behaviors and may facilitate the making of death threats, especially when the DTMs have access to a lethal weapon, such as a firearm or knife (MacDonald, 1968). In the SVP study, alcohol and illicit drug use was mentioned as a precursor to the incidents of violence among the DT victims in 25.9% of the incidents (see Appendix B—Study Results, Table B.6).

Domestic/Partner Violence

Domestic violence (DV) offenders are at risk of making homicidal threats (Straus, 1979; Marshall, 1992), and alcohol and illicit drug use is likely to trigger death threats by this group. The break-up of relationships also often leads to domestic violence against DT victims. According to the SVP, 31.5% of the partner violence incidents against DT victims were related to the break up of their relationship and 3.7% were related to divorce (see Appendix B—Study Results, Table B.6). However, there were no differences between DT victims and non-DT victims with regard to the prevalence of partner violence attributed to the break up of relationships.

Persons who fear the break up of their relationships may also make death threats. Mr. R, age 28, in SVP case A500, threatened to kill his ex-girlfriend, Ms. S, and himself if she "started to see someone else."

In the above instances, death threats and other forms of partner violence are often made as a response to the loss of attachment (Weiss, 1976; McClellan and Killeen, 2000). This loss of attachment can create intense separation distress, which often gives rise to intense anger toward the partner deemed responsible for the termination of the relationship. In fact, persons sometimes have murderous fantasies about their spouses. In one case a man read a newspaper article about a husband who, after a marital separation, shot his wife with a rifle. The reader believed that he too could take that action. In these situations the individuals believe that their anger is completely justified and they may be willing to harm their spouses. In other instances, however, the individuals may feel that their anger is incompatible with their true personalities and they seek to disavow the homicidal impulses.

Weiss (1976) points out even when persons feel the intense rage toward their partners they rarely completely suppress their positive feelings for them.

Partners with low self-esteem may be especially vulnerable to becoming intensely jealous and express their jealousy by physically abusing their partners (McClellan and Killeen, 2000). Figueredo and McCloskey (1993) suggest that men who abuse their partners may use coercion as a way of compensating for their own inadequacies. Male violence has been linked to low socioeconomic status, including low educational levels and lower income, which could result in feelings of inadequacy (Anderson, 1997).

DTMs, who are jealous, possessive, and overly controlling, often make death threats against their partners, friends, and acquaintances (McClellan and Killeen, 2000). According to the SVP study, partner jealousy was mentioned as a cause of violence in 13.9% of the incidents involving DT victims (see Appendix B—Study Results, Table B.6). In the SVP study as a whole, jealousy as a cause of partner violence did not differ significantly between DT victims and non-DT victims.

DTMs frequently become obsessed with their victims and stalk them. In the SVP, 36.7% of the death threat victims reported being stalked (see Appendix B—Study Results, Table B.5). However, in the sample as a whole, DT victims did not differ from non-DT victims in their prevalence of stalking victimization.

DV offenders will often threaten to kill or harm both their partners and their children or other family members. In SVP case A502, Mr. J threatened to kill his girlfriend, Ms. K, and her children.

Homicidal Threats, Child Custody Disputes, and Kidnapping

DTMs, especially those in domestic violence incidents involving child custody conflicts or who face potential or actual social losses, may threaten to kill their victims and also kidnap their children. In the SVP study, 25.0% of the violent incidents against DT victims involved child custody disputes (see Appendix B—Study Results, Table B.6). However, DT victims were not more likely to be involved in child custody disputes than non-DT victims.

In SVP case 134C, Mr. G, a 26-year-old man, reportedly had kidnapped his ex-girlfriend twice and had threatened to kill both her and her brother. For the SVP sample, as a whole, DT victims or their children (19.7%) were more than twice as likely to be threatened with kidnapping as non-DT victims (8.5%) (see Appendix B—Study Results, Table B.5). Likewise, female DT victims or their children (21.1%) were more than twice as likely to be threatened with kidnapping as female non-DT victims (8.6%) (see Appendix B—Study Results, Table B.10).

In trying to determine whether racial and ethnic factors may influence the link between death threats and parental-child and partner kidnapping, Morewitz (2003a,b), using the SVP database, found some racial and ethnic differences among perpetrators who threaten to murder their partners and those who threaten to kidnap their partners and their children. Among African-American offenders, threatening to kill their partners was positively related to threatening to kidnap their victims and their children, but among white and Hispanic offenders, there was no statistically significant relationship.

Recent and/or Chronic Stressors

Recent and/or chronic stressors, such as job loss, death of a family member, or business failure, may increase the risk of homicidal threats (MacDonald, 1968). In MacDonald (1968)'s study, more than 40% of the 74 adult males (18 years of age and older) in his sample had experienced either a job loss or a failed business. The DTMs may have problems dealing with school, work, family, and friends. In many instances, the individual is not able to deal with recent and/or chronic stressors. Persons who have immigrated to the U.S. may have difficulty adjusting to life due to differences in their language and customs and may suffer from chronic stressors as a consequence. For example, the Cho Seung-Hui, 21-year-old gunman in the Virginia Tech rampage, was a South Korean who came to the U.S. as a child. He reported having been bullied and teased as child and it is possible that he developed severe psychosocial problems as a result.

Having a Plan to Commit Homicide

MacDonald (1968) discovered that about 25% of the DTM patients in his psychiatric sample had planned to use firearms and an additional 25% of his sample had planned to use knives in carrying out their threats. Fourteen DTM patients were going to physically assault their victim: 3 were going to use an automobile; 3 were going to use poison; 1 had planned to use acid; and one had planned to hire drug addicts to do the "dirty work." Only a little more than 25% of the sample had no specific plan in mind.

Prior Homicidal Threats

DTMs who make repeated homicidal threats are at increased risk for continuing this pattern. DV perpetrators may make repeated threats to kill their victims, abduct the victims' children, and commit suicide, as in the case of SVP A100. When homicidal threats are uttered over a period of years, they may lose their significance for the victims, but the risks of homicide remain (MacDonald, 1968).

Parental Threats to Kill

Individuals whose parents threatened them or other family members are at increased risk of subsequently making death threats themselves. Ten of the 100 DTMs in MacDonald (1968)'s investigation had overheard a parent making a death threat against others; the same DTM parents had made threats against five of these patients. One of MacDonald's DTMs reported that his stepfather, when intoxicated, would threaten to murder all of his family members and would use a firearm to attempt to shoot the heels off his spouse's shoes.

Another DTM patient in MacDonald (1968)'s study stated that his father "went berserk," shooting high-powered guns in the basement when his stepmother threatened to leave because of her husband's physical abuse. The father was incarcerated when he threatened to shoot everyone. The patient also recalled that once his father had tried to smother his sixteen years old sister with a pillow, punched her and broke her jaw.

Pregnancy

Pregnant women and those who have recently given birth may make homicidal threats against their partners and children (MacDonald, 1968). In some of these instances, the women may be suffering from post-partum depression and psychosis. In MacDonald's (1968) study, four of twenty-five married women under the age of 40 years made homicidal threats when they were pregnant. A fifth woman had made death threats soon after giving birth. All of these women had made homicidal threats against their spouses and three of them had also made death threats against their children. All of these women had strong negative feelings about their pregnancy. They had either admitted their negative feelings or had evidenced depression in their prior pregnancies or had attempted to have abortions. MacDonald (1968) reported that each woman exhibited hostility toward her child, although she denied such hostility.

Two women in the study, who were not pregnant, had made homicidal threats against persons who had made negative comments about one of their children. A third woman had threatened to kill her spouse because of his lack of concern about his stepson's illness.

Emergency Evaluation of DTMs

MacDonald (1968) recommended that physicians consider the following factors in deciding whether to hospitalize these DTMs.

1. Demographic characteristics should be considered. Men between the ages of 18 and 40 have a high risk of committing homicide.
2. DTMs with the following clinical diagnoses are more at risk for committing homicide than other.

   (a) DTMs with psychotic depression and those with acute schizophrenia reaction or delirium should be hospitalized.
   (b) DTMs with mania do not often commit homicide but there may be other reasons for hospitalizing this person.
   (c) It is difficult to manage DTMs who suffer from chronic brain syndrome, chronic paranoia, or chronic schizophrenia. The persistence of paranoid delusions over many years does not preclude the possibility of violent behavior.
   (d) Sociopathic and passive-aggressive persons who exhibit poor impulse control are at higher risk than individuals with passive-dependent and hysterical personalities who have no history of assaults. If sociopathic and passive-aggressive individuals are unlikely to be compliant with outpatient therapy, hospitalization may be necessary to obtain their compliance.

Despite the advances in clinical diagnoses, diagnostic labels by themselves are insufficient for risk assessment. Instead, each individual case must be assesses and their total context considered.

3. The homicidal threat, itself, should be examined. A melodramatic death threat made by a hysterical individual is less likely to be ominous. However, death threats uttered quietly, but with conviction by sociopathic persons should be taken seriously. Repeated death threats even over many years should still be considered with caution, and it should be noted that conditional threats also can be dangerous.

MacDonald (1968) warns that DTMs who express guilt or shame may be avoiding blame on themselves. These perpetrators may be seeking rationalizations instead actually behaving more rationally.

4. Clinicians should inquire if the DTMs have a developed a method for carrying out their threats. DTMs should always be asked if they possess or have access to firearms. Hospitalization is necessary if the DTM has obtained a gun, poison, or other resource to carry out his death threat.

5. It is important for physicians to know if the DTM had ever committed a homicide, since this increases the risk of additional homicides (MacDonald, 1968). DTMs may not give this information voluntarily but may reveal it on direct questioning, or the physician may inquire of the police.

6. If the DTMs have a history of assaults and kidnapping, they should be asked if they have ever injured another person or tied anyone up with rope. Recent assaults and kidnapping behaviors by DTMs suggest the need for hospitalization.

7. Physicians should inquire about a history of attempted suicide. The lack of such a history suggests an increased risk of homicide, while a positive history of attempted suicide indicates a need to evaluate suicidal risks.

8. Clinicians should inquire if the DTMs have experienced any recent stresses, e.g., job loss, death of a friend, infidelity, threatened marital separation, since the stresses may weaken their self-control.

9. The clinician should ask questions that determine the level of family support for some family members may contribute the DTMs' homicidal behavior.

10. Physicians should determine if the DTMs made the death threats without provocation, since this increases the risk of homicide compared to threats made in response to intense provocation. Clinicians should take special precautions when children have been the recipients of threats, since they are more vulnerable.

Chapter 3
Death Threat Victims

Certain characteristics and behaviors of victims may increase their risk of receiving a death threat. This chapter discusses victim characteristics, the psychosocial impact of death threats, and the prevention of death threats made against partners, friends, acquaintances, and strangers.

Death Threat Victims' Gender

In MacDonald (1968)'s investigation, most of the targets of death threats were women. A majority (86.4%) of the death threat (DT) victims in the Stalking and Violence Project (SVP) also were female (see Appendix B—Study Results, Table B.3). There were no gender differences between DT victims and non-DT victims.

Gender differences may influence the type of threat made. Based on the findings of the SVP, Morewitz (2005) showed that among female domestic violence victims, being threatened with death was positively associated with parental-child, and partner kidnapping while there was no such association among male domestic violence victims.

DT Victims' Relational Status

Homicide victims are often family members or friends. The death threat makers (DTMs) may threaten their victims either some time before the homicide or at the time of the offense. Svalastoga (1956) studied 172 Danish killers and discovered that six out of every ten killers had murdered their own family members, three out of every ten had killed acquaintances, and one out of every ten had murdered a stranger. The findings also revealed that eight out of every ten Danish murderers had threatened their own family members and two out of ten had threatened friends or acquaintances. Police officers who came to the scene of the original threat and the relatives of one acquaintance were the only strangers who were threatened.

S.J. Morewitz, *Death Threats and Violence*, DOI: 10.1007/978-0-387-76663-8_3,

MacDonald (1968) reported that over 50% of the death threats involving family members were spouse-to-spouse threats and 15% involved parents making homicidal threats against their children. Threats to commit homicides most frequently were against spouses, children, mothers, siblings, fathers, and other relatives (in that order). This pattern of victimization was similar to those of an Ontario study of homicides and wounding (McKnight et al., 1966). Wolfgang (1958) discovered that homicides in Philadelphia were most frequently committed against spouses, children, and other relatives, followed by siblings, mothers, and fathers.

In the SVP, 34.0% of the DT victims were married (see Appendix B—Study Results, Table B.3).

About 67.4% of DT victims in the SVP were parents of at least one child (see Appendix B—Study Results, Table B.3).

In the SVP, about 28.6% of the DT victims in the SVP were in current or past dating or engagement relationships (see Appendix B—Study Results, Table B.3). In SVP case 13C, Mr. P, age 39, threatened to kick his ex-girlfriend's teeth down her throat and throw her out of her 14th floor apartment window.

There were no significant differences in relational status and parental status between DT victims and non-DT victims (see Appendix B—Study Results, Table B.3).

DT Victims' Race/Ethnicity

In the SVP, 50.4% of the victims of death threats were African-American, 24.8% Hispanic, 21.8% white, and 3% Asian and other racial and ethnic groups (see Appendix B—Study Results, Table B.3). There were no significant racial or ethnic differences between DT victims and non-DT victims.

DT Victims' Residential Socioeconomic Status

In the SVP, about 32.4% of the DT victims lived in census tracts with annual median household incomes of less than $20,000 (see Appendix B—Study Results, Table B.3). Fifty-nine percent of the DT victims lived in census tracts with annual median household incomes between $20,000 and $39,999 and 7.9% lived in census tracts with incomes between $40,000 and $59,999. Only about .7% of the DT victims lived in census tracts with incomes between $60,000 and $79,999. There were no significant differences in socioeconomic status between DT victims and non-DT victims.

Women who are pregnant or who have young infants may face an increased risk of being a target of homicide and other types of violence (Morewitz, 2004; Fildes et al., 1992; Dannenberg et al., 1995; Parsons and Harper, 1999; Horon and Cheng, 2001; McFarlane et al., 2002b).

Using a 10-city case-control design, McFarlane et al. (2002b) evaluated the odds of attempted and completed femicides (murder of females) for women abused during pregnancy. Four hundred and thirty-seven cases of attempted and completed femicides were obtained from police and medical examiner records. Interviews were conducted with the victims of attempted femicides and/or their proxies. The information thus obtained was compared with data from 487 randomly selected abused controls living in the same metropolitan area. The researchers discovered that 25.8% of the victims of attempted femicides had reported being abused during pregnancy, whereas 22.7% of the women, who were later murdered, reported abuse. Only 7.8% of the control group reported abuse during pregnancy. Five percent of the victims were killed during their pregnancy. The risk of becoming a femicide statistic was three times higher for women abused during pregnancy, after controlling for demographic, socioeconomic, and relationship status factors.

McFarlane et al. (2002b) examined racial differences and found that African-American women had more than a three-fold increase in risk of becoming an attempted or completed femicide victim than white women.

Controls and victims in the study who were abused during pregnancy also suffered more severe violence, compared to women not abused during pregnancy. The authors suggest that the link between abuse during pregnancy and attempted and completed femicide is very important and recommend universal abuse assessment of all pregnant women.

Since threatening behaviors may increase the risk of serious violence, it is important to evaluate the extent to which pregnant women are likely to be the target of death threats from their current or former partners. Data from the SVP revealed that 28% of the pregnant women reported that they had been the targets of homicidal threats (Morewitz, 2004). In SVP case X2, Mr. F, a 31-year-old man, made repeated telephone death threats to his pregnant partner and also threatened to abduct their older daughter.

Role of DT Victims

In MacDonald (1968)'s study of DTMs in 1966 and 1967, none of the DT victims was the first to display or use a deadly weapon or commit an assault after being targets of death threats. However, four of the death threat victims had previously threatened to murder the individuals who later threatened to kill them. In his investigation, one man had threatened to take away a patient's wife and shoot the patient between the eyes. The patient subsequently threatened to murder this man. In addition, three wives who first threatened to kill their husbands, were, in turn, threatened by their husbands.

Individuals who reject or may reject their current or former partners, girl friends/boy friends, and acquaintances run the risk that the rejected person will retaliate by threatening to kill them and their family.

DTMs who stalk their victims by repeatedly calling them and leaving harassing messages, following them, and coming to their home or workplace may threaten to murder these persons when they reject them (Morewitz, 2003a,b).

MacDonald (1968) discovered that some DT victims, through their own actions, seemingly provoked their offenders. In one case, when a patient asked his girl friend if she loved him, she replied: "If you don't know now, you never will." The patient overreacted by punching her on the back of her head, knocking her down, and then shooting her in the head, in each hand, and in the right shoulder, tried to drown her in the bathroom and later tried to smother her in the bedroom.

Telephoning the police during a domestic violence dispute can result in death threats against the caller. In SVP case 119C, Ms. R threatened to kill her mother after she called the police during a domestic violence incident. After her mother called the police, Ms. R said to her, "You think it's funny, but I'm going to kill your ass when I get you."

At times, the victims continue to make provocative comments long after they had first enraged the DTM. MacDonald (1968) noted that it was not just their provocative comments or gestures, but also their persistent insulting and sadomasochistic actions that had helped to trigger their victimization. For example, one wife told a patient after visiting him at Colorado Psychiatric Hospital, that maybe she would return to see him the next day, but that he should not expect her.

On the other hand, DTMs also may act in provocative ways. Many husbands in MacDonald's (1968)'s study reportedly acted in a provocative way by getting drunk, acting irresponsibly, and cheating on their spouses. Likewise, some wives enrage their spouses by flirting with other men or being promiscuous. For example, one patient's wife in the study had sex with another DTM patient at the psychiatric facility. Another wife, who had been the frequent object of assault and death threats by her husband, kept a gift from an ex-boyfriend prominently displayed in her living room.

Other wives react to husbands who threaten to kill them with firearms by making provocative statements. For example, some wives of the DTM patients in MacDonald (1968)'s investigation would ask their husbands if they "had the guts" to kill them.

Other family members also may make provocative comments when threatened with death. For example, a mother who was threatened by her daughter responded by telling her that she may kill her first (MacDonald, 1968).

In some instances, the arguments were about trivial issues, such as use of the bathroom or kitchen (MacDonald, 1968). However, frequently there was a history of longstanding conflict underlying these arguments.

Psychosocial Impact of Death Threats

Due to their exposure to death threats and other abuse, victims of such threats can suffer new psychosocial and physical health problems as well as a worsening of existing conditions. They live in suspense, for they never can be sure if their partners will carry out their threats. Those fears and anxieties are so intense and pervasive that the victims often are practically paralyzed by them. For example, in SVP case A501, Ms. H, was so fearful of her boyfriend's veiled and symbolic death threats (e.g., he sent black roses to her job) that she felt was unable to sleep, afraid to leave her apartment, or go to work.

Children living in the homes of DTMs are often physically abused and also suffer severe psychosocial stressors from living in that unstable environment. In SVP case 57C, a 7-year-old girl reportedly was so traumatized by her stepfather's death threats and other behaviors that she would hide behind furniture whenever he was around.

DT Victims' Use of Safety/Security Precautions

Domestic violence victims often fear for their lives and those of their children and of other family members (Morewitz, 2003a,b, 2004). The victims of domestic and partner violence often use various safety and security strategies. For example, the National Violence Against Women Survey found that 22% of the stalking victims reported taking extra precautions (NIJ, 1998b). Forty-five percent of them carried something to defend themselves and 17% obtained a firearm. In Pathe and Mullen (1997)'s investigation, 78% of the stalking victims took extra precautions such as using unlisted phone numbers, guard dogs, and security systems. Fremouw et al. (1997) discovered that carrying a repellant spray was one of the top five protective strategies of female stalking victims. The SVP findings revealed that 9.2% of the DT victims took safety/security precautions (see Appendix B—Study Results, Table B.7). In SVP case 12C, Mrs. O found a large kitchen knife under her bed on two separate occasions in one year. After meeting with the pastor to discuss her abusive husband, she again found a knife under her bed. After that, she began sleeping in her 18-year-old daughter's bedroom because she was afraid her husband would kill her in her sleep.

About 20.7% of the homicidal threat victims remained in the same residence with the DTM immediately following a partner violence episode (see Appendix B—Study Results, Table B.7). There were no significant differences between DT victims and non-DT victims in either their use of safety/security precautions, or in their decision to remain in the same residence with the DTM immediately after the episode of partner violence.

DT Victims' Use of Medical, Counseling, and Shelter Services

Little is known about the extent to which homicidal threat victims use medical care, counseling, shelter services and other resources to cope with death threats and related forms of violence. In his study of battered women treated in the emergency room, Pakieser et al. (1998) found that the most frequently used source of help was family and friends, followed by the police, and then the emergency room.

Guth and Pachter (2000), in their study of female homicide victims, discovered that a majority of the victims had been seen in the emergency department for prior partner-related injuries or had reported their injuries to the police. Individuals at risk for partner homicide often have been treated in the emergency room previously. Wadman and Muelleman (1999) showed that 44% of all of the female victims of domestic abuse-related homicide had been treated in the emergency room in the two years before they were killed. Twenty-one percent of all injuries requiring urgent surgery for women and 55% of all acute injuries were estimated to be a consequence of partner abuse.

Some researchers have found that domestic violence victims are reluctant to use counseling, shelter and/or medical services (Husni et al., 2000; Brookoff et al., 1997). For example, Husni et al. (2000) reported that 23% of domestic abuse patients refused ambulance services to the emergency department, compared to 4.7% refusal rate for the general emergency medical services population.

Domestic violence victims may be too frightened, embarrassed or ashamed to obtain counseling, shelter, or medical services, and many of them may lie about the real causes of their injuries. In a study of 528 abused women in the late stages of pregnancy, Stewart and Cecutti (1993) discovered that 66.7% had received medical services for their injuries but only 2.8% had told their health care providers about their abuse.

Many health care practitioners fail to routinely assess for domestic violence (Erickson et al., 2001). This is a critical problem because failure to assess for domestic violence may prove to be a missed opportunity to prevent a homicide. In a study of femicides in 11 U.S. cities, Sharps et al. (2001a,b) found that a majority of the victims had been abused by their partners (66%) and had visited a health care agency for either injuries or physical or mental health difficulties in the year prior to their murder.

In their survey of pediatricians and family physicians, only 8.5% indicated that they routinely screen patients for domestic violence. Clinicians frequently lack knowledge about screening guidelines. For example, Erickson et al. (2001) showed that 64% of health care providers surveyed indicated that they knew very little about the American Academy of Pediatrics Recommendation on Domestic Violence Screening.

When screening patients, health care providers should use both indirect and direct questions about possible violence (Mayer and Liebschutz, 1998; Chescheir, 1997). McFarlane et al. (1992) employed a 3-question Abuse Assessment Screen for pregnant women. Cowan and Morewitz (1995) developed a short psychosocial screening questionnaire to assess abuse and other problems facing college students at a university student health center.

The results from the SVP revealed that 11.5% of the DT victims reported that they had gone to the emergency department for their partner violence-related injuries (see Appendix B—Study Results, Table B.7). Almost 8% of the DT victims indicated that they had used shelter services and 8.5% had used counseling services.

For the SVP sample as a whole, there were no significant differences in the use of medical, counseling, and shelter services between DT victims and non-DT victims. However, DT victims who were hit by their DTM (93.3%) were more likely than non-DT victims (66.4%) to be treated in the emergency department for partner violence-related injuries (see Appendix B—Study Results, Table B.12). Likewise, DT victims who were attacked with a weapon and raped were more likely than non-DT victims to be seen in an emergency department.

Harris and Weber (2002) showed that having on-site crisis counselors for domestic violence victims in emergency departments improved referrals for victims who otherwise might be reluctant or unable to use community resources, and Muelleman and Feighny (1999)'s investigation, showed that an advocacy program at an urban county hospital emergency department increased use of shelters from 11% to 38%, and shelter-based counseling from 1% to 15%.

Additional health care provider training can also help domestic violence victims receive appropriate care. Jonassen et al. (1999) found that third-year medical student who participated in a domestic violence clerkship demonstrated a significant increase in domestic violence-related knowledge, attitudes, and skills.

"The Duty to Warn" Targets of Homicidal Threats

What happens when potential offender tells a counselor or therapist that they intend to kill someone? Generally, an individual has no legal "duty to warn" a third party about a death threat or other potentially dangerous behavior (Whitted, Cleary & Takiff, 2007). However, in many jurisdictions, case law has established exceptions to that rule if a special relationship exists, e.g., a relationship between a therapist and a patient.

The California Supreme Court, in a landmark case, *Tarasoff v. Regents of the University of California* (1976), ruled that a psychologist had a duty to use reasonable care to warn the intended victim since the psychologist knew that a patient had the intention to harm this person (*Tarasoff v. Regents of the University of California*, 1976).

The background of this case was that in August 1969, Prosenjit Poddar told a clinical psychologist at the University of California-Berkeley Hospital that he intended to kill Tatiana Tarasoff, who had rejected his romantic advances. The psychologist consulted with two psychiatrists and then the psychologist decided to commit Poddar for observation and report the death threat to campus police. The police detained him briefly and searched his apartment. However, eventually Poddar was released because he seemed rational and told authorities that he would stay away from Tarasoff. Poddar never went back to counseling and his psychologist's supervisor determined that no additional action should be taken to commit him or warn Tarasoff or her parents of his death threat. Poddar murdered Tarasoff on October 27, 1969, and her parents sued the University of California.

The California Supreme Court considered the importance of maintaining confidential psychotherapeutic communications, but the public interest in protecting the public from a known threat prevailed. The California Supreme Court asserted the need for confidentiality in the therapeutic relationship and noted that few threats of violence are ever carried out. The court indicated that therapists should not regularly reveal these threats since such disclosure would impair both the therapeutic relationship and the patient's relationship with the individuals threatened. Instead, therapists have a duty to disclose death threats only to avoid dangers to others. The therapists' disclosure of these threats should be done in such a way as to maintain patient confidentiality as much as possible. The California Supreme Court reversed the decision of the district court and remanded it back to the district court for a retrial.

Courts following the *Tarasoff* decision increasingly decided that those treating psychiatric patients had not only a right, but "a duty to warn" about a patient's potential dangerous behaviors (Whitted et al., 2007). However, the courts have decided that there are conditions under which a "duty to warn" is not required. For example, in another California case, *Thompson v. County of Alameda*, the court held that there was no "duty to warn" when there is no "readily identifiable foreseeable victim." In this case, a juvenile delinquent threatened to kill a youngster living in his neighborhood if he were let out of the institution. This court reasoned that the presence of an identifiable group of potential victims was not sufficient enough to create a duty to warn, especially since death threats are carried out infrequently and it is important to have free-flowing therapist-patient communication (*Thompson v. County of Alameda*, 1980).

Likewise, in *Brady v. Hopper* (1983), in which John Hinckley shot several people in his attempt to assassinate President Ronald Reagan, the court held that the therapist does not have a "duty to warn" the "world at large" and should not be held liable for injuries to third parties without specific threats to a readily identifiable person (*Brady v. Hopper*, 1983).

The courts have examined the foreseeability aspect of "the duty to warn" and have held that a therapist has an affirmative duty to investigate the possibility of a patient's dangerousness (Whitted et al., 2007). In *Bradley Center Inc. v. Wessner* (1982) the court ruled that a private hospital was held liable for failing to investigate in a more intensive way a patient's mental deterioration. In this case, the patient murdered his ex-wife while on a one-day pass (*Bradley*, 1982).

The court, in *Hedlund v. Superior Court of Orange County* (1983), found that the "duty to warn" is an essential component of the diagnostic process and that the therapist has the duty to first recognize the dangerousness of any patient. Therefore, the therapist has a duty to show initiative in assessing the patient's degree of dangerousness (*Hedlund v. Superior Court of Orange County*, 1983).

The Illinois Appellate Court, in *Eckhardt v. Kirts* (1989), set out three criteria for establishing the existence of a "duty to warn." First, the court held that the patient must make specific threats of violence. Second, the threats must be directed at a specific and identifiable victim. Finally, there must be a direct physician-patient relationship between the physician and the patient or a special relationship between the patient and the plaintiff (*Eckhardt v. Kirts*, 1989).

Cases involving death threats can also involve the doctrine of transferred negligence. The plaintiffs, in *Tedrick v. Community Resource Center Inc.* (2007), claimed that Teresa Street relied on several health care professionals to properly treat her husband, Richard Street, and prevent him from harming her. Yet despite her husband's paranoid delusions (he falsely accused his wife of adultery), hallucinations (he had hallucinations about being poisoned), declining mental condition, and repeated threats to kill her, the health care providers allegedly failed to protect her husband and herself by institutionalizing him. As a result of this negligence, Teresa was strangled by her husband. The Illinois Appellate Court in this case upheld the doctrine of transferred negligence, e.g., negligence toward a patient resulted in injury to a third person. The court concluded that a third party who is injured as a consequence of negligent acts performed against a patient could maintain an action against the health care professionals since a special relationship existed between husband and wife. In this case, Teresa and her husband had an intimate marital relationship, and she actively participated in her husband's care and offered information on her husband's moods and behaviors. Teresa also had consulted with her husband's health care providers regarding her concerns about whether her husband would act on his threats to kill her (*Tedrick v. Community Resource Center, Inc.*, 2007; Garmisa, 2007).

The "duty to warn" has been incorporated into various statutes. For example, at 740 ILCS 110/11, The Illinois Mental Health and Developmental Disabilities Confidentiality Act allows for records and communications to be disclosed "when and to the extent, in the therapist's sole discretion, disclosure is necessary to warn or protect a specific individual against whom a recipient has made a specific threat of violence where there exists a therapist-recipient relationship or a special recipient-individual relationship."

However, in 405 ILCS 5/6-103, the Illinois Mental Health Code allows for an exemption from liability for therapists who have made a "good faith effort" to fulfill the "duty to warn."

Practitioners should know the "duty to warn" requirements in their respective communities.

Chapter 4
Stalking and Homicidal Threats

Stalking or repeated and unwanted following, lying in wait, and other harassing and intrusive conduct first came to the public's attention in the late 1980s (Meloy, 1998, 1999; Morewitz, 2003a,b). This chapter analyzes the link between stalking and violence, including death threats and physical assaults.

The media's coverage of stalking incidents involving President Ronald Reagan, David Letterman, Jodie Foster, Rebecca Schaeffer, and other public figures played an important role in transforming stalking into a recognized social problem and legal issue. Stalking, however, is not a new behavior; it has existed since ancient times. Nevertheless, it is a vague and complex social phenomenon with varying legal and subjective definitions. Because of the diverse and complex nature of stalking, institutions of social control may be limited until the stalkers' behaviors are repeated frequently and/or they lead to crime-related physical injuries. The perceptions and beliefs of the victims, family members, police, courts, and others may affect whether the offender is arrested and prosecuted. Moreover, the responses of the stalkers affect how they are treated by the criminal justice system.

Prevalence and Risk Factors for Stalking

Because of the diverse and vague nature of stalking behaviors, its prevalence and impact can be difficult to measure (Turmanis and Brown, 2006). Using data from a national telephone survey of 8,000 men and 8,000 women, Tjaden et al. (2000) discovered that prevalence estimates increase when subjects are given an opportunity to define for themselves their stalking victimization.

In their analysis of repeated stalking incidents, Davis and Frieze (2000) found that the frequencies of stalking can vary, based on the sample and the precise definitions employed. They noted that self-definitions of stalking can be very different from legal definitions.

Despite its vague and complex nature and various definitions, researchers have investigated the prevalence and social patterns of stalking (NIJ, 1998b; Sheridan et al., 2003; Davis and Frieze, 2000). Based on data from the National Violence

S.J. Morewitz, *Death Threats and Violence*, DOI: 10.1007/978-0-387-76663-8_4, © Springer Science+Business Media, LLC, 2008

Against Women (NVAW) Survey, an estimated 8% of women and 2% of men in the U.S. are stalked at one time in their life. Annually, the NVAW survey estimated that 1% of women and 0.4% of men are stalked annually.

Other studies have documented gender differences in the prevalence of stalking victimization. Using data from the second Injury Control and Risk Survey in the U.S., Basile et al. (2006) showed that 4.5% of adults reported that they had ever been stalked. Women were more likely to report being stalked (7%) than men (2%). In other words, almost 1 in 22 adults (almost 10 million, about 80% of whom were women) in the U.S. were stalked at some time in their lives.

The prevalence of stalking has been analyzed outside the U.S. A postal survey of a randomly selected sample of 679 individuals, (400 women and 270 men) in a middle-sized German city, showed that almost 12% of those surveyed ($N = 78$, 68 women, 10 men) reported having been stalking victims (Dressing et al., 2005).

Stalking prevalence also may differ depending on the age of the victims. According to Davis and Frieze (2000), up to 62% of young adults are the victims of repeated stalking.

The social setting also may influence stalking prevalence. For example, Westrup et al. (1999) found that 30% of female undergraduate students and 17% of male undergraduate students reported being the victim of stalking.

Stalking can occur as individual try to cope with relationship problems related to friendship, dating, marriage, and relations with relatives. Based on the NVAW Survey, 14% of the female stalking victims reported being stalked by a current or former boyfriend or date (NIJ, 1998a). The results of the Stalking and Violence Project (SVP) revealed that 36% of the stalking victims who filed restraining orders were or had been in a dating or engagement relationship with the perpetrators (Morewitz, 2003a,b).

The NVAW Survey found that 10% of the female stalking targets reported being stalked by a current or former cohabiting partner, and that 38% of the female stalking victims indicated that they had been stalked by a current or former spouse (NIJ, 1998a). In the SVP, 25% of the spouses who filed restraining orders reported being stalked by their spouse (Morewitz, 2003a,b).

In Fremouw et al. (1997)'s study of undergraduate students, 80% of the stalking victims indicated that they knew their stalker and many had been romantically involved with the offender.

Based on an analysis of 1,785 domestic violence crime reports generated by the Colorado Springs (CO) Police Department, Tjaden et al. (2000) discovered that 16.5% of the domestic violence crime reports had evidence that the suspect had stalked the victim. Female victims had a greater likelihood than male victims to allege stalking by their current or former partners (18.3% vs. 10.5%). A majority of the stalkers were former intimate partners.

Using the findings of the second Injury Control and Risk Survey, Basile et al. (2006) showed that individuals who were never married or were separated, widowed, or divorced were more likely to have been stalked than those who were married or had a partner.

Persons with attachment problems and a history of having difficulties with relationships have an increased risk of becoming stalkers, especially as they deal with social losses (Meloy, 1992, 1996; Kienlen, 1998). According to Meloy (1992, 1996), stalking or obsessional following is a result of the pathology of attachment and he suggests that the childhood and adolescent attachment histories of stalkers should be analyzed. Kienlen et al. (1997), in an investigation of disturbances in childhood relationships among adults engaged in criminal stalking, discovered 63% (N=24) of the offenders had experienced a change or loss of a primary caregiver at age 6 years or younger. Parental separation or divorce was the most frequent reason for the disturbances in childhood relationships.

Kienlen et al. (1997) found that recent losses and social stressors may be a precipitating factor in stalking. Eighty percent (N=20) of the perpetrators in her investigation experienced substantial stressors, commonly losses within 7 months of the onset of the stalking. The stressors were: the breakup of a marriage or intimate relationship (48%); loss of a job (48%); and the potential loss of a child, e.g., child custody disputes (28%); or a seriously ill parent (8%). Forty-four percent of the stalkers had suffered more than one of these stressors before the onset of their stalking behavior.

Persons suffering from mental disorders and those with a history of violence and criminal behavior are likely to stalk (Dietz et al., 1991a, 1991b; Rothstein, 1964; Zona et al., 1993; Meloy and Gothard, 1995; Harmon et al., 1995; Meloy, 1998; Brewster, 2000; Morewitz, 2003a,b; Cupach and Spitzberg, 1998). Individuals who commit homicide-suicides may have a history of stalking their victims (Lecomte and Fornes, 1998). In a study of homicide-suicides in Paris, France, and its suburbs, Lecomte and Fornes (1998) found that some of the perpetrators had stalked their victims before murdering them.

People are influenced by other role specific norms, values, and expectations. For example, the media focus on the persistent male role may encourage date stalking (Sinclair and Frieze, 2000). Stalking is also affected by the context and circumstances. For example, the development of the Internet has facilitated Internet stalking or cyberstalking (Morewitz, 2003a,b).

Stalking, Death Threats, and Threats of Violence

Researchers have been delineating the link between stalking and threats of violence, including death threats and related violence (Pathe and Mullen, 1997; Meloy, 1998; Kamphuis and Emmelkamp, 2001; Morewitz, 2003a,b).

Meloy (1998) suggested that the link between stalking and violence is unclear. He noted that only about 50% of stalkers threaten their targets explicitly. Instead, stalkers create fear in their victims through their various stalking behaviors. Because of this, he believed it would be imprudent for stalking statutes to require explicit threats of violence. He suggested that a threat should be codified as either overt or implicit, and the latter can be determined by the offender's conduct that could create "reasonable fear."

Another issue is that threats may not predict violent behavior (Meloy, 1998). Some studies consisting of small or unusual samples have shown no association between direct threats and violence. Dietz et al. (1991a) found no link between explicit threats and the stalking of Hollywood celebrities, and Dietz et al. (1991b) showed a negative association between explicit threats and the stalking of members of the U.S. Congress.

According to Meloy (1998), group studies on threats may be less helpful in determining the risk of violence in individual cases of stalking. He suggested that it better to conceive of the relationship between explicit threats and violence in three possible ways. Threats

1. can block violence,
2. can inhibit violence, and
3. are not related to violence.

It is also useful to consider death threats as a prelude to violence. There are ample studies, which show that direct threats are more prevalent in instances in which the stalker becomes violent (Meloy, 1998, 1996; MacDonald, 1968; Zona et al., 1997).

Using a 50-item questionnaire, Pathe and Mullen (1997) found that a majority of the victims had suffered various types of harassment, including being followed, approached repeatedly and being the target of letters and telephone calls for periods ranging from 1 month to 20 years. Fifty-eight of the 100 stalking victims in their sample had reported receiving threats and 34 had been physically or sexually assaulted.

Based on a community investigation of 201 female stalking victims, Kamphuis and Emmelkamp (2001) discovered that seventy-four percent ($N=148$) reported having been threatened with violence and 55% ($N=111$) had been the victims of actual violence.

In their community-based investigation of stalking in Germany, Dressing et al. (2007) showed that the victims suffered a high rate of physical (31%) and sexual (19%) violence in addition to substantial psychosocial problems resulting from their stalking victimization.

One approach is to assess the risk of homicidal threats and associated violence among stalkers in different relationships and different contexts.

Acquaintance and Stranger Stalking

In acquaintance stalking, the victims and perpetrators know each other on a limited basis (Morewitz, 2003a,b). Victims and perpetrators may be neighbors, co-workers, or fellow members of organizations. People may engage in acquaintance stalking for diverse reasons, such as business conflicts and disputes over residential noise, trash, and landscaping. Some offenders may stalk someone because they desire a romantic relationship or are seeking revenge for a real or imagined injustice.

In SVP case 10C, acquaintance stalking resulted in physical violence and trauma to the victim and his family. Mr. C called the police and filed a restraining order against Mr. D, a 42-year-old man who resided in the same apartment building. The victim complained that the offender had verbally assaulted him on three occasions during the year. After being contacted by the police, the perpetrator agreed to stop cursing Mr. C. and move away. Later, during the same year, the offender returned to Mr. C's residence, ordered his children to waken him, and then he cursed and physically attacked Mr. C, bruising his kidneys. Both the victim and his family were traumatized by the assault.

In stranger stalking, the perpetrators and victims do not know each other personally, and the stalking result from the offenders' own sociopathology and psychopathy. Erotomania is one subtype of stranger stalking. Persons suffering from this disorder stalk their victims in the delusional belief or fantasy that their victim is in love with them (Esquirol, 1838; de Clerambault, 1921; Zona et al., 1993; Kurt, 1995).

In both stranger and acquaintance stalking, the perpetrators may hold paranoid and other delusional beliefs and will stalk and try to harm their victims as a result (Dietz et al., 1991a,b).

There are a variety of risk factors that may increase the probability that offenders who stalk strangers and acquaintances also will make death threats. Stranger and acquaintance stalkers may be more likely to suffer from mental disorders that increase their likelihood of also making death threats. Cho Seung-Hui, the Virginia Tech shooter, had a history of mental illness and had been taken to a mental health facility after exhibiting suicidal tendencies (Apuzzo, 2007; Dewan and Santora, 2007). He not only had stalked and harassed two female college students, but also reportedly had used a cell phone camera to secretly photograph or view the legs of female college students as they sat in class.

Persons may stalk and threaten to kill U.S. presidents, members of U.S. Congress, and other governmental officials (Dietz et al., 1991a; Rothstein, 1964). Dietz et al. (1991b), in their study of persons who threatened members of the U.S. Congress, discovered that their subjects had a lower probability of actually meeting their victims than those perpetrators who stalked their victims, but did not threaten them.

Both male and female stalkers can engage in violence. Using archival data on 82 female stalkers from the U.S., Canada, and Australia, Meloy and Boyd (2003) evaluated the characteristics of female stalkers and their propensity for committing violence against their targets. The authors discovered that the female stalkers were mostly single, heterosexual, educated, in the mid-30 age range, who had stalked their targets for more than a year. The female stalkers in their study frequently pursued men to create an intimate relationship, while most of the male stalkers pursued their targets in order to restore an intimate relationship.

Meloy and Boyd (2003) found that female stalkers, who threatened violence, had a greater likelihood of being violent. In their study, 25% of the female stalkers had been violent. However, they used weapons infrequently, and injuries were minor. Their stalking victims tended to be slightly older male acquaintances.

A variety of emotions and motivations, such as anger, obsessional thoughts, raging against abandonment, dependency, and jealousy were responsible for these behaviors.

Palarea et al. (1999) suggested that the stalker's level of proximity to the victim and threats toward the victim and property should be considered as predictors of violence.

Meloy and Boyd (2003) discovered that if the female stalkers had a previous sexual relationship with the victim, the risk of committing subsequent violence against their ex-partner was greater than 50%.

Based on an investigation of 100 cases of individuals charged with criminal harassment, Morrison (2001) discovered that stalkers with a history of violence, strong negative emotions, and who are obsessed with their victims may be at greatest risk of committing future violence.

Purcell et al. (2001) evaluated the characteristics and motivations of 40 female and 150 male stalkers referred to a forensic mental health clinic. They found that both female and male stalkers had similar demographic characteristics. However, male stalkers were more likely than female stalkers to have both a criminal history and higher rates of substance abuse. Compared to male stalkers, female stalkers had a greater likelihood of targeting professionals and a lower probability of stalking strangers. Female stalkers also were more likely than male stalkers to target victims of the same gender. A majority of female stalkers were motivated to stalk by their desire for intimacy with their victims, whereas male stalkers had more diverse motivations for stalking their victims. The duration of stalking and prevalence of related violence were similar in both groups.

Violence in acquaintance stalking may be related to the degree of familiarity and proximity between the perpetrator and victim (Morewitz, 2003a,b; Palarea et al., 1999). As acquaintances become more familiar with each other, there is an increased risk of offensive stalking behaviors and violent behaviors, including homicidal and suicidal threats. With greater familiarity, the interactions between the offenders and victims begin to resemble annoying and threatening dating relationships.

The emergence of the Internet has spawned online stalking on a widespread scale (Morewitz, 2003a,b). Godwin noted that there are two types of online stalking: stranger and known online stalking (Godwin, 2007). In stranger online stalking, neither the offender nor the targets knows each other. In contrast, in known online stalking, the offenders and victims had previously formed casual or friendly relationships and when their relationship deteriorates, they transfer their conflict online. Godwin suggested that stranger online stalkers are more likely to commit violence against their targets than nonstranger online stalkers.

Law enforcement agencies, including district attorney's and U.S. attorney's offices have received Internet stalking complaints (NIJ, 1999). The District Attorney's Office in Los Angeles estimates that 20% of the 600 cases in its Stalking and Threat Assessment Unit consist of Internet stalking incidents. In New York, the chief of the Manhattan District Attorney's Office, Sex Crimes Unit estimates that 2% of its cases involve Internet stalking incidents. According to the

New York Police Department's Computer Investigations and Technology Unit, almost 40% of its cases involve electronic threats and harassment.

A 22-year-old woman in Australia reported to the Queensland Police that she had been the target of several unwanted and threatening email communications (Australian Broadcasting Corp., 2000). The woman also reported the threatening emails to her Internet service provider, which closed the offender's account. Using a different Internet service provider account, the suspect then sent her a death threat.

In another case of online stalking, the victim, who met her offender in an American online chat room, was so afraid of her online stalker that she moved to another city (Morewitz, 2003a,b). The perpetrator stalked the woman in public and sent threatening online messages.

Individuals at work and on college campuses increasingly have been the targets of Internet stalking and threats. Park Dietz, president of Threat Assessment Group, Inc., in Newport Beach, CA, offers assistance to the victims of workplace stalking, harassment, and threats (Miller and Maharaj, 1999). Dietz's firm, between 1994 and 1999 has had thousands cases of workplace harassment, stalking, and threats. He noted that his firm's cases of electronic stalking and harassment increased from 0% to more than 25% during this period. If stalking, harassment and threats via pagers and faxes are included, the percentage increased to 50%.

In the U.K., a survey of employees at Novell, Inc. showed that 35% of those surveyed reported being the target of unwanted emails (Sanchez, 1999).

In North Hollywood, CA, Doug Lantz's Internet business was the target of death threats and other threatening email communications (ABCNEWS, 2000). One e-mail threatened to crush Lantz's skull and another warned him to close his business "or it would be another nail in his coffin."

Stalking and Death Threats in Dating and Intimate Relationships

Men who stalk their former or current female partners may have a higher probability of abusing them and also may be more likely to murder them than nonstalkers. Based on a study of 223 intimate and nonintimate stalking cases, Palarea et al. (1999) showed that intimate relationship stalkers engaged in more dangerous stalking activities than nonintimate relationship stalkers.

McFarlane et al. (2002a) used a case-control study of 384 female abuse victims and 437 attempted or actual murders of women by men to evaluate the extent to which heterosexual partner stalking and other threatening actions were related to an increased risk of potential or actual lethal outcomes for female partners. The results showed that women who were stalked by their male partners were more than two times as likely to become victims of attempted or actual murder. Women had a nine-fold increase in the risk of attempted or actual murder if the male partners had threatened to harm the victims' children if they broke up with them. The investigators conclude that women who are stalked and threatened by their male partners have an elevated risk of being killed.

Other studies have assessed the association between threats and stalking. Based on a random survey of adult men and women in the State of Victoria, Australia, Purcell et al. (2002) showed that the most frequently used methods of harassment consisted of unwanted telephone calls, intrusive approaches and stalking. Related threats (29%) and physical attacks (18%) often evolved from the stalking behaviors.

In SVP case 340C, Mr. Q, a single, 49-year-old man, stalked and threatened to murder Ms. R., his ex-girlfriend, and her children. Mr. Q reportedly had threatened Ms. R and her children with a dagger, but did not physically touch them with the weapon. Ms. R reported that Mr. Q stalked her "all the time."

Perpetrators who stalk and threaten to kill their partners also often physically attack them and vandalize their property. In SVP case A106, the death threat (DT) victim, Ms. J, indicated that Mr. I, age 69, had not only threatened her with death, but had tried to attack her with a hammer and rammed his automobile into her automobile three times.

Stalking and making death threats are not limited to those who have been in dating or engagement relationships. Spouses also stalk and make homicidal threats against their spouses (Morewitz, 2003a,b, p. 40).

Family Member and Relative Stalking

According to the NVAW Survey, 4% of women and 2% of men indicated that they had been stalked by a relative other than their spouse (NIJ, 1998a). Offenders who stalk family members and relatives may make death threats against them. For example, in SVP case 278C, Mr. X, a 38-year-old man, had stalked and threatened to kill his sister, Ms. W, because she had wanted him to leave their house so that another brother who was visiting from Puerto Rico could stay there (Morewitz, 2003a,b).

Risk Factors for Stalking and Making Death Threats

What factors increase the likelihood that partners will stalk and make death threats?

Stalkers who are overly controlling and jealous in their relationships with their partners may be at risk of making homicidal threats. In the SVP, jealousy on the part of the perpetrator was implicated in 13.9% of the cases in which the offender made death threats (see Appendix B—Study Results, Table B.6; Morewitz, 2003a,b).

In SVP case 159C, Mr. X frequently stalked his ex-girlfriend, Ms. Y, and had threatened to kill her and bury her in Indiana. He also accused Ms. Y of having sex with his brother.

In another stalking case, SVP case 157C, Mr. C, age 44, had a telephone conversation with his wife's boss, accusing him of being her boyfriend and cursing him.

Perpetrators who have been separated from their partners may be at increased risk of stalking and making homicidal threats as they try to resume the relationship. The break-up of a relationship can precipitate stalking and homicidal threats from the individuals who are devastated by the loss and are annoyed that they are unable to resume their relationship (Morewitz, 2003a,b). In SVP case 52C, Mr. B tried to persuade his ex-girlfriend, Ms. A, to resume their relationship. He had been very possessive of her and had stalked and threatened her previously. One day, Mr. B attempted to force his way into her home, threatened to cut her throat and murder anyone else who was inside her home (Morewitz, 2003a,b).

The SVP revealed that differences in stalking victimization between homicidal threat victims and nonhomicidal threat victims varied depending on the offender's race or ethnicity (see Appendix B—Study Results, Table B.14). If the perpetrators were White or Hispanic, DT victims did not differ from non-DT victims in whether or not they were stalked (Data are not included in the table.). However, if the offender was African-American, DT victims were more likely than non-DT victims to report that the perpetrator came to their home (52.0% vs. 38.0%).

In the SVP, stalking victimization between homicidal and nonhomicidal threat victims varied depending on the perpetrators' age group (see Appendix B—Study Results, Table B.11). If perpetrators were in the 26–40 year age group, DT victims were more likely than non-DT victims to be stalked (39.7% vs. 29.5%). There were no differences in stalking victimization between DT and non-DT victims if the offenders were in either the 18–25 (Data are not included in the table.) or 41–60 year age group.

Impact of Stalking and Death Threats

Stalking victimization is a significant public health problem, mainly for women, and is linked to many adverse health outcomes, including homicide (Pathe and Mullen, 1997; Westrup et al., 1999; Kamphuis and Emmelkamp, 2001; Davis et al., 2002; Morewitz, 2003a,b; Basile et al., 2006; Dressing et al., 2007). Dietz and Martin (2007) using the NVAW Survey, found that three-fourths of the women who were stalked felt fear. In their analysis, African-American women were less likely to report being fearful than white women.

The victims of death threats (and other threats of violence) and stalking can develop serious stress-related psychosocial and physical health problems (Bjerregaard, 2000; Kamphuis and Emmelkamp, 2001; Morewitz, 2003a,b). The persistence of death threats and stalking behaviors increase the fear and anxiety among the victims. Perpetrators who make repeated, threatening and abusive telephone calls to the victims' workplace and tell lies about the victim to their' co-workers worsen the victims' fear and anxiety. Bjerregaard (2000) found that feeling threatened by their stalkers is related to an increased likelihood of being physically attacked by their pursuer.

The negative health effects of being stalked and threatened with death are the same, regardless of the type of relationship. The victims of family and relative stalking and death threats also can suffer stress-related problems. In SVP case 278C, Ms. W indicated that she was unable to sleep because she feared that her brother, Mr. X, would come to her home and carry out his threats to kill her (Morewitz, 2003a,b).

Pathe and Mullen (1997) found increased levels of anxiety in 83% of the stalking victims, and intrusive thoughts and flashbacks in 55% of the victims. Moreover, difficulties sleeping, including nightmares, appetite problems, and depressive symptoms were frequently reported. Twenty-four percent of the stalking victims reported suicidal thoughts. Thirty-seven percent of the victims met the criteria for Post Traumatic Stress Disorder (PTSD) and 18% more had clinical features of the disorder but did not have a stressor consisting of threatened or actual physical harm.

Westrup et al. (1999), in their study of female undergraduate students, showed that stalking victims were more likely to suffer more PTSD symptoms and suffer more severe symptoms than individuals who were harassed or control subjects.

Using the 12-item General Health Questionnaire, the Impact of Event Scale, and other measures, Kamphuis and Emmelkamp (2001) revealed that more than 50% of the victims of stalking and harassment, including threats of violence, fulfilled the criterion for clinically significant pathology. The victims suffered symptoms related to PTSD that were similar to the findings in other investigations of traumatized individuals.

Gender differences in stalking victimization also have been documented (Davis et al., 2002; Kuehner et al., 2006). Davis et al. (2002), using the NVAW Survey, showed that female stalking victims were more than 13 times as likely to be "very afraid" of their perpetrators as the male stalking victims. However, the adverse consequences of stalking were similar for female and male stalking targets. Both female and male stalking victims were more likely than nonstalking victims to report poor current health status, depressive symptoms, injury, and substance use.

Stalking behaviors, combined with death threats, can be so disturbing to their victims and the victim's family members and friends that they will complain to the police, request a mental health intervention or contact other authorities. For example, two years prior to the Virginia Tech tragedy, a female student in November, 2005, complained to campus police that Cho had made annoying contact with her. A month later, a second female student complained to the police after Cho had sent instant messages to her (Dewan and Santora, 2007).

Victims and other persons will alter their behaviors to avoid these stalkers. One student who shared a dormitory room with Cho Seung-Hui, the Virginia Tech gunman, stated that he was so concerned about Cho's stalking and menacing behaviors that he told friends, particularly women not to visit him in his dormitory room. This student feared that Cho would then stalk his friends who came to visit him (CNN, 2007c).

DT victims who are also stalked often are fearful that they will lose their job because they are often stalked and harassed at work. In SVP case 40C, a DT victim, Mr. F, reported that Ms. G, his ex-girlfriend, had called him at work hundreds of times and he feared losing his job as a consequence.

Based on the NVAW Survey, Dietz and Martin (2007) showed that the frequency of stalking, being stalked by an intimate or family member or acquaintance or being stalked by physical or communication methods were associated with increased fear among the victims. In Turmanis and Brown (2006)'s study, increased stalking caused the victim to have increased anxiety, helplessness, PTSD, and depressive symptoms. Moreover, other factors such as the offenders' use of alcohol and drugs worsen the stress and fear among victims.

Help-Seeking Behaviors of Stalking and Death Threat Victims

With the passage of new laws to combat stalking and its emergence as a social problem, the victims of stalking and death threats may increasingly rely on family, friends, the police, courts, counselors, and others in dealing with these forms of violence (Morewitz, 2003a,b). To what extent does stalking victimization influence whether death threat victims will seek assistance from the police, courts, counselors, and friends, and others in dealing with their problems?

In the SVP, DT victims did not differ from non-DT victims in their requests for court protection against stalking (see Appendix B—Study Results, Table B.8). About 65% of the DT victims and 65.1% of the non-DT victims asked for such protection. Likewise, the courts did not differ in their granting of court protection against stalking. About 71% of the DT victims received court protection against stalkers, while 67.1% of the non-DT victims received such court protection. More research is needed to begin to address the issue of help-seeking strategies and organizational responses for the victims.

Chapter 5
Death Threats and Weapon Use

Children and adults frequently make death threats and/or use weapons in a variety of settings, including, schools, colleges, residences, workplaces, and various public settings. The presence or use of weapons weakens the ability of institutions of social control, such as the police, from maintaining that control through routine enforcement of laws. Individuals who carry or use weapons may take the law into their own hands and this often has lethal consequences.

Persons may have been threatened and carry weapons for protection, and others carry weapons so that they can threaten. The presence of weapons in schools establishes an atmosphere of threats and intimidation that may interfere with student learning (Aspy et al., 2004). In addition, the same situation exists in the workplace where it creates fear and impairs occupational functioning. However, there are limits to this process of domination since the use of weapons, especially guns, can lead to fatalities or serious injuries, which can trigger criminal justice interventions.

Firearms, Substance Use, and Increased Risk of Homicide

Tardiff et al. (1994) evaluated New York City medical examiner data from 1990 and 1991, and found that increased use of cocaine and firearms were linked to high homicide rates among young African Americans and Latinos. African-Americans, Latinos, and Asians had a higher probability than whites of being murdered by a firearm.

Tardiff et al. (1994) also showed that homicide victims aged 15–24 years old had a greater likelihood of being killed by a firearm than any other age group. Men were more likely than women to be murdered through the use of a firearm.

In addition, firearms-related homicide and associated drug use may be related to the location of the homicide. In Tardiff et al. (1995b)'s analysis, the most frequent locations of homicides were the streets and outdoor places (49.6%) and the victims' residences (19.3%). Firearms were the cause of death for 80.3% of victims murdered on the streets and other outdoor locations, and for 49.6% of the murders committed in residences. Homicide victims murdered on the streets were more likely to have used cocaine and ethanol than those murdered in their

S.J. Morewitz, *Death Threats and Violence*, DOI: 10.1007/978-0-387-76663-8_5,
© Springer Science+Business Media, LLC, 2008

residences. In addition, Tardiff et al. (1995a)'s analysis found that homicide victims who tested positive for cocaine and its metabolite, benzoylecgonine, were more likely to have been shot outdoors than victims who tested positive for opiates and ethanol.

School-Related Death Threats and Weapon Use

In an analysis of school-associated violent deaths, Kachur et al. (1996) found that homicide was the main cause of death, and that firearms were responsible for most of the deaths. In addition, there has been an increase in homicides perpetrated by juveniles, and this increase is associated with the use of firearms as the murder weapon (Snyder and Sickmund, 1999; infoplease.com, 2007b).

Miller et al. (2002a,b) evaluated juvenile deaths from 1988 to 1997 and showed that a disproportionately high number of children, ages 5–14 years, died from homicide, suicide, and unintentional gun-related deaths in states and regions of the U.S. where guns were more prevalent. Snyder and Sickmund (1999) reported that firearms were used in 54% of all homicides committed by juveniles between 1980 and 1987. These results support the traditional view that lax gun control laws increase the risk of school-related violent deaths (Klein, 2006).

The Centers for Disease Control and Prevention (CDC, 2003) analyzed school-associated violent death events between July 1, 1992 and June 30, 1999, and found that most of the firearms used in these incidents were obtained from the offenders' homes or from their friends or relatives.

What percentage of students brings weapons onto school property? The Youth Risk Behavior Surveillance System (YRBSS) asks students in grades 9 through 12 if they had carried a weapon, e.g., firearm, knife, or club anywhere or on school property in the previous 30 days (National Center for Education Statistics, 2006a). The survey revealed that in 2005, some 19% of the youngsters reported that they had carried a weapon anywhere, and about 6% indicated that they had carried a weapon on school property.

Between 1993 and 1997, the percentage of students who indicated that they carried a weapon anywhere declined from 22% to 18%. However, subsequently, there has been no significant change in the proportion of students who indicated that they carry a weapon anywhere. A similar trend was found for students who reported that they carry weapons on school property between 1993 and 1999; the rate declined from 12% to 7%. Between 1999 and 2005, there was no major change in the percentage of students who carried a weapon on school property.

Students are threatened or injured with weapons while they attend school and in other settings. The YRBSS asked students in grades 9 through 12 whether they had been threatened or injured with a weapon while on school property during the 12 months prior to the survey (National Center for Education Statistics, 2006b).

The percentage of students carrying weapons on school campuses may vary depending on different factors such as school characteristics. For example, a national study of alternative high schools using the YRBSS showed that 32.9% of the youths reported carrying a weapon during the 30 days prior to the survey (Grunbaum et al., 2000).

Individual risk factors also may influence whether a student carries weapons to school. Data from the YRBSS showed that boys are more than twice as likely as girls to carry a weapon, either anywhere or on school campuses (National Center for Education Statistics, 2006a). DuRant et al. (1997) evaluated weapon carrying and fighting on school property among high school students using the Massachusetts Youth Risk Behavior Survey. The researchers discovered that 15% of the male and 5% of the female high school students reported carrying weapons on school property 30 days before the survey.

Using data on 2,227 students from 53 middle schools in North Carolina, DuRant et al. (1999) revealed that increasing age, male gender, minority status, and substance use increased the risk that middle school students would carry guns on school property during school hours. In addition, they discovered that age, male gender, and substance use predicted carrying a knife or club on school property during school hours. Carrying a knife or club was also related to carrying a firearm, being threatened with a weapon at school, fighting, and substance use.

In their study of high school students, DuRant et al. (1997) showed that weapon carrying on school property was linked to: the prevalence of physical fights; being threatened or injured with a weapon; being the victim of theft or vandalism; substance use; and not attending school because of fear for their safety. The authors also found that high school students who participated in same-sex activity were more likely to carry a weapon on school property.

Death Threats and Weapon Use in Colleges and Universities

Based on a sample of 26,225 college students from the Core Alcohol and Drug Survey, researchers found that 7% of the students reported carrying a gun, knife or other weapon in the previous 30 days. The study also showed that college students who carry weapons were more likely than unarmed students to have suffered harassment, violence, or the threat of violence. Armed students were less likely than unarmed students to feel safe on campus (Presley et al., 1997).

Another investigation found that college students who possess firearms on campus were more likely to participate in activities, such as binge drinking and violent behavior after alcohol use, that place themselves and other persons at risk for injury (Miller et al., 2002a,b).

Workplace-Related Death Threats and Weapon Use

According to the U.S. Department of Justice, Bureaus of Justice Statistics study of job-related violence between 1992 and 1996, firearms were used to commit more than 80% of the job-associated homicides. The remaining 20% of the job-related homicides were caused by bombings, stabbings, or beatings (U.S. DoJ., 1998).

Death Threats and Weapon Use in Public Settings

Muggers often threaten their victims with firearms and other weapons in order to "persuade" them to part with their money and valuables. Individuals may "run amok" or go "berserk" and use weapons to kill or threaten to kill their victims and/or themselves. Stalkers may use weapons to threaten to kill celebrities and public officials in both public and private settings.

Death Threats, Weapons Use, and Domestic/Partner Violence

Individuals make death threats and use weapons to threaten or attack their victims in the context of partner and domestic violence (Rothman et al., 2005; Sorenson and Wiebe, 2004; Straus, 1979; Marshall, 1992). Most of the reported homicides in the U.S. occur between individuals who have had some previous relationship.

Because of cultural expectations and physical strength inequality, females are more likely to be the victim of violence rather than men. Abused women therefore are at increased risk of being killed by the male. Important risk factors for femicide are: having been previously threatened with a weapon; the male's easy access to a firearm; having the male's stepchild in the home; and separation from the abusive partner, especially from one who is overly controlling. Lower risks of femicide were related to having never having lived together and the male having been arrested for previous domestic violence (Campbell et al., 2003).

It is interesting to note that less than 15% of those arrested for homicide in the U.S. are females (U.S. DoJ., 1982, 1984). Although it is relatively rare, abused women have killed their abusive male partners, usually with a gun and often in self-defense following years of partner violence (Browne, 1987; Buda and Butler, 1985; Ewing, 1987; Walker, 1984; Dutton et al., 1994).

Walker (1984) compared battered women who murdered their abusive partners with battered women who did not kill their abusive partners and found that both groups had sustained major violence. Those women who killed their abusive male partners did so because they feared for their own lives and/or the lives of their family members. In this study, 57% of the abusers who were subsequently killed by their wives had previously threatened to kill their battered wives or close relatives (Walker, 1984).

Browne (1984) compared 42 abused women who had murdered their partners with a sample of 42 abused women who had not. This latter, comparison group had been drawn from a subset of battered women in Walker's (1984) earlier investigation. Eighty-three percent of the murdered men had previously threatened to kill their abused wives or their close relatives, compared to 39% in the non-homicide group.

These findings are supported by other studies such as Browne (1987)'s study, where 60% of the murdered men were assaulting or threatening to kill or harm their wives at the time of their own murder. Women who kill their abusive male partners often report that their partner had abused their children as well (Ewing, 1987).

Roberts (1996a,b) compared the prevalence of death threats based on a prison sample of 105 women who had killed their partners and were serving sentences at the Edna Mahon Correctional Institution for Women in Clinton, New Jersey, with a community sample consisting of 105 women (50 women from two police departments in suburban New Jersey and 55 women from two battered women shelters in New Jersey). The imprisoned women were more likely to report that a weapon had been used against them (39.7%) than those in the community sample (18.8%). About 66% of the incarcerated women reported that their abusive partner had threatened to kill them, 16 or 15.2% reported that he had threatened to kill children, and 20 or 19% claimed that he had threatened to kill a relative. In the community sample, 70 or 66.7% indicated that their abusive partner had threatened to murder them, 24 or 22.9% said he had allegedly threatened to kill children, and 33 or 31.4% said he had threatened to kill a relative.

O'Keefe (1998) was interested in the impact that the type and amount of violence suffered by battered women during the last year that they lived with their partner had on their future actions. He compared 50 abused women who had been incarcerated for homicide and serious assault against their male partners (42 convicted of different charges of spousal/partner homicide, 4 convicted of assault with a deadly weapon against their partners, and 4 convicted of conspiracy to kill or attempted murder) with 26 abused women convicted of other offenses such as forgery, grand theft, petty theft, prostitution, drug offenses, and child mistreatment. Using the Violence subscale of the Conflict Tactics Scale (Straus, 1979), the researcher discovered that compared to abused women incarcerated for other crimes, abused women who murdered or seriously assaulted their abusive partners were more likely to have been threatened by their partners with a firearm or knife and felt that their life was in jeopardy.

Pakieser et al. (1998) studied the prevalence of homicidal threats received by women, ages, 19–65 years, who presented to 10 emergency departments in two cities. They discovered that 55% of the women who disclosed a domestic battery incident stated that the offender had made a homicidal threat against them at some time.

Results from the Stalking and Violence Project (SVP) revealed that death threat (DT) victims were more likely than non-DT victims to be the target of weapons-related abuses (see Appendix B—Study Results, Table B.5). DT victims (19.1%) were more than three times as likely as non-DT victims (5.1%) to be threatened with a weapon, e.g., had a handgun pointed at them, and were more likely than non-DT victims to have had a weapon actually used against them, e.g., were assaulted with a blunt instrument (25.9% vs. 14.9%).

The availability of firearms and societal attitudes toward gun use may affect the incidence of homicide-suicides, which vary considerably among different countries (Aderibigbe, 1997). Countries with strict handgun control policies and negative societal attitudes toward gun use have lower homicide-suicide rates than those with liberal handgun control policies and positive societal attitudes about using guns.

In a study of homicide-suicides in Paris, France, and its suburbs, Lecomte and Fornes (1998) showed that in 80% of the cases, the perpetrator used a firearm for both the homicide and suicide. The offender used a knife in 4 homicides, and strangulation was used in 4 murders. Poisoning, beating, or arson was employed in only one case each. The perpetrator used a different weapon for the homicide and suicide in 9 homicide-suicides.

Hanzlick and Koponen (1994) examined the characteristics of murder-suicides in Fulton County, Georgia, between 1988 and 1991, and discovered that firearms (all handguns) were used in 92% of the deaths. An intimate relationship existed between the offender and victim in 67% of the homicide-suicides in this sample.

Investigators have constructed scales and questionnaires to measure violence, including different types of threats made against individuals (Straus, 1979; Marshall, 1992; Campbell, 1986; Hudson and McIntosh, 1981). These scales and questionnaires have helped to elucidate the prevalence, type, severity, and predictors of homicidal threats and other forms of violence that occur in the contexts of domestic violence and intimate partner relationships. They have been used to assess the prevalence and type of homicidal threats made against vulnerable groups, such as pregnant women and individuals in dating relationships. In addition, these scales are used to assess changes in the prevalence of homicidal threats over time to assist in predicting homicidal risks and to measure the effectiveness of violence intervention programs.

Straus (1979) included the item, "Threatened with a knife or gun," as a measure of violence in his widely validated and used Conflict Tactics Scale. The Violence Against Women Scales include homicidal threats: "Threatened to kill her," "Threatened her with a knife or gun," "Threatened her with a weapon" (Marshall, 1992).

The Danger Assessment Scale contains the item: "He has threatened to kill you or think he could" (Campbell, 1986). This scale also includes items dealing with other violent behaviors, such as violent jealousy, and threats to commit suicide by either the offenders or victims.

Owning a gun also may be a risk factor for making death threats (Rothman et al., 2005; Sorenson and Wiebe, 2004; MacDonald, 1968). Based on data from 8,529 men participating in certified batterer intervention programs in Massachusetts between 1999 and 2003, Rothman et al. (2005) found that gun ownership in the three years before the study began was a risk factor for threatening an intimate partner with a gun.

Other factors increase the likelihood that individuals will threaten their partners with a gun. For example, Rothman et al. (2005) showed that drug and alcohol abuse, homicidal behavior, and threatening with a knife were risk factors for threatening an intimate partner with a handgun. More data are needed to determine the characteristics of offenders who own, have access to, and use firearms against death threat victims.

Based on structured, in-person interviews with 417 women from 67 women's shelters, Sorenson and Wiebe (2004) showed that one third of the battered women had a firearm in their residence and in two thirds of these homes, the partner used the guns against the victim. Of these individuals, 71.4% reportedly used the gun (s) to threaten to shoot/kill the women and 5.1% of the offenders used the gun (s) to threaten to shoot at them.

In Pakieser et al. (1998)'s investigation of domestic battering incidents, a gun was used in 5% of the attacks, a knife in 4% of the attacks, and another object in 12% of the attacks. Offenders may use potentially lethal weapons, such as firearms, to make dramatic death threats. The use of these weapons bolsters the intensity of their threats and associated emotions.

In MacDonald (1968)'s sample, 51% of the psychiatric patients who made death threats owned a total of 81 firearms. As mentioned in Chapter 2, a number of patients in his sample had plans for committing suicide and these plans included the use of firearms, knives, and other weapons.

DT victims also face being threatened with other types of lethal weapons, and more research is needed to evaluate the prevalence, risk factors, and etiology of different weapons-related threats against DT victims, as well as the likelihood that weapons-based threats result in actual weapon use against DT victims.

Victims in Long-Term Relationships

The frustrations and pressures of dealing with the constraints of married life can result in a spouse's violent reaction that culminates in a death threat. Substance abuse, whether it be alcohol, or drugs can reduce a spouse's inhibition level to the point that he/she loses control and "on the spur of the moment" uses a weapon to threaten his/her partner. In other instances the irritated spouse may have developed a long-term plan to kill his wife. There are cases of sexual abuse within a long-term intimate relationship where the male partner uses the threat of a weapon to enable him to sexually assault his partner, and sometimes physically and verbally and sexually abuse his children as well.

In SVP case A101, Mr. B, was very upset with their 3-year-old daughter and his wife and threw his 3-year-old daughter's food into the garbage, smashing the pot at the same time. He complained that his wife couldn't do anything right, and that he was going to kill her with a knife. The tirade lasted for more than an hour, and the children ended up crying.

It is common for one spouse to make death threats against the other spouse at the time the latter is seeking a separation or divorce. The abusive spouse frequently damages or destroys the partners' personal property.

In SVP Case # 367C, Mrs. G, a 30-year-old woman, came to her estranged husband's apartment, tried to kick the door down, and threatened to f… him up and shoot him.

Other factors may be present that cause the offender to plan extensively his use of a weapon to kill his spouse.

In SVP case 0012C, Mr. N, a 56-year-old man, told a counselor that he had been ready to kill his wife a number of times when she was sleeping, but stopped when he thought of the children. In this same case, his wife reported that he raped her several times a week. "He wants to have sex, I tell him no, but he forces himself on me anyway." In addition, Mr. N was accused of having sexually abused his wife's young daughters, and physically and verbally abused all of her children.

Victims in Current or Previous Dating or Engagement Relationships

Those in dating relationships are at increased risk of weapons-related death threats, physical assault, and verbal harassment when they end or try to end the relationship. In many instances, the perpetrator threatens future use of a weapon, but does not actually display the weapon. The cases described below illustrate these behaviors:

In SVP case A104, Mr. F, a 41-year-old man, threatened to kill his girlfriend with a "shank" the next time that he saw her because she had refused to talk to him.

In SVP case A106, Mr. I, a 69-year-old man, tried to hit his ex-girlfriend with a hammer when she told him that she was ending their dating relationship. Mr. I verbally abused her and used third parties to harass both her and her family members.

DTMs' Gender

While both men and women have been known to threaten to kill their current or former partners and acquaintances with a weapon, men far outnumber the women in this type of scenario.

DTMs' Race/Ethnicity

Ethnic and cultural styles and traditions may influence the offenders' use of weapons against DT victims. In the SVP, if the offenders were white, DT victims were more than 21 times as likely as non-DT victims to be threatened with a weapon (21.1% vs. 0%) (see Appendix B—Study Results, Table B.14). DT victims had more than a four times greater chance than non-DT victims of being threatened with a weapon if the offenders were African-American (18.7% vs. 4.3%). If the perpetrators were Hispanic, DT victims were more than three times as likely as non-DT victims to be threatened with a weapon (19.4% vs. 5.2%).

However, White offenders were 13 times more likely to use a weapon against DT victims (22.6%) than non-DT victims (1.7%). In contrast, there were no differences between African-Americans and Hispanics in their use of weapons against DT and non-DT victims (Data are not included in the table.).

DTMs' Age

The DTMs' age may affect whether or not they use a weapon when threatening to kill their targets. In the SVP, if the DTMs were in the 18–25 year age group, DT targets were about 21 times more likely to be threatened with a weapon than non-DT targets (21.1% vs. 0%) (see Appendix B—Study Results, Table B.11). In the 26–40 year age group, DT victims were more than four times likely than non-DT victims to be threatened with a weapon (20.5% vs. 4.9%). The DT victims also were more likely to have had a weapon used against them if the offenders were in the 26–40 year age group (28.2% vs. 16.0%). However, in the 41–60 and 60 + age groups (Data are not included in the table.), there were no differences between DT targets and non-DT targets regarding threats to use a weapon or actual use of a weapon.

Victims' Assistance-Seeking Behaviors
for Weapons-Related Offenses

The findings of the SVP revealed that DT victims who were attacked with a weapon (73.3%) were more than 3 times as likely as non-DT victims (21.6%) to be treated in an emergency department for partner-associated injuries (see Appendix B—Study Results, Table B.12). DT victims in the SVP who were threatened with a weapon were not more likely than non-DT victims to be treated in the emergency department for partner-related injuries (data are not included in the table; see Appendix B—Study Results, Table B.12).

There were no differences in being threatened with a weapon or attacked with a weapon and being involved in police contacts (see Appendix B—Study Results, Table B.13).

Preventing Weapons-Related Deaths and Injuries

Nguyen et al. (2002) believe that prevention strategies can be effective in reducing weapons-associated deaths and injuries. In examining the period, 1985–1999, the researchers found that BB/pellet gun-associated injury rates increased from the late

1980s until the early 1990s and then declined until 1999. The authors also discovered a similar trend for fatal and nonfatal firearm-associated injury rates. They believe that the decline in BB/pellet- and gun-associated injury during this period is linked to the increased number of prevention strategies and programs designed to reduce injuries to children that result from youth violence and unsupervised access to guns. They recommended that further program studies at the local and state levels are needed to evaluate if these prevention efforts are continuing to be effective in reducing injuries to and deaths among children.

Chapter 6
Substance Use and Abuse, and Homicidal Threats

There is extensive research, which shows that substance use and abuse contributes to an increased risk of homicide. Alcohol and drug use, including cocaine, opiates, and methamphetamines, have been implicated as triggering or facilitating factors in homicides, including partner homicides and severe domestic violence incidents (Wolfgang, 1958; Sharps et al., 2001a,b; Cunradi et al., 2002; Kantor and Straus, 1989; Bailey and Shaw, 1989; Tardiff et al., 1994, 1995a; Harruff et al., 1988). Alcohol and drug intoxication is also linked to workplace violence (Tolhurst et al., 2003). Drugs and alcohol weaken the social control process as they lead to impairment in judgment, memory, and trigger rage, hatred, and associated violence.

As mentioned in Chapter 2, certain types of drugs are associated with behavior problems which can result in homicidal impulses and threats. Chronic use of high doses of methamphetamines can lead to hallucinations and delusions that are similar to a paranoid psychosis and not distinguishable from schizophrenia (Hanson et al., 2006). It also can produce disorganized patterns of thought and behavior, irritability, suspiciousness, and irrational fear. These behaviors increase the risk of police involvement. Withdrawal from methamphetamines after chronic high-dose use can lead to depression and suicide attempts.

Wolfgang (1958) found that alcohol was a factor in 64% of homicides and in 44% of the homicides both offenders and victims had been drinking. MacDonald (1961) discovered that one third or more of homicide offenders were drunk at the time of the homicide. Riedel et al. (1985), in a study of 8 cities in the U.S., showed that the percentage of homicide victims who had tested positive for alcohol ranged from 38.4% to 62%. Alcoholic intoxication also may actually lead to amnesia so that individuals may not remember that they had made homicidal threats while in an intoxicated state (MacDonald, 1968).

Cocaine use and firearms have been associated with high rates of homicide. In their study of homicides in New York City, Tardiff et al. (1994) discovered that 31.0% of the homicide victims tested positive for cocaine metabolites. The researchers found that African Americans, Latinos, and victims in the 25–34 and the 35–44 year age groups had a greater likelihood of testing positive for the cocaine metabolite than other groups. Firearms were involved in about three fourths of all the homicides.

S.J. Morewitz, *Death Threats and Violence*, DOI: 10.1007/978-0-387-76663-8_6,

Other studies have documented cocaine and/or amphetamine use among homicide victims (Bailey and Shaw, 1989; Harruff et al., 1988; Zhu et al., 2000). In a study of cocaine- and methamphetamine-associated fatalities in San Diego County in 1987, Bailey and Shaw (1989) showed that cocaine use was involved 66 fatalities (39 homicides and 27 accidental overdoses and methamphetamines in 10 cases (4 homicides and 6 accidental overdoses).

In a study of cocaine use and homicide in Memphis and Shelby County from 1980 to 1986, Harruff et al. (1988) reported that 46 of the 87 cocaine-associated fatalities were homicides. In 1986 alone, the researchers found 87 cocaine-associated deaths and 31 cocaine-associated homicides. Research has shown that some homicide victims were using multiple drugs at the time of their death (Tardiff et al., 1995a; Bailey and Shaw, 1989).

In addition, drugs and alcohol may increase the probability of homicide-suicides (Centers for Disease Control and Prevention (CDC), 1991). In a study of homicide-suicides in Kentucky, between 1985 and 1990, available postmortem results revealed that 21% of the perpetrators of homicide-suicides were legally intoxicated. Chronic alcoholism was detected in 16 of 56 homicide-suicides in Paris and its suburbs, between 1991 and 1996 (Lecomte and Fornes, 1998).

Persons who are taking prescription drugs for mental disorders, such as psychosis and depression, may be at risk both for making death threats and carrying out those threats. Even under medication, some of these individuals may still behave erratically, or violently, while others may show no signs of either. There are reports that the gunman in the Virginia Tech massacre, Cho Seung-Hui, may have been taking medication for depression, and that he was becoming increasingly violent and erratic before he went on his lethal rampage at the campus.

MacDonald (1968) substantiated the association between substance abuse and homicide. In his psychiatric in-patient sample, he discovered that 60% of the adult non-psychotic males and 60% of the adult non-psychotic females had been drinking alcohol before making homicidal threats. On the other hand, he found that 80% of the adult psychotic females and none of the adult psychotic males had been consuming alcohol before making death threats. He also showed that 50% of the adult non-psychotic patients had a history of heavy alcohol consumption and alcohol-related impairment in social or work functioning. In contrast, almost 25% of the psychotic patients had a history of excessive drinking and related occupational or social impairment.

Substance use is linked to weapon carrying or firearm possession among middle school, high school, and college students (DuRant et al., 1999, 1997; Presley et al., 1997; Miller et al., 2002a,b). In their investigation of 2,227 middle school students in North Carolina, DuRant et al. (1999) showed that weapon carrying (including a knife or club) was linked to early onset of smoking cigarettes as well as the frequent use of alcohol, marijuana, and cocaine. DuRant et al. (1997) also found that among 3,054 high school students:

1. Substance use at school, including cigarette use, chewing tobacco, smoking marijuana, and drinking alcohol, predicted weapon carrying.

2. There was a stronger association between alcohol use and carrying a weapon on school property among students who were afraid to go to school than those who were not fearful.
3. Students who had been offered, provided, or sold illegal drugs at school had a greater probability of carrying a weapon on school property.
4. Students who engaged in same-sex sexual behaviors had a greater likelihood of carrying a weapon to school than those who did not participate in those behaviors.

In Presley et al.'s (1997) study of 26,225 students, weapon-carrying male college students were more likely than unarmed male college students to consume more alcohol, binge drink, use other drugs, and suffer negative effects from substance abuse. However, the associations between substance abuse and outcomes were less consistent when comparing armed female college students and unarmed female college students.

Based on a sample of 10,000 undergraduate students, Miller et al. (2002a,b) showed that binge drinking and high-risk and violent behaviors after drinking were linked to gun possession. The authors conclude the college students who report having guns at college are more likely to state that they participate in behaviors that put them and others at risk for injury.

Research is needed to evaluate whether perpetrators who use alcohol and drugs are more likely to commit a variety of physical, sexual, emotional, and mental abuses against death threat victims due to the disinhibiting effects of substance use. For example, Boeringer (1996) found that alcohol and drug intoxication increased the likelihood that male fraternity members in college would engage in sexual aggression and coercion against women.

Substance Use and Partner Violence

In a study of alcohol use in intimate partner female homicide (femicide) in 10 cities, Sharps et al. (2001a,b) showed that problem drinking among offenders was related to an eight-fold increase in partner violence and a two fold increase in the risk of femicide/attempted femicide.

Using a multiethnic sample of 1,613 married and cohabiting couples, Cunradi et al. (2002) discovered that alcohol-associated problems among men and women and other drug use among women are associated with the severity of intimate partner violence.

Based on data from a national sample of 6,002 households, Kantor and Straus (1989) showed that the husband's drug use, a history of paternal abuse in the wife's family of origin, the husband's intoxication, low income and the woman's intoxication predicted wife abuse. The researchers found that women who abuse alcohol had a higher likelihood of being the victim of minor violence, but women's abuse of any type of substance did not predict severe violence.

Different causal processes may underlie the link between substance use and spouse abuse in Kantor and Straus (1989)'s study and other research. The pharmacologic impact of alcohol and other drug use by victims may increase their risk of being assaulted. This may take place because of impaired judgment, memory, or misinterpretation of the partner's behavior or statements. Intoxicated victims may be less able to protect themselves from their abusive partners or avoid their abusers in a conflict.

Other researchers have demonstrated that substance abuse can trigger increased aggressiveness (Kantor and Straus, 1989; Powers and Kutash, 1982). According to Kantor and Straus (1989), alcohol is a central nervous system depressant, nevertheless they note that the physiological impact of alcohol on abusive behaviors depends on the social meanings and scripts that alcohol users have learned to relate to feeling intoxicated.

Kantor and Straus (1989) assert that hallucinogens, central nervous system stimulants or combinations of drugs may more often trigger aggressive behavior (Kantor and Straus, 1989; Tinklenberg, 1973). However, a person's mental status and the social context of drug use shape all drug responses.

Conflict over substance abuse may increase family conflict and thus indirectly increase spouse abuse. The drug bond shared by the couple can provide a way of coping with stress and yet also be a source of conflict for them (Kantor and Straus, 1989). Other studies have shown that many of the narcotic-dependent women are attacked by their substance-dependent partners (Rosenbaum, 1981).

Gender differences in norms concerning alcohol and drug use may contribute to wife abuse (Kantor and Straus, 1989). Drinking and intoxication are considered macho, while women who engage in these same behaviors may be viewed as having questionable morals. Women who violate these gender norms may open themselves up to physical abuse and rape. Sandmaier (1980) gives an example of a husband who assaulted his wife if he smelled alcohol on her.

Women who drink alcohol may violate other gender roles since, like their male counterparts, women may become more aggressive when they consume alcohol (Kantor and Straus, 1989). However, in contrast to men, women are supposed to be passive. Therefore, when women drink and become verbally aggressive, they may lose the protection traditionally afforded to "ladies" (Young et al., 1975).

It is important to note that that substance abuse may be a consequence of physical violence. For example, an analysis of hospital records revealed that abused women are more likely to have drug problems than nonabused women (Stark et al., 1981).

In MacDonald (1968)'s investigation of 100 psychiatric in-patients who made death threats, 60% of the adult non-psychotic males and 60% of the adult non-psychotic females had been consuming alcohol before making the death threats. In his sample, 0% of the adult psychotic males and 80% of the adult psychotic females had been drinking alcohol before making the death threat. He noted that 50% of the adult non-psychotic patients had a history of alcohol impairment, while almost 25% of the adult psychotic patients had such a history.

Findings from the Stalking and Violence Project (SVP) showed that, according to the victims of partner abuse, alcohol and illicit drug use was associated with

25.9% of the cases involving homicidal threats (see Appendix B—Study Results, Table B.6). However, alcohol and illicit drug use as a cause of partner violence did not differ between DT victims and non-DT victims.

Offenders who are intoxicated often engage in other harassing behaviors and physical violence, including child abuse and abuse of pets, and vandalism.

In SVP case 157C, Mr. C reportedly came home intoxicated almost every night and frequently made death threats against his wife. She also reported that while intoxicated, her husband often damaged household items, attacked their dog and cats, and verbally abused her and her stepchildren. He also reportedly slashed her automobile's tires.

Chapter 7
Death Threats and Violence at Schools and Colleges

This chapter examines the nature of death threats and other violence against schools and universities. Death threats and violence against schools and universities reflect the inability of families, schools, universities, and other social institutions to regulate the behavior of children, adolescents, and adults. Access to lethal weapons, inadequate family socialization, school bullying and teasing, mental disorders in young children, adolescents, and adults, plus media-oriented "copy-cat" violence may increase the risks for school and university shootings. In these instances, students transform private rages and mental disorders into school-and university-related tragedies. Individuals who feel powerless and downtrodden use school shootings to regain their power and take revenge against the world. In this way, private, individual problems are turned into an institutional problem, which requires new adaptive responses by parents, instructors, school and university administrators, law enforcement personnel, and political leaders.

Death Threats and School Shootings

School-related death threats, threatening comments, and school shootings have occurred with regularity since the 1960s, and these incidents continue to cause public concern about the safety of school-age children and adolescents (Kachur et al., 1996; Anderson et al., 2001; infoplease.com, 2007a; Wikipedia, 2007d; CNN, 1999a,b; Mushinski, 1996; Dobnik, 2007).

Based on an analysis of two online news databases, police reports, medical examiners' records, and interviews with police and school administrators, Kachur et al. (1996) evaluated trends in school-associated deaths in the United States between July 1, 1992, and June 30, 1994. The authors estimated the incidence of school-related violent deaths was 0.09 per 100,000 student-years. The researchers concluded that school-related violent deaths were more prevalent than previously estimated.

The Centers for Disease Control and Prevention (CDC, 2003) analyzed school-related violent death events between July 1, 1992 and June 30, 1999, and discovered that 323 violent death events took place, resulting in 358 deaths.

S.J. Morewitz, *Death Threats and Violence*, DOI: 10.1007/978-0-387-76663-8_7,
© Springer Science+Business Media, LLC, 2008

Anderson et al. (2001), using data collected from media databases, state and local agencies, and police and school officials, analyzed school-related violent deaths in the United States between July 1, 1994 and June 30, 1999. They discovered that there were 220 events that resulted in 235 deaths. One victim was killed in each of 202 events and multiple fatalities occurred in 18 of the incidents. The median number of victims in the multiple-victim incidents was two. A majority of the incidents were homicides ($N=172$), followed by suicides ($N=30$), combined homicide-suicides ($N=11$), legal intervention deaths ($N=5$), and unintentional firearm-associated fatalities ($N=2$).

The researchers found that the incidence of single-victim student homicides actually decreased significantly during the study period (Anderson et al., 2001). However, the rate of multiple-victim student homicides increased significantly.

In many of the student homicides ($N=120$), there was a threat, note, or other action that may have revealed a risk for violence before the shooting incident (Anderson et al., 2001). For example, one of the assailants in the Jonesboro school massacre had made a death threat prior to going on a shooting rampage (*Wikipedia*, 2007b). On March 24, 1998, Mitchell Johnson, age 13, and Andrew Golden, age 11, were two middle school boys who committed the Jonesboro school massacre, close to northwestern Jonesboro, Arkansas. The two boys murdered four female students and one teacher and wounded 9 other students and a teacher The two shooters dressed in army-style camouflaged, stole a van from the Johnson's home and had 7 weapons, including two semi-automatic rifles which they had stolen from Golden's grandfather's home.

Both shooters had come from broken homes (*Wikipedia*, 2007b). Johnson's mother was a guard at a prison, and she had remarried an inmate from the facility. Johnson reportedly had a good relationship with his stepfather and siblings. He was described by adults as quiet and respectful and had attended church regularly and sang in the choir. However, fellow students of Johnson described him as a braggart and a bully. Johnson reportedly had talked of wanting to join gangs and smoke marijuana. He also reportedly talked about "having a lot of killing to do."

Andrew Golden, according to his fellow students, previously had shot a classmate in the face with a pellet gun (*Wikipedia*, 2007b). Golden reportedly once had killed a friend's cat and dumped it in the trash. However, no charges had been made against him. There was also a report that both Johnson and Golden were fascinated with rap music, guns, and violent television programs.

While in custody after the massacre, the media reported that both boys cried and exhibited remorse (*Wikipedia*, 2007b). However, guards at the Jonesboro jail reported that they were faking remorse and that the two boys slept and ate well and seemed to be mostly unaware of the severity of their crimes. At a facility where they were later confined, fellow inmates reported that the two boys bragged about their crimes, especially the murder of Shannon Wright.

The Jonesboro school massacre was a major media event, and it seemed to trigger copycat school incidents or threats to attack schools. One year later, on

April 20, 1999, the Columbine High School massacre occurred in Littleton, CO, in which 14 students and a teacher were killed in a gun and bomb assault on the school campus (CNN, 1999b,e). Two seniors at the school, Eric Harris and Dylan Klebold were the killers, who proceeded methodically through the school grounds and building killing their victims before killing themselves. The shooters were reported to have been the targets of repeated bullying and teasing.

There were reports that Eric Harris and Dylan Klebold belonged to the "Trenchcoat Mafia," a loosely organized group of so-called outsiders at the school (Bronski, 1999). The Trenchcoat Mafia members reportedly wore swastikas and other Nazi symbols, but this was disputed by some Columbine students.

Before the Columbine massacre, Harris reportedly had been prescribed an anti-depressant medication, Luvox, which is often used in the treatment of obsessive-compulsive disorders (CNN, 1999c). The Marine Corp reportedly had rejected Harris because he was under the care of a physician and had been treated with an anti-depressant medication.

Police and school officials were informed that one of the shooters, Eric Harris, had been detonating pipe bombs and talking about killing people around the time of Jonesboro school massacre and more than a year before the Columbine High School massacre. The parents of a fellow student of Harris, Randy and Judy Brown, filed a police report in March 1998 and turned over messages from Harris' web site which discussed bomb making and murder. One of the messages said "I can't wait until I kill all you people."

Deputy Neil Gardner, whose jurisdiction covered Columbine High School, was informed of these threats and began monitoring Harris and Klebold. Deputy Gardner also notified a dean at Columbine about Harris' threats.

The Browns filed another police report one month later, stating that their son had received an anonymous e-mail threat and received a death threat on Harris' web site. Judy Brown also asked for help from an investigator in the District Attorney Office, who suggested contacting the sheriff's department and obtaining a restraining order against Harris. According to David Thomas, Jefferson County District Attorney, there is no evidence that a restraining order was ever obtained.

Harris and Klebold were in a juvenile offenders' diversion program after being charged with burglary at the time that the Browns had filed their police report (CNN, 1999e). However, the prosecutors were not informed about the Browns' complaint at the time since the two boys had not been charged with a crime for making threats.

The police did not file charges against Harris at that time because they could not find his web site. Lt. John Kiekbusch of the Jefferson County, Colorado, Sheriff's Department reported that even if the police had located Harris' Web site it is apparently not illegal to post threats on the Internet. Lt. Kiekbusch further noted that the police had done everything reasonable, given its workload and policies (CNN, 1999e).

School Violence Resulting from Imitation: Impact
of the Media Coverage of the Columbine School Massacre

Widespread media attention devoted to the highly dramatic Columbine school massacre may have led to other school incidents, threats, and hoaxes (Dobnik, 2007; Kostinsky et al., 2001). After the school shootings in Littleton, Colorado, school officials, police, and the media reported many bomb threats and threats of other school violence that were thought to be due to imitation.

In Jefferson County, Colorado, about ten days after the Columbine massacre, the police arrested one individual for an alleged bomb threat and arrested another for making a hoax threat related to the Columbine massacre (CNN, 1999e). A hardware store employee, Gary Sowell, told the media and police that he had sold propane tanks, wire, screws, and other items to someone. According to District Attorney Thomas, the police examined store sales records and believed that Sowell was lying. He was arrested for providing false information about a crime to the police.

The police also arrested Rae Holt for making a false bomb threat over the phone directed at Pomona High School, another school in the Denver, Colorado area. Holt, who is a parent of a Pomona student, was charged with false reporting of explosives and felony menacing, both of which carry a sentence of up to 4 ½ years in prison. Apparently she was angry over the way school officials were treating her son, and left a telephone message at the school threatening the students and the school. She went on to say that this is not a joke. School officials recognized her voice on the recording and notified the police who arrested her.

District Attorney Thomas noted that school officials are experiencing many false reports of school threats and as a result they are going to punish those who make false reports (CNN, 1999e). Both of the above mentioned incidents, according to Thomas, had diverted attention and resources away from investigating the Columbine massacre.

Nine days after the Columbine massacre, five boys at McKinley Junior High School in Brooklyn, New York, were charged with conspiracy to blow up their school (CNN, 1999d).

Kostinsky et al. (2001) evaluated the threats of school violence in Pennsylvania following the Columbine shooting rampage. The investigators measured the frequency of threats in that state based on the numbers of threats of school violence that had been reported to the Pennsylvania Emergency Management Agency, Harrisburg, Pennsylvania, during the 50 days following the Columbine shootings. They sought to determine if the clustering of threats of school violence were due to imitation and which factors predicted the likelihood of threats. The authors discovered that during the 50 days after the Columbine shootings, there were 354 threats of school violence. These results far exceeded the 1 or 2 threats per year school officials estimated they received before 1999. Over time, the frequency of school violence threats developed a crescendo-decrescendo pattern. On or before the 10th day following the Columbine massacre, 56% of the threats had been made. On the 8th through the 10th days following the shootings, more than one third of the threats had taken place. The researchers identified two factors predictive of threats: schools with a higher proportion of white students and those with larger school population. These findings suggest that threats of school violence following a massacre are significantly influenced by imitation. The two assailants in the Columbine incident were white and Columbine had a large student population at the time of the massacre, indicating that students who share similar characteristics as the two shooters could relate to them and attempt to follow their lead in their own schools.

From April 20, 1999, the date of the Columbine massacre, through January 3, 2007, thirty-three school shootings occurred in different states and several countries, and most of them resulted in fatalities. Victims in these school shootings have included students, teachers, administrators, a guidance counselor, etc. All but one of the offenders was male. The suspects were mostly teenagers who reportedly acted alone in carrying out their attacks. The assailants frequently used firearms, such as a 9mm semiautomatic handgun (December 6, 1999, Fort Gibson, Oklahoma) and a .32-caliber handgun (February 29, 2000, Mount Morris Township, Michigan) (infoplease.com, 2007a).

In two school shootings, the assailants were reported to have shown symptoms of depression. One of the shooters, Elizabeth Catherine Bush, age 14, shot and wounded another student, Kimberly Marchese at Bishop Neuman High School. The shooter was reportedly depressed and often had been teased by other classmates (March 7, 2001, Williamsport, Pennsylvania). Another assailant, Thomas Solomon, age 15, was reportedly depressed after breaking up with his girl friend (May 20, 1999, Conyers, Georgia).

Christopher Williams, age 27, was looking for his ex-girl friend at the time he reportedly shot two teachers at Essex Elementary School, killing one teacher and wounding another (August 24, 2006, Essex, Vermont) (infoplease.com, 2007a).

Assailants in several of the school incidents reportedly were frequently teased and ostracized and a few of them had been expelled or had dropped out of school. On February 19, 2002, in Freising, Germany, a man killed the headmaster at the technical school in Germany from which he had been expelled. On April 28, 1999, eight days after the Columbine massacre, a 14-year-old boy killed one student and wounded another at the W.R. Myers High School in Taber, Alberta, Canada. The boy had dropped out of school after being ostracized by fellow students (infoplease. com, 2007a).

In two of the school shootings, the offenders took hostages. In one school shooting, the assailant, Chris Buschbacher, 17-years-old, took two hostages at the Caro Learning Center before killing himself (November 12, 2001, Caro, Michigan). In the other incident, an adult male took six students hostage at Plate Canyon High School and then shot and killed Emily Keyes, age 16, and himself (September 26, 2006, Bailey, Colorado).

Another shooter, Christopher Williams, 27-years-old, killed his victim during a fight. Williams had murdered his ex-girlfriend's mother before going to the school and killing one teacher and wounding another (August 24, 2006, Essex, Vermont).

On March 21, 2005, in Red Lake, Minnesota at the Red Lake Indian Reservation, a 16-year-old boy, Jeff Weise, killed his grandfather and his grandfather's girlfriend, and then went to his school, where he murdered five students, a teacher, a security guard, and then committed suicide. Weise, like some of the other suspects in school shootings, was characterized as a misfit, a loner, and a troubled boy, who enjoyed violent short stories and animations. Like the Columbine shooters, Eric Harris and Dylan, Weise favored neo-Nazi culture. It was reported that Weise had been teased and bullied repeatedly by his classmates (infoplease.com, 2007a; Lee, 2005).

In some of these school shootings, the assailants committed both homicide and suicide (infoplease.com, 2007a).

Risk Factors for School-Related Violent Deaths

Although school-associated violent deaths are rare, they occur with enough regularity that certain risk factors and characteristics may be identified (Anderson et al., 2001).

Based on a descriptive case series of school-related violent deaths between 1992 and 1994, Kachur et al. (1996) found that both victims and perpetrators tended to be young and male. Studies show that young males tend to be more aggressive than other groups.

Being the victim of violence increases one's risk of becoming an offender in school-related violent deaths (Lee, 2005). Boys who grow up exposed to domestic and partner violence may be at increased risk. Boys who experience neighborhood and community violence may also have a higher probability of becoming violent.

Students in secondary schools had a greater probability of dying in school-associated violent deaths than students in elementary schools. Students from racial and ethnic minority groups were at greater risk of dying in school-associated violent deaths than nonminority students (Kachur et al., 1996).

With regard to perpetrators, Kimmel and Mahler (2003) assert that white boys might be more likely than African-American boys to initiate school shootings.

Students in urban school districts had a greater chance of dying in school-related violent deaths than those from nonurban school districts. Homicide was the main cause of death in these school-related violent deaths, and firearms were responsible for most of the deaths (Kachur et al., 1996). Access to and availability of firearms increases the risk of deaths from homicide, suicide, and unintentional firearms-related juvenile deaths (Miller et al., 2002a,b).

Most events took place around the start of the school day, the lunch period, or at the end of the school day (Anderson et al., 2001). The Centers for Disease Control and Prevention (CDC, 2001) tracked school-related violent deaths in the U.S. since the 1992–1993 school year and discovered that student homicide rates are highest near the beginning of the fall and spring semesters and student-associated suicides are highest during the spring semester.

Offenders are more likely than victims to show some type of suicidal behavior before the event (Anderson et al., 2001). A note, death threat, or other activity that potentially indicated a risk for violence is a risk factor. They may write about their suicidal thoughts or write a suicide letter. Prior to the Columbine school massacre, one of the shooters, Eric Harris, wrote about rigging up explosives all over a town and detonating each one of the explosives. He indicated that he did not care if he lived or died in the shooting rampage. Harris just wanted to kill and injure as many individuals as possible (Immelman, 1999).

Young males may be more likely than others to feel challenged about their manhood. Children, especially boys, who are teased and bullied by their classmates about being gay or other stigmatizing conditions may be at increased risk of becoming shooters (Anderson et al., 2001; Klein, 2006; Kimmel and Mahler, 2003). A number of the shooting incidents involved boys who had been teased and bullied repeatedly about being gay even though there was no evidence that they were actually gay. Klein (2006) noted that many of the shootings occurred after classmates, both "preps" and "jocks" had relentlessly teased and bullied the assailants about being gay.

Kimmel and Mahler (2003) suggest that the perpetrators retaliated against these threats to their manhood. Similarly, Klein (2006) proposed that boys, who feel that they should be respected, and are instead cruelly teased and bullied by their class-mates, may seek to avenge the wrong by going on school shooting spree. Thus, the so-called "boy code," a culture in which anti-gay teasing and bullying are accepted as "boys being boys," may be a major risk factor for school shootings (Lee, 2005).

In this culture, aggression and violence are viewed as appropriate ways to express one's masculinity. Kimmel and Mahler (2003) found that the school shoot-ers in their study of 28 random school incidents were examples of "overconform-ists" to the notion that it is essential to aggressively defend one's manhood when it is being sullied by cruel and repeated teasing and bullying. However, this viewpoint may be over-simplified (Lee, 2005). Boys' homicidal and suicidal responses to teasing and bullying reflect more than just tensions over masculinity. They occur when boys have a reduced self-identity.

Kimmel and Mahler (2003 indicate that most boys who are teased or bullied develop psychosocial resilience that enables them to cope with these repeated traumatic events without turning to violent acts. However, assailants in school shootings may not have developed the resilience to endure relentless threats to their self-esteem and identity. Barry Loukaitis, age 14, the offender in the Frontier High School, Moses Lake, Washington, shooting, stated during his trial that he had planned to murder his classmate, Manuel Vela, after Vela had repeatedly called him a "faggot" a month before the shooting (Lee, 2005).

The two shooters in the Columbine school massacre often were called gay by athletes at the school. One football player at the school told *Time* magazine that Harris and Klebold were homosexuals and that if you want to "get rid of someone," you keep teasing them.

Shooters who were teased and bullied about being gay had other characteristics that may have increased their risk of being harassed (Lee, 2005). For example, Luke

Woodham, age 16, the assailant in the Pearl High School, school shooting in Pearl, Mississippi, had been repeatedly teased because of his weight and was called a fag and gay. Charles Andrew Williams, age 15, the assailant in the Santana High School shooting in Santee, California, was a new student at the time of the incident and was teased about being gay.

The teasing and bullying can go on for years. Michael Carneal, age 14, the assailant in the Heath High School shooting in West Paducah, Kentucky, reportedly had suffered years of anti-gay harassment after the school newspaper published a rumor that he was in love with another male student (infoplease.com, 2007a).

Shooters in the Columbine school massacre were characterized as outsiders who had an affinity for the Neo-Nazis and "The Trenchcoat Mafia" and a fascination with violence. Boys who are socially marginal may be at risk to become school shooters.

Another risk is exposure to media violence and having role models who emphasize the use of gratuitous weapons-related violence (Klein, 2006; Lee, 2005). Boys' extensive exposure to violence in the media, computer games, and videos is thought to promote school-associated violent deaths as they model their aggressive behaviors based on socially approved role models who are violent (Lee, 2005).

In addition, boys who grow up in broken homes and who have parents who are unable to effectively socialize or supervise them are also at risk for becoming offenders in school shootings (Klein, 2006). Teenage use of alcohol and drugs can impair judgment, lead to other risky behaviors, and reflect nonconformity with societal values. Other possible risk factors for children include poverty, inadequate educational opportunities, and social isolation.

Psychosocial Impact of School-Associated Violent Deaths

Widely publicized school shootings such as the Jonesboro and Columbine school massacres can have a major psychosocial impact on students, teachers, and staff. The Columbine shooting rampage appeared to have significant psychosocial effects on students and others (Brener et al., 2002; Schubert and Seiring, 2000). One study analyzed nationally representative data from the 1999 Youth Risk Behavior Surveillance System (YRBSS) to assess the effect of the Columbine school massacre on students' violence- and suicide-associated behaviors. The study found that students who completed the survey after the Columbine incident were more likely to indicate that they felt too unsafe to attend school and less likely to be planning to commit suicide than those who completed the YRBSS before the school massacre (Brener et al., 2002).

Given the potentially worldwide impact of the media, it is possible to assess the effects of school shooting in different countries. German researchers noted the significance of current and often dramatized media reports of school shootings and decided to evaluate the experiences and approaches in Berlin. They found that students often felt threatened by other teenagers (Schubert and Seiring, 2000).

To what extent can school shootings lead to Post Traumatic Stress Disorder (PTSD) in community residents? Palinkas et al. (2004) analyzed the psychosocial impact of two separate school shootings among community residents. A sample of 85 community residents was asked about their responses to shooting incidents at two different high schools within the same school district in San Diego East County. The researchers discovered three patterns of responses among community residents. First, about 53% of those interviewed indicated that they had intrusive reminders of the school shootings due to the media's extensive coverage of the events and subsequent threats of school violence, rumors, and hoaxes. Second, about 45% of the community residents sampled stated that they had tried to avoid thoughts, feelings, discussions, or locations related to the school shootings. These residents also reported having negative views of the media portrayal of the school incidents and felt that these incidents generally cannot be prevented. Finally, about 31% stated that they were angered, hyper-vigilant, and showed other evidence of increased arousal. In addition, about 27% of those interviewed reported fear, anxiety, depression, drug use, and other related symptoms in themselves or in other people. The authors conclude that widely publicized school shootings can trigger symptoms of PTSD among community residents (Palinkas et al., 2004).

Both the Jonesboro and Columbine shooting rampages reveal that emergency personnel will have to be prepared to handle future tragedies that result in multiple casualties (Hospital Security and Safety Management, 1999).

Fighting, School Bullying, and Weapon Carrying

In the U.S., violence is prevalent and youth, ages 10–29, are disproportionately affected. In 2003, 5,570 persons, ages 10–24, were killed. Eighty-two of these homicide victims were murdered with a firearm. More than 750,000 individuals, ages 10–24, were treated in emergency departments for violence-related injuries in 2004 (CDC, 2006).

Youth violence involves the use of physical force or power, threatened or actual (Mercy et al., 2002). It includes fighting, school bullying, teasing, and weapon carrying. In addition to perpetrators and offenders, bystanders may be exposed to incidents of violence (Stueve et al., 2006).

Students engage in a variety of violent behaviors at school as well as away from school. They may make death threats or threats of physical harm. In many instances, youth will use weapons in making these threats, while in other cases they will make death threats and other threatening comments or gestures without the use of weapons (Alikasifoglu et al., 2004; Mushinski, 1996).

Some students fear youth violence, including the threat of violence, and some students carry weapons to school in order to protect themselves. According to Schubert and Seiring (2000), research shows that students are willing to arm themselves for self-protection.

Based on data from the MetLife annual survey, Mushinski (1996) found that students in urban schools had the greatest likelihood of reporting behaviors such as gang violence, fighting between students, threats or violent behaviors or hostile/ threatening comments as major issues in their schools. The survey results also revealed that almost 20% of the students surveyed noted that they were at least somewhat afraid of being assaulted in or near their schools. Fear of being attacked was higher in urban (27%) than in non-urban schools (15%). Minority students were twice as likely as white students to view gang conflict and turf battles as a serious issue.

A national study of high school students in the U.S. revealed that 33% indicated that they had been in a physical fight at least once in the 12 months before the survey (CDC, 2004). The results also showed that 17% reported carrying a weapon, such as a firearm, knife, or club, on one or more of the 30 days before the survey.

Using the results of the National Alternative High School Youth Risk Behavior Survey (a component of the YRBSS), Grunbaum et al. (2000) evaluated the incidence of weapon carrying in a sample of students in grades 9 through 12 in the U.S. They discovered that 32.9% of the students surveyed reported that they had carried a weapon during the 30 days before the survey.

In a study of 1,720 Turkish high school students, 42% stated that they had been in a physical fight in the last 12 months before the survey, and 7% indicated that they had been involved in a fight, which necessitated medical treatment (Alikasifoglu et al., 2004).

Researchers have identified risk factors that increase the probability that youth will engage in violence (Department of Health and Human Services (DHHS), 2001; Lipsey and Derzon, 1998; Resnick et al., 2004; Mercy et al., 2002; Centers for Disease Control and Prevention, Youth Violence: Fact Sheet). These risk factors include individual (e.g., history of violent victimization, exposure to domestic violence), family (e.g., low parental involvement, inconsistent discipline), peer/school (e.g., differential association, poor academic achievement), and community (e.g., socially disorganized communities, low socioeconomic status).

Some studies have examined individual risk factors. For example, Smith-Khuri et al. (2004) in their cross-national study, discovered that smoking, alcohol use, irritability or bad temper, and a history of being bullied were significantly related to fighting. Based on the results of a survey of Turkish high school students, Alikasifoglu et al. (2004) found that being male, sexually active, smoking cigarettes, illegal drug use, bullying, being bullied with a weapon, carrying a weapon and not wearing automobile seat belts were related to fighting. They also found one social risk factor, spending more time with friends, to be associated with fighting.

Other investigators have emphasized the contributions of community, family, and school variables to student victimization, including being threatened. One study evaluated students and their families using a nationally representative sample of 10,400 Israeli students in grades 7 through 11 in 162 schools (Khoury-Kassabri et al., 2004). The researchers showed that higher levels of student victimization were associated with overcrowded classes, but school size did not predict victimization. They also discovered that the socioeconomic status (SES) of the school's neighborhood and students were moderately predictive of student victimization.

A number of protective factors may limit a person's risk of becoming violent (DHHS, 2001; Lipsey and Derzon, 1998; Resnick et al., 2004; CDC, 2007). These protective factors include individual (e.g., positive social perspective, religiosity), family (e.g., good communication with parents, frequent participation in activities with parents), and peer/school (e.g., commitment to school and participation in social activities).

Researchers have also focused on bullying as a form of youth violence. Some studies have shown a link between Machiavellian beliefs and school bully/victim problems. One investigation involving 186 students in grades 4 through 6 found that both bullying and being a victim are associated with most of the following factors: lack of faith in human nature, manipulation, dishonesty, and distrust. Bullying and victimization were also related to measures of overall Machiavellianism and self-efficacy (Andreou, 2004).

Based on a representative sample of 15,686 students in grades 6 through 10 in U.S. public and private schools, Nansel et al. (2001) evaluated bullying behaviors using the World Health Organization's Health Behaviors in School-aged Children survey. The investigators discovered that 29.9% of the students surveyed indicated that they were moderately or frequently involved in bullying. Thirteen percent had been a bully, 10.6% had been bullied, and 6.5% had been involved in both.

Smith-Khuri et al. (2004) evaluated violence-related behaviors based on a cross-national survey of youth in five countries (Ireland, Israel, Portugal, Sweden, and U.S.). The researchers discovered that the prevalence of bullying differed significantly among youth in the five countries (14.8% for Sweden to 43% for Israel). However, the prevalence of physical fighting among U.S. children and adolescents (39.8%) was similar to that of all of the other countries. The frequency of carrying weapons among U.S. youth (10.4%) and fighting that resulted in injuries (15.5%) also were similar to that of the other four countries.

In a study of school bullying among 1,756 Korean middle school students, Kim et al. (2004) evaluated school bullying using the Korean-Peer Nomination Inventory. The researchers discovered that 40% of the students surveyed indicated that that they had been involved in school bullying. In their study, 14% were victims of school bullying, 17% were offenders and 9% were both victims and offenders.

Yang et al. (2006), in study of bullying in South Korean primary schools, found that 5.3% were victims, 12% were bullies, and 7.2% were perpetrator-victims.

In their study of Turkish high school students, Alikasifoglu et al. (2004) showed that 19% of those surveyed reported that they had bullied other students at school during the last school term. Thirty percent of the students in the sample indicated that they had been bullied at school, 7% reported being bullied with a weapon on school property, and 8% stated that had carried a weapon on school property.

Research shows that boys are more likely than girls to be more involved in bullying (Seals and Young, 2003; Nansel et al., 2001; Yang et al., 2006). In Nansel et al. (2001), boys were more likely than girls to bully others and to be bullied by others. Similarly, Yang et al. (2006) found that boys were more likely than girls to be bullies and bullies/victims.

In a study of 6 classes of 8–9 year-olds and 6 classes of 11–12 year-olds, Boulton and Underwood (1992) discovered that a majority of the boys were bullied by other boys, whereas girls were more likely to be bullied by either boys or girls.

Bullying may vary based on the students' grade level. According to Spector and Kelly (2006), children as young as kindergarten age are involved in bullying. Nansel et al. (2001) showed that the prevalence of bullying was higher among students in grades 6 through 8 than among students in grades 9 and 10.

According to Boulton and Underwood (1992)'s investigation, fewer younger students than older students reported being bullied by same-age students, and more of the younger students reported being bullied by older ones.

In their study of school bullying in Korean middle schools, Kim et al. (2004) discovered that students with either high or low SES were more likely to be involved in bullying. In addition, they found that bullying was more prevalent among students who lived in nonintact families.

In terms of the site of bullying, some studies have shown that bullying is more likely to take place away from school than in school (Nansel et al., 2003). For example, Nansel et al. (2003) showed that weapon-carrying related to bullying was more likely to occur away from school than in school.

Youth involved in bullying, both as offenders and victims, tend to have problems in psychosocial functioning. Nansel et al. (2001) discovered that those who bully and those who are bullied have worse psychosocial adjustment than those not involved in bullying. In Kim et al. (2006)'s investigation of two Korean middle schools, youth who were the victims of bullying at the start of their study were at higher risk of developing social problems ten months later. Those who bullied others exhibited increased aggressive behaviors and those who were both victims and offenders showed increased aggression and externalizing problems.

Yang et al. (2006) also found psychosocial problems associated with school bullying. In their multivariate analysis, bullying and being bullied by others were related to higher levels of depression, lower self-esteem, higher trait anxiety, and total difficulties based on the Strengths and Difficulty Questionnaire results.

Using a sample of 3,530 students in grades 3 through 5, Glew et al. (2005) discovered that victims, bullies, and bully-victims had a greater likelihood than bystanders to feel unsafe at school. Victims and bully-victims were more likely than bystanders to say that they do not belong at school and to have low academic performance. Bullies and victims were more likely than bystanders to report feeling sad most days.

Similarly, Seals and Young (2003), using a study of 7th and 8th graders, showed that both bullies and victims had higher levels of depression than those who were neither bullies nor victims. However, they discovered no differences in self-esteem between bullies and victims and those who were neither.

Death Threats and Violence Against School Teachers, Principals, and Other Staff

In addition to student-on-student violence, teachers, principals, and other staff are at risk of being victims of violence. Teachers and school principals may be especially vulnerable because students view them as authority figures and violence is used to challenge authority.

Student violence against teachers may be due to a combination of risk factors, including the influences of parents, involvement from school staff and police, peer pressure, students' preoccupation with and access to weapons, and the media (Ruff et al., 2004). Individual student risk factors such as a history of violence, gender (male), and SES may increase the likelihood of student violence against teachers, principals, and other staff.

Teachers' perceptions of student-teacher violence may influence teacher performance. Based on a survey of 393 elementary, middle, and high school teachers in a suburban school in central Pennsylvania, Fisher and Kettle (2003) assessed teachers' perceptions of school violence. The results indicated that 56% of the teachers surveyed felt that violence or the threat of violence had a direct influence on the quality of teaching that they are able to offer. According to the findings, elementary school teachers were more likely than middle and high school teachers to be physically assaulted by a student. Elementary school teachers also were more likely than other teachers to fear parents.

Although teachers may fear being assaulted by students, many teachers may underestimate the extent of school bullying in their schools. Similarly, many parents may frequently under report the prevalence of school bullying. Stockdale et al. (2002) assessed students', teachers', and parents' perceptions of bullying in seven rural elementary schools. 739 students in the 4th, 5th, and 6th grades, 37 teachers, and 367 parents participated in the survey. The results showed that students reported a higher frequency of bullying than did teachers or parents. Aggressive behaviors, attitudes toward aggression, and views on school safety were related to perceptions of bullying.

Teachers Who Bully Students

In addition to student-student bullying, teachers also bully students. Teachers who were bullied themselves when young may have a greater likelihood of bullying students and being bullied by students (Twemlow et al., 2006; Twemlow and Fonagy, 2005). Based on an investigation of 116 teachers from 7 elementary schools, Twemlow et al. (2006) discovered that teachers who were bullied when they were young were more likely to both bully students and be bullied by students in and outside the classroom. A sadistic bully type and a bully-victim type were two types of bullying teachers identified in this study.

School characteristics may influence whether teachers bully students. For example, Twemlow and Fonagy (2005) revealed that teachers from schools with high school suspension rates indicated that they bullied more students, were more likely to be bullied when they were student, had worked with more bullying teachers in the previous three years, and had noticed more bullying teachers in the previous year.

Hate-Crime-Related Death Threats in Schools

Hate-crime-related death threats and other types of violence have been committed against students, teachers, and administrators in schools (Wing and Richter, 1999; Delos, 2002; Minnesota Advisory Committee, 2002).

In April 1999, two Little River High School students in Little River, Kansas, were arrested for making hate crime-related death threats and rape threats at the high school (Wing and Richter, 1999).

After 9/11, Muslim, Arab-American, and South-Asian students and faculty have been subjected to hate-based harassment and intimidation, including death threats. For example, at South Lakes High School in Reston, Virginia, Arab and Muslim students have been harassed and intimidated since 9/11 (Delos, 2002). They have been exposed to a range of intimidation from dirty looks to death threats because of their race and religion. Nadia Akhtar, a sophomore of white and Pakistani descent at South Lakes High School, discovered a death threat note in her locker a few days after the 9/11 attacks (Delos, 2002). She was in shock for about five minutes since it was something that she had never expected. Ms. Akhtar reported the death threat to her assistant school principal, who then filed a police report. Ms. Akhtar's mother also found about the death threat made against her daughter and decided to pick her up from school early that day because she did not think her daughter was safe.

Death Threats and Violence on College and University Campuses

Death threats, including bomb threats, and other type of violence have been made against, college/university students, faculty, and administrators/staff. Individuals may send death threats, including bomb threats to universities and colleges. These threats can be in the form of letters, emails, telephone calls, or other forms of communication. The offenders may provide details, e.g., specify where the bomb is and when it will explode or they may leave no details. Law enforcement authorities will evacuate affected areas, investigate these threats and take other precautions to protect people in and around these areas. Typically, law enforcement authorities will ask the public, university staff, and students to be extra vigilant and report any suspicious packages, letters, notes, or behaviors.

The California State University, East Bay (CSUEB) reported a bomb threat of the University's student union buildings and bookstore on its Hayward, CA, campus (CSUEB, 2007). The CSUEB police evacuated the buildings and areas, investigated the bomb threat, and blocked nearby traffic. The police asked that individuals remain vigilant and watch for suspicious packages or unusual behavior.

Certain groups, such as women, lesbians, gay men, transgendered persons, and racial and ethnic minorities, may be at increased risk of being victimized on college and university campuses. In a survey of 125 gay men and lesbians in a university community, D'Augelli (1989) discovered that almost 75% of those surveyed reported verbal abuse, 26% were threatened with violence, and 17% had their property vandalized. The survey findings indicated that students and roommates were most frequently the perpetrators, and men were more frequently victimized than women. A majority of the harassment and abuse were not reported and many respondents indicated that they altered their daily activities to avoid further violence. More than 50% of the respondents were fearful for their own safety and their fear was associated with the level of prior abuse and vandalism.

The findings listed above suggest there is a continuity of abuse from childhood through adulthood. Children who threatened other children based on their perceived or actual sexual orientation and minority status continue to commit these types of offenses as adults.

College students who carry weapons on campus may threaten persons with these weapons. Based on the Core Alcohol and Drug Survey of 26,225 on 61 campuses in the U.S., Presley et al. (1997) discovered that 11.1% of the men and 4.3% of the women indicated that they had carried a weapon such as a firearm or knife in the last 30 days. Compared to a matched sample of students who did not carry weapons, a greater percentage of armed students reported being harassed and/or the victims of violence and threats of violence. Weapon-carrying students also reported feeling less safe on their campuses than unarmed students.

In another survey based on more than 10,000 undergraduate students from 119 four-year colleges, Miller et al. (2002a,b) found that 4.3% of those surveyed indicated that they possessed a working firearm on campus. The results showed that 1.6% of the students surveyed reported being threatened with a firearm while attending college.

Several risk factors have been associated with college students having firearms at college and being threatened with a firearm. Being male, living off-campus, binge drinking, participating in high-risk and aggressive behavior after alcohol use, and going to college in regions of the country where firearms are prevalent in households increase the likelihood that students will have firearms and/or be threatened with these weapons (Miller et al., 2002a,b).

Researchers are evaluating factors such as fraternity membership, participation in athletics, and male living arrangements to see if they increase the risk of sexual violence. For example, one survey of 477 male undergraduate students at Southeastern University found that some types of self-reported sexual violence were more prevalent among fraternity members (Boeringer, 1996). Fraternity members were less likely to report the use of physical violence or threats in their perpetration of sexual violence. However, alcohol and drug intoxication did increase their likelihood of engaging in sexual aggression.

Some college and university students may make direct threats, such as bomb threats. They may also write essays, plays or leave notes in their college residences that provide clues as to their motivations for committing violence. They may also exhibit bizarre and erratic behaviors.

Cho Seung-Hui, the gunman in the Virginia Tech massacre, the deadliest shooting rampage in recent U.S. history, had written screenplays full of bizarre violence, stalking, sexual molestation, and obscenities as part of his playwriting class at the University (Apuzzo, 2007). One of his English professors at Virginia Tech was so alarmed about Cho's bizarre and disturbing behavior and writings that she repeatedly sought counseling and other interventions for Cho (Apuzzo, 2007; CNN, 2007a). The professor stated that she had gone to the police and university officials requesting that something be done about Cho's threatening and strange behaviors. Because of his threatening writings, Cho reportedly was referred to counseling at Virginia Tech, but it is not known if he ever entered campus counseling or elsewhere (Apuzzo, 2007).

In the three weeks before Cho Seung-Hui went on his lethal shooting rampage, Virginia Tech received two anonymous bomb threats, and Cho may have been the sender. A note containing a bomb threat was left at one of the scenes of the massacre (Apuzzo, 2007). After the school massacre, a note was found in Cho's dormitory room in which he railed against rich kids, debauchery, and deceitful charlatans, and he wrote: "You caused me to do this."

Cho sent a package to NBC headquarters in New York between his two killing sprees. In the 1,800-word manifesto, photos, and videos railed against society and expressed his desire to kill (CNN, 2007b). His manifesto paralleled Eric Harris's writings before Harris committed the Columbine massacre.

Not surprisingly, there were other aspects of the Virginia Tech tragedy that reflected the Columbine massacre. In Cho's manifesto, he described martyrs like "Eric and Dylan" who also killed a large number of people and themselves on April 20, 1999, in Littleton, Colorado (CNN, 2007b). Cho committed his shooting rampage around the anniversary of the Columbine shootings. He used two hand-guns with multiple rounds of ammunition in order to inflict as much death as possible in a manner similar to that of Eric Harris and Dylan Klebold.

Perpetrators in both the Virginia Teach and Columbine shooting rampages had been isolated from their peer groups, family and acquaintances. They were alienated and marginalized by being teased and bullied while they were growing up. The shooters in both incidents probably were suffering from severe mental disorders and they exhibited extreme, anger, hostility and other anti-social behaviors.

Researchers are beginning to evaluate a possible continuity of violence victimization from elementary school to college. Using a sample of 119 undergraduate students, Chapell et al. (2006) assessed the continuity in being a bully, victim, or bully-victim as students go from elementary school through college. The researchers found some evidence that being a bully and victim in college are linked to having been both a bully and victim in elementary school and high school.

Universities and colleges have also been the site of hate crime-based death threats. These threats have been made against Muslim, Arab-American, and South Asian college students and faculty. A campus chapter of the American Arab Discrimination Committee was the target of threatening letters and telephone calls as the organizations' leaders tried to organize an Arab Awareness Week. Two individuals assaulted the president of the campus chapter on campus, apparently because they wanted to discourage the organization's attempts to organize such an activity (Leadership Conference on Civil Rights, 2002; Minnesota Advisory Committee, 2002).

At the University of Minnesota after 9/11, many Muslim, Arab-Americans, and South Asian students were targets of many acts of harassment, and the president of the Arab Student Association received a voicemail death threat (Minnesota Advisory Committee, 2002). One Iranian woman was called a terrorist while in a class at the University of Minnesota.

An Augsburg College professor received a death threat in a note placed on his automobile at home (Minnesota Advisory Committee, 2002).

Death threats on college and university campuses can have particularly lethal consequences since college-age students who are over 18 years old may have the legal right to purchase firearms which they can then use to make and carry out death threats (Eaton and Luo, 2007).

Chapter 8
Workplace Homicidal Threats and Violence

Death threats are a major concern to employers, employees, customers, and others. Disgruntled employees, employers, clients, litigants, criminals, terrorists and other people make workplace-related death threats. These persons threaten to kill individuals on the job or blow up the work facilities. From 1992 through 1996, 2 million persons were the victims of violent crimes or threatened with a violent crime on the job (U.S. DoJ., 1998).

As in the case of school- and university-related death threats, workplace-associated death threats involve the transformation of individual rage and mental disorders into an institutional problem, requiring employers to develop new safety and security procedures to adapt to these threats and requiring new responses from law enforcement officials and political leaders. Workplace-related death threats also lead to the social construction of the phenomenon as a social problem.

Death threats are now viewed as part of the larger problem of workplace violence. The International Labour Organization and other organizations have defined workplace violence as incidents where employees are abused, threatened, or assaulted in situations associated with their work. These incidents may include commuting to and from work, as well as at the workplace, and involve situations that threaten their safety, health, or well-being (ILO, ICN, WHO and PSI, 2002).

In California, the Division of Occupational Health and Safety, Department of Industrial Relations cited surveys that show that 6.6 million employees have been threatened at work and 16 million have reported being harassed (IME, 1997).

Northwestern National Life Insurance Company, in a survey, found that in 1992 an estimated 2 million workers were physically attacked on the job and more than 22 million had been threatened with violence or harassed in the workplace (Northwestern National Life Insurance, 1993; Kitzmiller, 2002).

A study of workplace violence was conducted by a market research firm, Prince & Associates, and sponsored by a threat management company, Risk Control Strategies (2003). Their study showed that senior management received more threats than other employees and larger companies received more threats than smaller companies. The results revealed that 17.1% of the incidents of workplace violence in the previous 12 months involved electronic assault/death threats against senior management in companies with 300 to 500 employees, and 36.2% of the

S.J. Morewitz, *Death Threats and Violence*, DOI: 10.1007/978-0-387-76663-8_8,
© Springer Science+Business Media, LLC, 2008

incidents of job-related violence involved electronic assault/death threats against senior management in companies with 500 to 900 employees. The survey findings also showed that 9.4% of the incidents of workplace violence in the last 12 months involved electronic assault/death threats against other employees in companies with 300 to 500 employees, and 18.6% of the incidents of workplace violence against other employees involved electronic assault/death threats against other employees in companies with 500 to 900 employees.

According to a study of job-related violence between 1992 and 1996, an estimated 1.5 million of the incidents of violence victimization (75%) involved simple assaults, but 1,000 were homicides (U.S. DoJ., 1998). Homicide was the second leading cause of death on the job following job-related highway fatalities during this period. In more than 80% of the job-associated homicides, firearms were used. Twenty percent of the job-related homicides were due to bombings, stabbings, or beatings.

Data from the National Traumatic Occupational Fatalities Surveillance System revealed that 9,937 homicides occurred on the job from 1980 through 1992 (CDC, 1996a). In the 1980s, job-related homicides decreased, but in the 1990s the rate began to increase. During this period, 80% of the workplace homicides occurred among male workers.

Hate crimes have invaded the workplace and community. Individuals of Middle-Eastern or South Asian descent who work in retail and other settings which are readily accessible to the public are at risk of receiving hate crime-related death threats and death related to 9/11.

After 9/11, Arab-owned businesses in Minnesota were targeted for extensive verbal threats and harassment. In the aftermath of 9/11, the FBI conducted voluntary interviews with Arab-Americans and Muslims. The FBI also interviewed their neighbors, friends, and co-workers without giving the interviewees advanced notice. This procedure may have aroused fear and suspicion among their co-workers, neighbors, and friends, resulting in an increase in hate mail and death threats (Minnesota Advisory Committee, 2002; Stephens, 2002).

Workplace Violence and Different Occupations

Individuals in certain occupations are more likely to be the victims of violent crimes or threatened with violent crimes in the workplace than those in other occupations.

Between 1986 and 1997, more than 40 individuals were killed in at least 20 incidents involving U.S. Postal Service (USPS) workers (*Wikipedia*, 2007f). The slang term, "going postal," has been used to describe workplace murders perpetrated by workers in acts of job-related rage. Although these USPS worker incidents have received widespread media coverage, researchers have shown that the homicide rates at USPS facilities (0.26 per 100,000 workers) have been lower than at other work settings. In major industries, retail companies had the highest rate (2.1

homicides per 100,000 workers), followed by public administration, including police officers (1.6 homicides per 1000,000 workers). The most dangerous occupation was taxi driving (31.54 per 100,000 workers).

Law enforcement officers, correctional officers, and taxicab drivers had the highest rates of violence victimization from 1992 through 1996 (U.S. DoJ., 1998).

The British Crime Survey has found that out of all occupations, law enforcement personnel have the highest exposure to violence. One British study showed that the assaults against police officers were most likely to be related to circumstances where the police had to deal with public disorders, disputes, and traffic stops (Brown, 1994). In addition, other circumstances in which police had a high probability of being assaulted were: detaining individuals who have allegedly committed offenses; taking part in organized operations, such as searching premises or arresting suspects wanted on warrants (Waddington et al., 2006; Bragason, no date).

A study of 397 police officers in Iceland revealed that about 70% of those surveyed reported having been threatened or assaulted while on duty in the past five years). Most of the police officers who reported being threatened or assaulted indicated that this had occurred five times or less in the past five years. About 40% of the police surveyed reported that the assault resulted in no serious physical injury. Threats and assaults against police officers were much less prevalent when they were off-duty (Bragason, no date).

Among those on-duty officers who were threatened with assault but did not sustain physical injury, chief superintendents and superintendents received fewer threats than lower level police officers. Officers who had been employed for five to nine years were more likely to be assaulted than those who had worked for 15 years or longer. The police officers were arresting a suspect in more than 50% of the incidents involving assaults (Bragason, no date).

Judges and attorneys are also targets of death threats and other violence. Data from U.S. Marshals Service revealed that death threats as well as general threats of violence and other inappropriate communications against federal judges have quadrupled between 1996 and 2005. In 1996, there were 201 incidents while in 2005, there were 943 incidents reported. From January to July 2006, there were 822 incidents of threats and inappropriate communications. Threats generally involved direct references to using weapons and violent acts to kill or harm the federal judge. The inappropriate communications ranged from rambling messages to accusations of bias to envelopes containing feces (Sherman, 2006).

The U.S. Marshals Service attribute part of the increase in the rate of threats to the heightened awareness of judges and their staff regarding threats, after U.S. District Judge Joan Lefkow's husband and mother were killed in Chicago by an unemployed electrician (Sherman, 2006). Prior to these murders, the white supremacist leader, Matthew F. Hale, had been arrested for plotting to murder Judge Lefkow, who had issued an injunction forbidding Hale's church from using the term, "Church of the Creator" (*Wikipedia*, 2007a). Hale then sued Lefkow and around this time, Judge Lefkow was the target of threats on the Internet, and her home address and photographs of her husband and children were posted on the Stormfront.org website.

Another federal judge was reported to have been threatened by an inmate who had appeared before her. This judge had received dozens of letters from the inmate over a 6-month period, but left them unopened. After the murders of Judge Lefkow's family members, the judge sent the letters to the U.S. Marshals Service, who revealed that the inmate had claimed the judge as his bride and had written in detail about the bizarre sex acts that he was going to perform on her (Sherman, 2006).

Other judges have been the targets of death threats. In February 2006, U.S. Supreme Court Justice, Ruth Bader Ginsburg, indicated that she and former Justice, Sandra O'Connor were threatened in 2005 by a person who made a request on the Internet for the immediate "patriotic" murders of the justices (Sherman, 2006). At the time, Justice Ginsburg blamed lawmakers for triggering "the irrational fringe" (Mears, 2006).

Controversial cases can trigger death threats against judges. U.S. District Court Judge Michael B. Mukasey received death threats when he handled the trial of the so-called blind sheik, Omar Abdel Rahman, who was convicted and sentenced to life in prison for his role in plotting to blow up the United Nations and other New York City landmarks (Shenon and Weiser, 2007).

A number of trends may have contributed to the increased rate of death threats and other inappropriate behaviors against federal judges (Sherman, 2006). There are an increased number of lawsuits filed in state and local courts by individuals (without attorneys) who have naïve notions about the law and the justice system. Persons who file and lose multiple lawsuits may be more likely to be emotionally unstable and therefore may be more likely to make death threats against federal judges or make other threatening attacks on federal judges. Federal courts are now hearing more cases involving violent crimes than state and local courts handled ten years ago.

Following the Lefkow family homicides, some judges criticized the U.S. Marshals Service for their unresponsiveness to the security needs of judges (Sherman, 2006). Moreover, in 2004, a Justice Department Inspector General's report revealed weaknesses in the U.S. Marshals Service's system for assessing threats. John Clark, the head of the U.S. Marshals Service, has increased the numbers of marshals trained to investigate threats and plans to open a 24-hour assessment and analysis center. The U.S. Congress has now set aside $12 million to implement security systems in the residences of judges. Approximately, 1,700 judges have requested alarms for their residences. However, only about 500 have received them.

Persons in other regulatory and law enforcement-related occupations also face death threats and other forms of violence. Safety inspectors are at increased risk of death threats, physical assaults, and murders. A Workplace Violence Prevention Taskforce 2000 was established in the U.S. Department of Agriculture to identify possible causes, risks, and contributing factors to violence in the work environment of USDA employees and to implement preventative measures (U.S. DoA., 2000). The Taskforce has developed a number of recommendations including changing the culture, e.g., addressing the sometimes tense relationship between industry and the USDA, identifying safety and security measures, offering violence prevention training, designing a systems approach to responding to workplace violence incidents, and using civil and criminal penalties to respond to workplace violence.

Tom Billy indicated that the following factors have resulted in major changes in the way USDA employees perform their jobs:

1. The increased prevalence of school violence.
2. The effects of the Oklahoma bombing on security practices in federal facilities.
3. The assaults on the former Secretary of Agriculture.
4. The increased conflicts resulting from the changes in the USDA's regulation of businesses (U.S. DoA., 2000).

Other occupations that have high rates of violence victimization include private security guards, bartenders, mental health professionals, gas station attendants, and convenience or liquor store clerks. An average of 330,000 retail workers were victimized each year between 1992 and 1996 and 84,000 workers were robbed while on the job (U.S. DoJ., 1998).

Workplace violence, including threats of violence, also occurs at government sites. A study of 96,000 federal workers employed by a U.S. government agency and its contractors used two surveys to measure the incidence of violence in the workplace. One survey of occupational medicine directors showed that there had been 43 incidents involving verbal threats or verbal abuse among federal workers, and the second survey of human resource directors showed that there had been 60 incidents involving verbal threats or verbal abuse (Eisele et al., 1998).

The risk factors and motivations underlying workplace-related death threats and other forms of violence vary by occupational setting. Many workers are at increased risk for workplace-related death threats and other violence because they work in jobs that place them at risk for robbery. Having a mobile workplace, such as a taxicab or police cruiser, working at jobs that involve the exchange of money, working late at night or during the early morning hours, guarding valuable property or possessions, and working in high-crime areas increase employees risks for robbery-related death threats (CDC, 1996b).

Employees who work with unstable or volatile persons, such as those who work in health care, mental health, social services, or criminal justice organizations are at increased risk for work-related death threats (CDC, 1996b). Medical, mental health, and social services professionals have been assaulted, threatened with violence, and sexually harassed by patients or clients and other individuals (McKenna et al., 2003; Magin et al., 2005; Duncan et al., 2001; Godfroid, 2001; Kaye et al., 1994).

Working in emergency departments, mental health settings, providing care after hours, working in low socioeconomic status areas, being female, and young also increases the risk of different forms of violence (Kowalenko et al., 2005; McKenna et al., 2003; Tolhurst et al., 2003; Magin et al., 2005; Godfroid, 2001). Drug and alcohol intoxication by patients and clients also increases the likelihood of violence against physicians, counselors, etc. (Tolhurst et al., 2003).

Using a mailed survey of emergency physicians in Michigan, Kowalenko et al. (2005) found that 74.9% of the emergency physicians reported having had at least one verbal threat in the preceding 12 months. About 28% of the emergency physicians surveyed reported having been physically assaulted; 11.7% had been confronted outside of the emergency department; and 3.5% had been stalked during this period. Emergency physicians who were threatened tended to have less experience than those who were not threatened (11.1 years vs. 15.1 years in practice), as were those who were physically assaulted compared to those who were not physically assaulted (9.5 years in practice vs. 13.1 years). Female emergency physicians were more likely to be exposed to physical forms of violence, but not other forms of violence.

In addition, 81.9% of the emergency physicians surveyed indicated that occasionally they were afraid of job-related violence, while 9.4% were often afraid of workplace violence. Forty-two percent noted that they used some of the following types of protection because of actual or perceived violence: obtaining a firearm (18%), carrying a knife (20%), having a concealed weapon license (13%), carrying mace (7%), carrying a club (4%), or having a security escort (31%).

According to Godfroid (2001), psychiatrists are at risk of being assaulted during their first contacts with the patients, especially in emergency departments, with both verbal and non-verbal threats. Female psychiatrists have been subjected to sexual harassment by patients.

Other physicians face verbal and non-verbal threats and physical violence from their patients and third parties (Magin et al., 2005; Godfroid, 2001). Based on a cross-sectional survey of occupational violence in Australian urban general practice, Magin et al. (2005) found that 63.7% of 528 general practitioners surveyed had encountered violence in the previous year. About 23% of the general practitioners surveyed reported being the targets of threats, 9.3% had been the victims of sexual harassment and 2.7% had been the targets of physical abuse.

In a survey of Australian rural general practitioners, Tolhurst et al. (2003) revealed that 73% of the general practitioners surveyed had been exposed to some type of violence from patients, and 20% had been the targets of physical abuse sometime during their career in rural practice.

Nurses and social workers are also exposed to a range of threats of violence, physical assault, and sexual harassment (Duncan et al., 2001; Williams, 1996). In a survey of 8,780 registered nurses in 210 hospitals in Alberta and British Columbia, Duncan et al. (2001) showed that 46% of nurses surveyed had suffered one or more forms of violence in their last 5 work shifts. Nineteen percent reported being threatened with assault, 18% reported being physically assaulted, 7.6% reported being the target of verbal sexual harassment, and 0.6% reported being sexually assaulted. In addition, 70% of those who had encountered violence indicated that they had not reported the violence.

Williams (1996), in a study of 345 registered nurses in Illinois, showed that 57% of those surveyed reported experiencing sexual harassment and 26% reported being the victim of physical assault in the workplace. Approximately one third of the registered nurses who reported sexual harassment also reported physical assault. In this study, patients/clients were the most frequent perpetrators of unwanted sexual advances and physical assault.

Another investigation by Gunnarsdottir et al. (2006) showed that nurses (19%) were more likely to suffer threats, bullying, and physical violence on the job than flight attendants (12%), whereas flight attendants (31%) had a greater likelihood of suffering repeated sexual harassment on the job than nurses (8%) or female primary school teachers (4%).

Based on a survey of 551 registered nurses in their first year of practice, McKenna et al (2003) discovered that the first-year registered nurses most frequently reported work-related verbal threats (35%), followed by verbal sexual harassment (30%), and physical intimidation (29%). The nurses surveyed reported 22 incidents of assault that required medical treatment and 21 incidents of being stalked by patients.

Certain types of nurse practices and specialization may increase the risk of workplace violence. For example, based on a survey of nurses in Poland, Merecz et al. (2006) discovered that psychiatric nurses were exposed to a higher rate of violence than non-psychiatric nurses. In their survey, the most frequently reported form of violence was verbal abuse, but the nurses had also been threatened and physically assaulted.

Other health care providers face sexual harassment and other forms of violence, but not because of their involvement in socially and politically sensitive activities. In a survey of 285 dental hygienists in Virginia, Pennington et al. (2000) discovered that 54% suffered sexual harassment at work. Of these individuals, 50% had experienced it four or more years ago, 23% one to three years ago, and 28% within the last year.

Based on a survey of 86 nurses in the emergency department, intensive care unit, and general floor of a 770-bed acute care medical center in Florida, May and Grubbs (2002) showed that 88% reported being verbally assaulted by patients, their family members or visitors and 74% indicated that they had been physically assaulted at work in the past year.

Persons who work in socially and politically controversial fields are at increased risk of being threatened with death. Abortion providers and abortion clinics have been harassed, threatened, and attacked by pro-life supporters (Grimes et al., 1991; Henshaw, 1995; Hern, 1994; Anonymous, 1993). Dr. Warren Hern, a former medical director of the Boulder (Colorado) Abortion Clinic (1994) noted in 1994 that every physician in the U.S. who performs abortions "lives under a death threat." Hern (1994) reported being harassed while at home and at work when he was the medical director of the clinic. When he left the clinic to start a private practice specializing in abortions, the pro-life supporters followed him and continued to harass him. After he published a textbook on abortions, the publisher was forced to withdraw the book because of extensive hate mail and boycott threats.

In a survey of violence committed against abortion clinics, Grimes et al. (1991) describe an epidemic of violence directed at these facilities. The authors reported 110 cases of arson, firebombing, or bombing between 1977 and 1988. In 1984, the epidemic of violence reached its peak, when there were 29 attacks on abortion clinics. Organizations in 28 states and the District of Columbia were targeted. The national rate of violence against abortion providers was 3.7 per 100 abortion providers and 7.2 per 100 non-hospital providers. The National Abortion Federation reported the following acts of violence perpetrated against abortion clinics during the study period: 222 invasions of clinics, 220 acts of vandalism, 216 bomb threats, 65 death threats, 46 assault and batteries, 20 burglaries, and 2 kidnappings. These acts of violence resulted in $7.6 million in direct cost. This does not include the cost of the facilities that were destroyed but were not rebuilt, and it does not include the cost of attorneys, security, increased insurance, etc.

Intense investigations and successful prosecution of offenders seems to have slowed the epidemic of violence. The longest sentence handed down was 30 years and the largest fine was $350,000 (Grimes et al., 1991).

However, Henshaw (1995) discovered that the epidemic of violence against abortion clinics did not subside. This author reported that in 1992, 86% of the clinics which offered 400 or more abortions were targeted for anti-abortion harassment. Between 1988 and 1992, anti-abortion personnel increased their picketing of abortion clinics and the homes of abortion clinic staff members. In addition attacks of abortion facilities with butyric acid increased during this period. The murders of providers, escorts, and staff reflect a gradual increase in violence, while the incidence of bomb threats decreased between 1988 and 1992.

According to Hern (1994), the violent attacks on abortion clinics increased when Reagan was elected. Hern (1994) reported that shots were fired into his waiting room. The head of the pro-life group, Operation Rescue, Randall Terry, reportedly prayed for Dr. Hern's death at a protest rally in front of his clinic.

One of the most extreme instances of anti-abortion violence occurred in March 1993, when a pro-life supporter killed Dr. David Gunn. By the time of Dr. Gunn's assassination, there had been more than 1,285 incidents of violence against abortion clinics, and more than 100 clinics had been destroyed (Anonymous, 1993; Hern, 1994).

Animal rights and radical environment activists have threatened, harassed, and attacked numerous individuals and organizations for two decades (animalrights.net; naiaonline.org). These activists employ a variety of techniques, including threatening phone calls and emails, arson, and theft and murder of animals. In the United Kingdom, the National Extremism Tactical Coordination Unit (Netcu) in April 2007 warned that animal rights activists are attacking farmers at a rate of one incident every nine days. These incidents included threatening telephone calls and emails, arson, white powder mailed to farmers (to appear to be anthrax), and burglaries (Netcu, 2007).

In Iowa, extremists had killed a dozen cows and had vandalized farm equipment, buildings, and livestock construction sites. Iowa farmers have reported receiving threatening letters and telephone calls. Investigators are not sure if an organized group is carrying out these threatening activities.

Extremists write threatening messages on websites in addition to vandalizing the homes and other possessions of individuals employed by targeted organizations (naiaonline.org). For example, after vandalizing the home and automobile of a Wachovia financial advisor in the Portland, Oregon, area, a threatening message claiming responsibility for the attacks was posted on the Animal Liberation Front (ALF) website. The message indicated that "things are going to get much worse" and that they have the names and addresses of the top executives. The ALF is an extremist organization that has claimed responsibility for thousands of incidents of violence against organizations and their staff involved with animals. In the 1970s, the ALF was founded in Great Britain and later became influential in the U.S. and elsewhere. Activists threaten and attack targets and then label their actions as part of ALF. Unfortunately, the ALF is an informal organization. Therefore it is difficult for law enforcement to prosecute it (Wikipedia, 2007e).

Politicians and celebrities are the targets of death threats and other forms of violence from people unhappy with their political goals and strategies, as well as from stalkers and other persons suffering from mental disorders (Morewitz, 2003a,b).

Journalists and other members of the media in many countries face death threats and other types of violence, including assassination by terrorists and other criminals. They are especially at risk since their job involves publicizing illegal or unethical activities and criticism of individuals in authority or others who may be unhappy with this public attention. In 1998, Amnesty International reported that there has been an increased frequency of attacks, death threats and harassment against journalists and others working for the media in Argentina. They reported that there were more than 120 incidents involving attacks and death threats against journalist and media personnel in Argentina between 1992 and 1993. In several instances, the attacks and death threats were carried out with the involvement or acquiescence of Argentina's security forces. Among those journalists in Argentina who were attacked and threatened with death in 1997 and in previous years were: Hernan Lopez Echague, Santo Biasatti Magdalena Ruiz Guinazu, Gabriela Cerrutti, and Daniel Straga. According to Amnesty International, the attacks occurred at different times and in varying settings. In September 1993, President Carlos Menem nominated a Special Attorney, known as Procurator Fiscal, to investigate the attacks against journalists and media personnel and make sure that those found responsible were prosecuted. However, a majority of those cases have remained unsolved (Amnesty International, 1998).

Journalists who investigate and detail the violence in their communities may find themselves to be targets of death threats. For example, several Palestinian journalists in the West Bank received death threats for several days because of their reporting of the armed conflicts between Fatah and Hamas in the Palestinian Authority-dominated areas. The Deputy Information Minister Ahmed Suboh stated that multiple press offices had received mailed death threats (*The Jerusalem Post*, 2007).

One journalist stated that his colleagues who had been threatened were taking the threats very seriously and were frightened (*The Jerusalem Post*, 2007).

In the television industry, the airing of controversial broadcasts can trigger death threats against media personnel. J. Sri Ranga, the director of Tamil-language Shakthi Television, received death threats soon after the station broadcasted a talk show about the assassination of a Tamil National Alliance parliamentarian. Ranga reportedly had been the target of previous death threats because of his broadcasts of sensitive political topics on his weekly show, Minnal. The Free Media Movement, an affiliate of the International Federation of Journalists, notes that there has been little success in investigating these death threats (TamilNet, 2006).

In the Philippines, journalists, including Allan Dizon, have been assassinated. Dizon, a photojournalist for "*The Freeman*," a daily, and the tabloid, "*Banat News*," reportedly had been reporting on drug trafficking in a Cebu neighborhood. According to the World Association of Newspapers, 9 journalists had been murdered in the Philippines in early 2004 and a total of 45 had been assassinated since the beginning of their democracy in 1986 (UNESCO, 2004).

It's not only the journalists, but their family members have also been targeted for death threats and other violence. Allan Dizon's widow, Amelina, filed a police report with the Cebu City Homicide Section, indicating, that she had received multiple telephone death threats on her mobile phone and landline. These death threats came a year after her husband had been murdered on his way home. Amelina stated that ever since the murder trial of the man charged with her husband's death, she has been getting death threats. In one of the telephone messages, the caller told her that she may not "make it" to the anniversary of her husband's death (Awit, 2005).

A survey of police officers in Iceland showed that 15% of the officers indicated that a member of their family had been the target of threats. In 100% of these cases, it was the police officer's child who was threatened and in an additional 35 cases a spouse was also threatened. Only 25% of these incidents were reported to superiors (Bragason, no date).

In the 1998 Bureau of Justice Statistics' investigation, 67% of all job-associated victims of violent crimes or threats of violence were male and 33% were female. Approximately 12% of the victimizations produced injuries, and in about 50% of these cases, injured individuals obtained medical treatment (U.S. DoJ., 1998).

Partner and Domestic Violence Spill-Over into the Workplace

There has been increased concern about individuals bringing partner and domestic violence into the workplace. Perpetrators often know where and when their victims work and they will stalk, threaten, and physically attack them at their place of employment. The victims are trapped by their necessity to work on fixed work schedules.

How often does domestic and partner violence carry over into the workplace? The prevalence of the spill-over phenomenon has not been studied extensively. The U.S. Bureau of Justice Statistics report in 1998 found that the perpetrators of workplace threats and other violence were more likely not to be partners, boyfriends or girlfriends. The researchers found that while 37% of the victims of workplace violence stated that they knew their perpetrators, only 1% was victimized by a current or former spouse, boyfriend or girlfriend. On a nationwide basis, intimate partners produce 21% of all violence against women and 2% of all violence against men (U.S. DoJ., 1998).

In one publicized case of partner violence spilling over into the workplace, Roger Hargrave set his estranged wife, Yvette Cade on fire at work. Cade stated that at 2:30 a.m. on October 10, 2005, Hargrave called her and threatened to fry her like Crisco grease. She was fearful that she would lose job at the Clinton, Maryland, mobile phone store if she failed to show up for work in the morning. Therefore, Cade went to work as scheduled and an hour after she arrived, her estranged husband stormed in the store doused her with gasoline and set her on fire. Cade suffered third-degree burns over 60% of her body and she reported that her lip was actually melted to her chin. In 2006, Hargrave was convicted of attempting to murder Cade (Daly, 2007).

In the Stalking and Violence Project (SVP), there are a number of instances in which perpetrators who threatened to kill their partners also harassed them at work.

In SVP case A111, Mr. A, a 40-year-old man, came to his ex-girlfriend's workplace and started arguing with her. When the phone rang, and she went to answer it, he became enraged. He knocked her out of her chair and began hitting her. During the altercation, he threatened to kill her and her family. The supervisor had to break it up, and the police were called. She filed a police report against Mr. A for Aggravated Battery.

DTMs may use the phone, email and other forms of communication to stalk and threaten their victims at work. Besides the primary targets, supervisors, co-workers and other third parties in the workplace can be targets of abuse and threats.

In SVP case 157C, Mr. C, a 44-year-old man, interrupted a phone call between his wife and her supervisor regarding possible overtime work. He verbally abused the supervisor and accused him of being his wife's boyfriend. Mr. C had made death threat against his wife, slashed her automobile tires, physically attacked her dog and cats, and tried to throw their oldest stepchild out of the house. In addition, the wife reported that Mr. C came home intoxicated almost every night and he would make death threats and break household items.

Jealousy, alcohol and drug abuse exacerbates aggressive tendencies and can be a major contributor to death threats and other forms of partner and domestic violence in the workplace. Alcohol and drug abuse is especially significant, since it reduces a person's inhibitions and impairs one's judgment. Intoxicated persons and those under the influence of certain drugs have a greater likelihood of stalking, harassing and threatening to kill their victims regardless of their locations.

Psychosocial Impact of Death Threats on Occupational Functioning

Death threat victims can suffer severe impairment in their occupational functioning. They are at increased risk of suffering severe anxiety, depression, and other stress-related health problems and may be at risk for engaging in suicidal behaviors. These substantial stressors reduce the victims' ability to concentrate at work and can result in dismissal from the job.

Chapter 9
Crime, Culture, and War

In this chapter, the role of death threats in crime, cultural traditions, and wars and other conflict is discussed. It describes how death threats are embedded in the norms, values, and beliefs, in societies and as a result, death threats can become institutionalized as patterns of behavior among both legitimate and illegal groups and organizations. This process of institutionalization allows groups and governments to make death threats themselves and evade sanctioning under certain conditions.

Death Threats, Crime, and Culture

Criminals resort to death threats to achieve their illegal goals, such as obtaining payment for activities related to blackmail, extortion, kidnapping, drugs, prostitution, gambling, bribery, and other criminal enterprises (MacDonald, 1968). Extortionists and loan sharks routinely threaten to kill individuals to obtain money and other goods and services. Sex offenders and murderers may threaten to kill their victims before carrying out their threats. Kidnappers frequently threaten to kill the abducted persons to reinforce their demand for a ransom or to obtain other criminal objectives.

Certain types of offenders may be at higher risk for criminal recidivism if they make death threats. For example, in a Swedish study of young sex offenders, Langstrom and Grann (2000) discovered that the perpetrators' use of death threats was associated with their increased risk of general but not sexual recidivism.

Celebrities and wealthy individuals are especially vulnerable to death threats related to blackmail, extortion, and kidnapping since criminals seek to extract large sums of money from them. Even Berlin's celebrity polar bear cub, Knut, has received a death threat (Partridge, 2007)!

Criminals use homicidal threats in an attempt to dissuade crime victims from pursuing a criminal investigation against them. They also employ homicidal threats against the police, judges, journalists, politicians, attorneys, and the general public to intimidate them so that they would not interfere with their illegal activities. For

S.J. Morewitz, *Death Threats and Violence*, DOI: 10.1007/978-0-387-76663-8_9,
© Springer Science+Business Media, LLC, 2008

decades, journalists have been the targets of homicidal threats and other violence from criminal gangs and armed extremists (Rosenberg, 2007).

In many countries, those involved in illicit drug and sex trafficking and other criminal activities often use death threats, kidnappings, and murder to intimidate the public, law enforcement officials, rival criminal groups, to keep them from interfering with their activities. According to a report by The Hiscox insurance group, Columbia, Mexico, the Former Soviet Union, and Brazil had the highest rates of kidnappings for ransom for the period between 1992 and 1999 (Pharoah, 2005). Kidnapping for ransom is a heterogeneous and changing phenomenon, but is most prevalent in countries characterized by high crime rates, corruption, a weak justice system, and history of instability and conflict. In Mexico and Columbia, where cocaine trafficking is extensive and corruption is prevalent, criminal organizations use death threats, kidnappings, and murders against those who try to oppose their activities. In many instances, these criminal organizations are successful in intimidating the supporters of the law (Vinas, 1997).

Criminal gangs make death threats to achieve or reinforce their dominance over rival gangs and individuals and organizations who try to oppose them. These gangs may commit hate crimes and make racial and ethnic-based death threats against rival gang members and members of the community. Data from the National Crime Victimization Survey showed that 7% of the victims of violent hate crimes believed that gang members had attacked them. This is about the same percentage of victims of non-hate-based violent offenses who thought that their attackers had been gang members (Harlow, 2005).

Archibold (2007) reported that criminal gangs in Los Angeles had participated in a wave of hate crimes, including a murder of a 14-year-old African-American girl following a confrontation between gang members and an African-American man. Some attribute this increased rate of gang-related hate crimes to rivalries between African-American and Latino gangs, especially in areas where the African-American population has been declining and the Hispanic population has been increasing.

Hate crimes, including making death threats can be part of a criminal gang's initiation rituals (Leadership Conference on Civil Rights, 2002). On July 16, 1995, a gang assaulted a rabbi's son in Cincinnati. The gang members chased the boy for about a block before catching up with him outside a synagogue and beating him until he fell down. At his sentencing, one of the gang members involved in the attack told the judge that they did it as part of their gang initiation and the victim was chosen because he was Jewish.

Criminals employ homicidal threats to achieve other objectives, such as intimidating witnesses of crimes, so that they will be too frightened to testify against them in court. Criminals make homicidal threats against judges, journalists, and politicians to dissuade them from intervening in their criminal activities and trying to prosecute them for their crimes.

As noted in Chapter 1, criminals may also resort to homicidal threats to enforce discipline among against other criminals. MacDonald (1968) discussed the case of an individual who was an illicit drug user. He was selected by criminals to kidnap a person who was engaging in open sales of marijuana since this was increasing the risk of police arrests of drug sellers in the community. He kidnapped the reckless drug seller and took him to a lake in a quarry and threatened to throw him into the lake with "concrete shoes" if he did not leave the area.

Sex trafficking facilitates kidnappings, death threats, and other types of violence against vulnerable groups, especially girls, boys, and women, who attempt to resist their sexual, physical, and economic exploitation. Silverman et al. (2007) analyzed the experiences of sex trafficking victims in Mumbai, India, and discovered most of the victims were trafficked as minors, and a majority of the traffickers were previously known to them. The researchers found that the most frequently used method to lure their victims was to promise them financial rewards (55%). Traffickers also kidnapped the victims by using drugs or force (26.3%). They also found that 49.4% of the sex trafficking victims indicated that some form of family disruption led to their victimization. The most common types of family disruption reported were family violence involving a husband or other member (38%) and marital separation or abandonment (32.9%).

Other cultural norms, such as the perpetuation of the male-dominated power system may permit the physical and sexual abuse of many girls and women within their families (Armstrong, 1994; Everett, 1997; Kumari, 1995; Ouattara et al., 1998). In rural areas of India, girls have no power to control their sexuality or reproduction, making them susceptible to sexual exploitation and death threats (Kumari, 1995). Girls are not allowed to go out alone or stay outside in the evening. They are expected to get married and have children. In this society, the fathers shift their control of female sexuality to the husband. Likewise, cultural norms in part of West Africa permit child marriages (Ouattara et al., 1998). These types of cultural norms increase the girls' risk of violence, especially being threatened with death, if they violate these strongly-held cultural norms.

In Lesotho, South Africa, many girls suffer physical and sexual violence within their families because of the cultural norms, family structure, and economic pressures (Armstrong, 1994; Everett, 1997). Poor girls in Lesotho are frequently placed as servants in the homes of more prosperous extended families, increasing their risk of additional sexual abuse. In addition, in Lesotho, women are coerced into having sex as a prelude to marriage. These women are often kidnapped and raped by their prospective bridegrooms (Armstrong, 1994; Everett, 1997; Muleta and Williams, 1999).

In Ethiopia and in other countries, such as Kyrgyzstan, cultural traditions, known as bridal kidnapping, also allow men who cannot afford a wife to kidnap and rape their prospective brides (Smith, 2005; Lom, 2004; Report of the Committee on the Elimination of Discrimination Against Women, 2004; Stoddard, 2007; Muleta and Williams, 1999).

One investigation evaluated the post-coital injuries of 91 women who were treated at the Addis Ababa Fistula Hospital between 1991 and 1997. The researchers showed that 78 had been sexually abused under the guise of marriage, 9 were abducted with the intent of marriage, raped and then abandoned by their prospective husbands, and 4 women were "just" kidnapped and raped (Muleta and Williams, 1999).

The victims of sexual violence are coerced or threatened with death to induce them into engaging in a range of unwanted sexual behaviors and forced sex. Offenders often threaten and intimidate their victims and may threaten to kill them if they do not comply with their sexual demands. A study of 939 sexually active women, aged 18–35, in two urban areas of Lesotho revealed that boy friends most frequently had forced or attempted forced sex (66% and 44%, respectively) with the women, while 52% of the other males in the community were most likely to touch and/or fondle the women against their will (Brown et al., 2006).

Individuals frequently are exposed to or witness incidents of violence in the community, including the use of death threats and physical assaults. Studies have found that exposure to community violence has a significant adverse impact on social, family, school, and educational functioning (Samms-Vaughan et al., 2005).

Death Threats During Wars and Conflicts

During times of war, political and social unrests, and other conflicts, there is often an increased number of murders, torture, kidnappings, sexual violence, death threats, and other forms of violence and human rights abuses, especially against vulnerable groups, such as women, girls, members of ethnic and racial groups, and refugees (Amowitz et al., 2004, 2002; De Silva et al., 2001; Wandita, 1998; Anonymous, 1996a,b).

Wandita (1998) suggests that during periods of political unrest, men are more likely to regard women as sexual property. Moreover, women from racial-ethnic minority groups are especially susceptible to threats and related violence. During the May 1998 student demonstration in Jakarta, Indonesia, the sexual assault of Chinese-Indonesian women support this view. There were 152 documented cases of rape in Jakarta and 20 deaths associated with rapes. Nationwide publicity about these rapes led to additional reports of violence against women from minority groups, which reportedly were perpetrated by members of the paramilitary and military and civilians in positions of power.

During the war in Rwanda, it was estimated that between 15,700 (the Rwandan government's estimate) and 250,000 women (the United Nations Special Representative's estimate) were raped (Anonymous, 1996a,b). Men gang-raped and sexually mutilated women, forced fathers to rape their daughters, and sons were forced to rape their mothers. Women were kidnapped and taken to refugee camps as sex slaves and many women wrote to their families that they were married to Hutu militia men.

In countries with male-dominated and corrupt, totalitarian regimes, political conflicts, and war, women are faced with increased violence in different forms (Amowitz et al., 2004; Pharoah, 2005). Countries with high levels of crime, poorly trained and corrupt police, and a weak justice system also facilitate death threats and other violence against women and other vulnerable groups (Pharoah, 2005).

Based on a cross-sectional random survey of 1,991 Iraqi men and women, Amowitz et al. (2004) evaluated the extent of human rights abuses and concerns about women's health in southern Iraq. The survey results revealed that 47% of those interviewed indicated since 1991 that household members experienced one or more of the following: torture, kidnappings, hostage-taking, disappearance, gunshot wounds, ear amputation, forced conscription, and killings. It was reported that ninety-five percent of the offenders were affiliated with the Baath party regime. Fifty-three percent of the violence took place between 1991 and 1993 after the Shi'a uprising and an additional 30% occurred between 2000 and the first half of 2003. Seventy percent of the abuses reportedly occurred in residences. Some respondents, both male and female, also favored restricting women's freedom of movement, their associations with individuals of their choosing, and their freedom to refuse sex. About half of the women and men (54% and 50%) indicated that men have the right to assault their wives if they disobey them. Fifty-three of those surveyed indicated that there are justifications for limiting educational opportunities for women (Amowitz et al., 2004).

During wartime, children may be conscripted into armed conflicts and when they try to resist, they can be threatened with death. Based on a study of former child soldiers, De Silva et al. (2001) discovered that child soldiers who attempted to or did run away were threatened with death or received other punishments, such as beatings, imprisonment or kitchen duty.

Death threats and other forms of violence are especially prevalent during periods of political instability, especially in countries with corrupt and ineffective political regimes. The disruption of political leadership by in countries can trigger an increase in human rights abuses and criminal activity. Kolbe and Hutson (2006) found extensive acts of violence in Haiti following the departure of the elected president in 2004. Using a random survey of 1,260 households and 5,720 persons in the Port-au-Prince area, the authors discovered that 8,000 were reportedly killed in that area in a period of 22 months. The respondents revealed that almost 50% of the murders were committed by government personnel or outside political representatives. The survey results also indicated that about 35,000 women and girls had been sexually assaulted and more than 50% of the victims were under 18 years. While criminals committed the majority of the rapes, 13.8% of the rapists were Haitian National Police officers and 10.6% of the rapists were from armed anti-Lavalas groups. During this 22-month period, death threats, threats of sexual assaults, physical threats, kidnappings, and illegal detentions were also found to be prevalent.

Ritu Sharma, of the Women's Edge Coalition, an alliance of 40 U.S. development and human rights organizations, noted that in post-Taliban Afghanistan there has been an increase in sexual violence against Afghan women resulting from the lack of security outside of Kabul. Afghan women have increasingly suffered sexual assaults, physical assaults, abductions, and other types of violence. According to Sharma, many Afghan women and girls who live outside of Kabul cannot go to school or work without facing the possibility of violence and fearing that their lives will be endangered (Lobe, 2004).

Violete Krasnic, of the Autonomous Women's Center Against Sexual Violence in Belgrade noted that the war in the former Yugoslavia increased domestic violence against women, especially in inter-ethnic marriages, where death threats against women, rape, and threats with weapons were common. Krasnic suggested that men's exposure to nationalistic propaganda during the war increased their use of violence against their wives, and other women (Anonymous, 1996a,b).

The decade-long war in Sierra Leone resulted in many human rights abuses among internally displaced individuals. Based on a survey of women who offered information on 9,166 households, Amowitz et al. (2002) discovered that 1,157 household members indicated that war-related abuses took place in the last ten years. Those surveyed reported incidents of war-associated killings, beatings, kidnappings, sexual assaults, and other human rights violations (Amowitz et al., 2002).

Paramilitary groups, political representatives, and organizations may use killings, death threats, kidnappings, and other forms of violence to achieve their political goals and objectives (Fog, 2006; Manson, 2007a). For example, in Columbia, there have been reports of an increased number of death threats and related violence at public universities. The Columbian Association of University Students (CAUS) notes that during 2004 and 2005, there were three murders and dozens of incidents of threats, violence, and attempted kidnappings against university faculty, staff, and students. The CAUS suspects that paramilitary groups have infiltrated state university campuses and are to blame for this violence. Violence against public universities in Columbia has existed for many years but it seems to be increasing in prevalence. Hugo Vega, a geneticist at the National University, fled Columbia in July 2006 after being the target of persistent death threats that accused him of being a member of a guerrilla organization. Other members of Vega's research team also received threats, and they were forced to terminate their research activities. Vega believes that the death threats against him occurred because of his team's success in publishing a study in the journal, Nature Genetics. He suspects that one of his colleagues paid a paramilitary group to force him out of his job, his research team, and his country under the pretext that he is a guerrilla. In June 2006, Gustavo Loaiza, a professor of mathematics at the University of Antioquia, was murdered (Fog, 2006).

Psychosocial Impact of Death Threats and Other Violence

Persons who are exposed to oppressive totalitarian regimes, war-associated trauma, life-threatening human rights abuses, and forced relocation to refugee camps are especially at risk for severe psychosocial and physical health problems.

Individuals who are threatened, attacked, kidnapped, or tortured often suffer severe physical and psychosocial problems (Olsen et al., 2006; Keller et al, 2006; Rasekh et al., 1998; Favaro et al., 2000; Van Ommeren et al., 2001; Basoglu et al., 1994). In a study of 325 refugees and survivors of torture seeking treatment services, Keller et al. (2006) found that 81.1% of these patients had symptoms of anxiety, 84.5% had depressive symptoms, and 45.7% had symptoms of Post Traumatic Stress Disorder (PTSD). Higher levels of anxiety and depression were found in women who had suffered death threats as part of their victimization. Being threatened with death predicted having PTSD symptoms, but these symptoms were also associated with having been a rape victim, having been subject to family torture, one's religion, and age. The findings also revealed that women had higher levels of anxiety and depression than men.

Based on a study of 418 torture and 392 non-torture Bhutanese refugees living in camps in Nepal, Van Ommeren et al. (2001) showed that torture refugees were more likely than non-torture refugees to have higher 12-month rates of PTSD, somatoform pain disorder (physical symptoms that mimic a medical condition), and dissociative (amnesia and conversion) disorders. (Conversion disorder is a type of condition in which emotional conflicts are repressed and converted into sensory, motor, or visceral symptoms having no underlying organic causes, such as involuntary muscular movements and paralysis.) Compared to torture men, torture women had higher life-time generalized anxiety disorder, persistent somatoform pain disorder, affective disorder, and dissociative (amnesia and conversion) disorders.

Torture survivors can suffer from pain symptoms years after the torture had occurred. A study of 69 refugees who had been tortured with both psychological methods (e.g., death threats) and physical methods (e.g., beating) revealed that torture victims continued to suffer from pain (e.g., pain in the head, back, and feet) more than ten years after the torture had taken place (Olsen et al., 2006).

Being kidnapped also can cause severe psychosocial and physical health problems and symptoms, including PTSD and the Stockholm syndrome during captivity (Favaro et al., 2000; Navia and Ossa, 2003). In a study of 55 abducted and released persons and 158 of their family members, Navia and Ossa (2003) evaluated family functioning, coping, and psychosocial adjustment in victims and their family members 2–4, 5–8, and 9–15 months following kidnapping. The authors found that the period of captivity was the most stressful period.

Based on an investigation of 160 women who lived in Kabul, Afghanistan, under the Taliban regime, Rasekh et al. (1998) discovered that most of the women indicated that their physical and mental health had deteriorated (71% and 81%, respectively) and that they had reduced access to health care (62%) during the last two years of living in Kabul. Forty-two percent of the women had symptoms of PTSD, 97% had symptoms of major depression, and 86% had significant anxiety symptoms.

Chapter 10
Hate Crimes

Persons, groups, and organizations threaten to kill and intimidate individuals because of their national origins, cultural, ideological, religious, and political beliefs and traditions, ethnic/racial background, and sexual orientation. They frequently make death threats in order to keep their targets in subordinate roles and make them change their behaviors, such as moving out of town.

Hate crime laws have been passed to combat this form of bigotry. Hate crime laws consist of several types:

1. Laws that define bias-motivated behaviors as crimes.
2. Laws that provide criminal penalty enhancements for the commission of hate crimes.
3. Laws that create a civil cause of action for hate crimes.
4. Laws that require administrative agencies to collect data on hate crimes.
5. Laws that emphasize war crimes, genocide, and crimes against humanity. Prohibitions against these activities are limited to public officials (*Wikipedia*, 2007g).

Individuals have attempted to challenge the legality of hate crime laws. However, in the U.S., the U.S. Supreme Court has upheld the constitutionality of hate crime statutes. For example, the high court, in *Wisconsin v. Mitchell* (1993), upheld a Wisconsin hate crime statute that was based on model legislation that was originally drafted by the Anti-Defamation League in 1981 (*Wisconsin v. Mitchell*, 1993; ADL, 2001).

Hate crime-related death threats are an age-old problem in society. During the Spanish Inquisition, Jews were threatened with death and then murdered if they refused to convert to Christianity. In the U.S., during the Jim Crow era after the Civil War, African-Americans frequently were the targets of death threats, sexual violence, torture, lynching, and church burnings and vandalism by whites (Ogletree, 2002; PBS, 2006; Leadership Conference on Civil Rights, 2002). More than 4,700 persons were lynched in the United States between 1882 and 1968 (Ogletree, 2002). Records from the Tuskegee Institute revealed that 4,730 persons were lynched nationwide between 1882 and 1951, and 3,437 were African-Americans (Wyatt, 2007).

S.J. Morewitz, *Death Threats and Violence*, DOI: 10.1007/978-0-387-76663-8_10,
© Springer Science + Business Media, LLC, 2008

Myrdal (1944) asserted that lynching in the Jim Crow era was used by whites as a tool to support racial caste differences and keep African-Americans in subordinate positions. Lynching eliminated those blacks who may have broken white norms and also offered a powerful incentive for African-Americans to remain subordinate and passive.

In recent times, the term, hate crime (also known as bias crime), has been coined to characterize death threats and other forms of harassment and physical violence that are motivated by the offenders' hatred of individuals because of their actual or perceived disability, race, ethnicity, sexual orientation, religion, or national origin (Harlow, 2005; Sun, 2006). In addition, some individuals also consider gender-based crimes as hate crimes (McPhail and Dinitto, 2005).

The Internet, since it is a channel for world-wide electronic communication, has helped to promote hate crimes. Deirmenjian (2000) suggests that hate crimes on the Internet have become increasingly widespread. However, few studies have been conducted to measure the prevalence of electronic hate crime-based death threats.

Hate crime-based death threats take on different forms, depending on the type of hate crime target. Death threats may emphasize the supposed low income and unsanitary life style of ethnic and racial minorities, e.g., "Death to all of you dirty Mexicans." Death threats against gays and lesbians may involve alleged sexual behaviors. "I am going to kill you, you HIV-infected gays." In the above instances, the death threats are used to identify the targets for the death threat maker (DTM) using certain criteria, e.g., clean vs. dirty, HIV-negative vs. HIV-positive, prostitute vs. sexually appropriate. These criteria reflect emotionally laden and socially desirable behaviors such as the need to be clean, healthy and control one's sexual behaviors. At the same time, these death threats dehumanize and stereotype individuals.

Death threats against racial and ethnic minorities may also involve telling the targets to go back to their original homeland. Death threats may contain a number of images. For example, a death threat may be: "Go back to Saudi Arabia, or die, you lousy Arab."

Death threats made in public settings depend on the perceptions, demeanor, clothes, and behavioral cues of the offenders and targets. How does one know who is a certain racial or ethnic minority? How does one know if a person is gay or lesbian? How do you determine if someone is Jewish? Certain groups may be more recognizable than other groups. However, there are times when doubt or mistakes occur. For example, a person can be black and be from Haiti but not be African-American. Similarly, DTMs may not be able to distinguish Muslims and Arab-Americans from Hindus, Whites or other groups. Devout Muslim women's clothing, which consists of traditional Muslim covering, headscarves, and long, flowing dresses, for example, can make them more of a target than Muslim men who may wear more western-style clothes (Minnesota Advisory Committee, 2002).

What Motivates Hate-Crime Offenders?

What motivates a person to commit a hate crime? A large percentage of offenders may be young thrill-seekers and not extreme bigots (Leadership Conference on Civil Rights, 2002). A study conducted for Northeastern University in 1993 showed that 60% of the perpetrators committed hate crimes for the thrill related to the attack. Offenders often hope to gain increased status among their friends and this explains why gangs of youth commit hate crimes. For example, one "gay basher," who was interviewed, explained that he and his friends participated in the crimes to show each other how tough they were.

The second most prevalent DTM type is the reactive offender, who commits hate crimes because he feels insulted (Leadership Conference on Civil Rights, 2002). DTMs also may feel that certain behaviors or conditions threaten their own values or identity. They may feel insulted or threatened by interracial couples, gays, lesbians, and bisexuals, or individuals with other characteristics.

Fanatics or extremists who maintain an ideology of racial, religious, or ethnic hatred are the least prevalent DTM type (Leadership Conference on Civil Rights, 2002).

External Factors and Hate-Crime-Related Death Threats

It is not surprising that external factors influence the prevalence of hate-crime related death threats and other types of hate crimes. The 9/11 attacks and the emergence of Islamic terrorist acts against the U.S. can give rise to death threats against person who may be considered responsible for or allied with these terrorist efforts.

Researchers have analyzed the role of economic conditions in triggering hate crimes. The increased prevalence of hate crimes is often attributed to downturns in the economy (Green et al., 1998). The worsening economic conditions in Czarist Russia during the late 19th and early 20th centuries led to the pogroms against the Jews just as the post–World War I conditions in Germany led to the Holocaust where millions of Jews, Gypsies, homosexuals etc. were slaughtered. Historical and time-series investigations have found a link between economic downturns and the lynching of African-Americans in the South during the pre-Depression era. However, similar techniques have not found an association between economic conditions and hate crimes against minorities using data for the late 20th century.

Impact of Hate Crimes

Like the lynchings in the Jim Crow era, hate crimes in recent decades have the function of keeping people in subordinate and inferior roles because of some attribute. Death threats are used to terrorize the hate crime victims and to remind them that their very identities violate the dominant values and beliefs in society.

Hate crimes tend to put a figurative fence around some of its victims. People may change their daily activities, limit their social interactions, and change their life and career choices—all in an effort to remain safe. Yet other hate crime victims refuse to let these crimes change their daily lives, and fight back, using any means they can—publicity, organizations, criminal justice system, etc.

Hate crimes don't affect only individual victims but also have community-wide effects (Leadership Conference on Civil Rights, 2002).

Characteristics of Hate Crimes

With the passage of the 1990 Hate Crime Statistics Act, the U.S. Attorney General was charged with the duty to collect data on hate crimes based on race, ethnicity, religion, or sexual orientation (Harlow, 2005). An amendment was added in 1994 to include disabled persons in the list of groups to be monitored. Nationwide data on hate crimes now come from two sources: the National Crime Victimization Survey (NCVS) consisting of a nationally representative sample of about 77,600 individuals who are interviewed biannually and the FBI Uniform Crime Reporting Program. The NCVS's definition of a hate crime requires that there must have been evidence that the perpetrator used derogatory words, left hate symbols, or that the police corroborated that a hate crime had occurred.

According to estimates derived from victim reports to the NCVS, an average of 210,000 hate crime victimizations took place from July 2000 through December 2003 (Harlow, 2005). An average of 191,000 incidents of hate crimes involving one or more victims occurred during this period. Victims indicated that 92,000 of these hate crime incidents were reported to the police.

Type of Hate-Crime Offenses

Aggravated assault, and being threatened with a weapon constituted 13.5% of hate crimes during this period, compared to only 3.1% of other crimes. Simple assault and verbal threats constituted 28% of hate crimes, compared to only 6% of other crimes. It is not known which percentage of the above threats were death threats.

Between July 2000 and December 2003, about 84% of the hate crimes reported to NCVS were violent offenses, e.g., sexual assault, robbery, or simple or aggravated assault compared to 23% of other crimes reported to the NCVS The NCVS data also revealed that hate crimes involved a higher percentage of less serious violent offenses compared to other crimes reported to the NCVS. Victims were threatened or assaulted without being injured or threatened with a weapon in about 46% of the hate crime victimizations, compared to only 12% of the nonhate crime victimizations.

Hate crimes were less likely to involve property crimes than nonhate crimes. About 13% of the hate crimes and 63% of the nonhate crimes involved theft of a motor vehicle or anonymous theft of property or household goods.

   Although per capita victimization rates in the NCVS did not vary by race or ethnicity, most of the hate crime victims identified race as the perpetrators' motivation for committing the crime (56% of the victimizations). Ethnicity was perceived to be the offenders' motivation in 27.9% of the victimizations. In 30.6% of the victimizations, the victim's association with individuals who have certain characteristics, e.g., multiracial couples was thought to be the perpetrators' motivation (Harlow, 2005).

Offenders

According to the NCVS findings, 68% of hate crimes consisted of incidents where one person abused the victim or victims. Hate crimes, which involved violent offenses, were more likely to be committed by two or more offenders (32.5%) than violent crimes unmotivated by hate (18.5%). Hate crime offenders were mainly male. About 79% of the victims reported that at least one of the perpetrators was male, compared to 83% of perpetrators in non-hate-oriented violent offenses (Harlow, 2005).

   Steinberg et al. (2003), in their review of the literature, noted that single or small groups of young males commit hate crimes. Moreover, studies have shown that these young males often are not affiliated with organized hate groups.

   Hate-crime offenders in the NCVS study were more likely to be White (43.5%), followed by African-American (38.8%), other race (11.9%), and more than one race (5.7%). About 26% of the hate crime perpetrators and 33% of nonhate crime violent offenders were described by victims as being 20 years or younger. Most of the victims (52%) of hate crimes were attacked by strangers or those they recognized only by sight, compared to 45% of the victims of non-hate-based violent offenses. [Hate crimes can also be committed against acquaintances, intimate partners, or family members (Leadership Conference on Civil Rights, 2002).]

   The NCVS study also showed that about 24% of the victims of both hate crimes and non-hate-related violent offenses reported that the perpetrator used a weapon, such as a firearm, knife or other sharp or blunt object. About 31% of hate crime victims and non-hate crime victims believed that the perpetrators were intoxicated or high on drugs at the time of their crimes. Approximately 7% of the hate crime victims and about 6% of the victims of non-hate crimes believed that their attackers had been gang members. The perceived motivations of hate crime offenders did not vary by the gender of the offenders.

Victims

In the NCVS, the per capita rates of hate crime victimization did not vary based on the victims' gender, race, ethnicity, or educational level. However, higher rates of hate-crime victimization were reported by young individuals, those never married, separated, or divorced, those with low incomes, and people living in urban areas (Harlow, 2005).

Another aspect of hate crimes is whether they involve most single attacks or do they often consist of a series of attacks. Barnes and Ephross (1994), in a study of 59 hate crime victims, including African-Americans, whites and Southeast Asians, discovered that more than 50% of the victims reported suffering a series of hate crime attacks.

Death Threats Against African-Americans

Before the Civil War, African-Americans were subjected to various forms of racially motivated violence, including death threats and assaults, and their churches were burned and vandalized. Slavery was outlawed after the Civil War, however African-Americans were increasingly targeted by racially motivated hate crimes, such as lynching, church fires, vandalism, etc. (Leadership Conference on Civil Rights, 2002). Beginning in the 1950s, civil rights activism resulted in school desegregation and the racial and ethnic integration of neighborhoods, workplaces, and other institutions. These advances in civil rights actually promoted race-based death threats and other hate crimes against African-Americans. In recent times, the U.S. has become more ethnically and culturally diverse, causing an increased frequency of racial hate-based death threats and related crimes (Willis, 2004).

Rapid racial, ethnic, and socioeconomic changes occur in many neighborhoods and communities in the U.S. (Taub and Wilson, 2006), leading to increased racial and ethnic tensions among residents who believe that their neighborhoods and communities had been taken over by lower socioeconomic status minority groups. These conflicts can trigger hate-based death threats and other forms of intimidation against these groups (Archibold, 2007; Leadership Conference on Civil Rights, 2002).

Of the 4,831 racially motivated hate crimes reported to the FBI in 1995, 2,998 or 62.1% were against African Americans. Such hate crimes take on a variety of forms. For example, on March 29, 1996, Bridget Ward, an African-American woman, and her two young daughters, Jamila and Jasmine, moved into Bridesburg, an almost all-white neighborhood of Philadelphia. That night, Ms. Ward heard a group of young people marching down the street, cheering: "Burn, mothf_____, burn." The next morning Ms. Ward found racial slurs smeared on her house, ketchup was splattered on her front sidewalk and back porch, and an oily substance was smeared in the rear of her house.

In another incident, a white man threatened an African-American couple in Harper Woods, Michigan, telling them that he would murder and cut their bodies into parts if they moved into his neighborhood (Leadership Conference on Civil Rights, 2002).

Weapons are also used to make racial hate crime-motivated death threats. For example, an automobile driven by an African-American woman in

Berwick, Pennsylvania, was hit repeatedly by a white man who made racial slurs and threatened to murder her and her son (Leadership Conference on Civil Rights, 2002).

The epidemic of suspicious African-American church fires in the 1990s appeared to be racially motivated hate crimes designed to terrorize the African-American community. The church burnings are of special concern because African-American churches are considered to be the most important institution in the African-American community. The safety of African-Americans has been threatened since those who attack African-American churches often also attack African-Americans.

Hate groups, such as the Ku Klux Klan (KKK), criminal gangs, and those who sympathize with these groups have made hate-based death threats against African-Americans, target African-American churches for arson and vandalism, and engage in other forms of racially-motivated intimidation against African-Americans. The first recorded arson of an African-American church occurred in South Carolina in 1822. In Cincinnati in 1829, white mobs set African-American churches on fire. During the 1830s in Philadelphia, whites also torched African-American churches. The KKK sought to restore white supremacy after the Civil War by burning down and vandalizing African-American churches.

During the civil rights period, the 16th Street Baptist Church in Birmingham, Alabama, was bombed and four young girls were killed. Another African-American church, St. John Baptist Church in Dixiana, South Carolina, illustrates the history of attacks on African-American churches. The church, which was established in 1765, has been attacked during the eras of slavery, the Civil War, Reconstruction, segregation, and civil rights. During church services in 1983, a group of white people shot out the windows of the church and later that day wrote "KKK" on the church door, defecated on the sacrament cloth, and committed other acts of vandalism against the church. The church was burned down on August 15, 1995, and in May 1996, three white teenagers were charged with the crime.

Since January 1, 1995, the St. John Baptist Church has been one of at least 73 African-American churches that have had suspicious fires or were targeted for acts of desecration. Although white churches were also targeted, the rate of African-American church arsons was twice the rate of white church arsons. Most of African-American church arsons occurred in the South. Two geographic clusters were identified: (1) a 200-mile oval in western Tennessee, Alabama, and Mississippi, and (2) North Carolina and South Carolina, but other areas were also targeted. Members of the "Fourth Reich Skinheads" were convicted for planning to attack the historic First African Methodist Episcopal Church in South-Central area of Los Angeles. The hate group had hoped that the church attack would spark a race war (Leadership Conference on Civil Rights, 2002).

In addition to African-American churches and other organizations, civil rights leaders have been targets of death threats. Dr. Martin Luther King, Jr. faced death threats for leading civil rights demonstrations. King organized and led these demonstrations despite these death threats (*Wikipedia*, 2007c).

Death Threats Against Hispanics

Hispanics have been the victims of death threats and other forms of intimidation and violence. A 1995 report revealed that of 814 hate crimes that were based on ethnicity or national origin of the victim, 63.3% were against Hispanics. Longstanding antagonisms between Hispanics and other racial and ethnic groups have occurred in California and throughout the Southwest.

Hate crimes against Hispanics, like those against other minority groups, are part of a long history of racial, ethnic and religious hatred. During periods of nativism in California and throughout the Southwest, both new immigrants and long-time U.S. residents of Hispanic descent have been criticized for various social and economic troubles. About 500,000 citizens and non-citizens of Mexican heritage were the victims of mass deportations during the economic Depression of the 1930s. A paramilitary operation with the derogatory name, "Operation Wetback" in the early 1950s resulted in the deportation of tens of thousands of Mexicans from California and several southwestern states.

Decreased employment opportunities and defense cutbacks, coming during an economic recession, have led to renewed efforts to restrict legal immigration and pass punitive laws against undocumented immigrants. Fifty-nine percent of California voters approved controversial Proposition 187 in November, 1994, which made undocumented immigrants ineligible for a majority of public services such as non-emergency care and public education. Hate crimes, including hate speech and hate-based violent offenses, against Hispanics increased during the emotional debates over Proposition 187. After the proposition was passed, there was also an increase in civil rights violations of Hispanics, including U.S. citizens and permanent legal residents. In 1994, the Los Angeles County Human Relations Commission reported an 11.9% increase in hate crimes against Hispanics in the Los Angeles metropolitan area.

Hate crimes against Hispanics have not been restricted to California and the Southwestern states. Hispanics have been the targets of attacks from the Midwest, to the Northeast, to Florida. Those who have been targeted include Mexican-Americans, Puerto Ricans, Cuban-Americans, and Central American and South American immigrants (Leadership Conference on Civil Rights, 2002).

In 1995, Allen Adams and Tad Page were sentenced to prison for their shooting of four Hispanics in Livermore, Maine. Adams and Page taunted the individuals, three of whom were migrant laborers, with ethnic epithets, telling them to: "Go back to Mexico or we'll send you there in a body bag." After the migrant laborers drove away, Adams and Page chased them by automobile, firing 11 rounds from a handgun into the laborers' automobile. One victim was shot in the arm and another bullet hit the driver's headrest, narrowly missing the driver. In the same year, arsonists burned down a Hispanic family's home in the area of Palmdale, California. The arsonists spray painted the house with the slogans: "White power" and "Your family dies."

Hispanics have also been the target of severe police beatings. Two Riverside County, California sheriff's deputies in April 1996 were videotaped assaulting two suspected undocumented Mexican immigrants. The videotape showed the deputies beating the man and woman with batons and grabbing the woman by her hair and using her hair to force her to the ground. Leaders of Hispanic rights organizations assert that Hispanics are frequently attacked by private citizens and law enforcement officials. They believe that this trend is due in part to a hostile political atmosphere that targets anyone who appears to be an immigrant and subjects them to excessive law enforcement actions.

Since 9/11, the emergence of so-called undocumented immigration as a major national policy controversy has triggered death threats and forms of violence against suspected undocumented individuals. One of the issues underlying the controversy over undocumented immigrants is the belief that undocumented immigrants are taking jobs away from those who are lawfully in the U.S. (Leadership Conference on Civil Rights, 2002).

Undocumented immigrants become visible when they congregate in groups at building supplies stores, and on streets looking for jobs as day laborers. This visibility may encourage local residents to voice death threats and commit other types of violence against them.

The controversy over undocumented immigrants is also tied to concern about threats to homeland security, especially since the attacks on 9/11. Since undocumented immigrants can enter the U.S. through its porous borders, there is fear that many of these illegal "border crossers" are criminals or terrorists who pose a threat to U.S. citizens. These fears may be the provocation for some death threats.

Death threats have also been made against government officials because of their ethnic and racial backgrounds, or against those who either have expressed contrary views about, or who are carrying out immigration policies.

California Lt. Governor Cruz Bustamante and Los Angeles Mayor Antonio Villaraigosa and other elected officials of Mexican descent have been targets of death threats during the national debate over immigration. California Governor Arnold Schwarzenegger told reporters that his Lieutenant Governor, Cruz Bustamente, received a postcard from Pasadena, CA, which essentially said: "All you dirty Mexicans should go back to Mexico. The only good Mexican is a dead Mexican." Subsequent to his appearance with Mayor Villaraigosa at some immigration rallies at the end of March 2006, he began to receive "nasty e-mails" (Williams, 2006).

Death Threats Against Asian Pacific Americans[1]

As with other minorities, throughout history Asian Pacific Americans have been subjected to discrimination, death threats, and related violence. Since they first came to the U.S., Chinese, Japanese, and other Asian Pacific Americans faced cycles of discrimination and intimidation. In the nineteenth century, Chinese-Americans provided cheap labor for the mining industry and the building of the

---

[1] Where no other references are cited, the information was obtained from the Leadership Conference on Civil Rights, 2002.

railroads. Other workers resented them, and as a result discriminated against them and intimidated them. The courts began to regard Chinese-Americans as second-class citizens. For example, in 1854, Chinese-Americans were prevented from testifying in a murder case involving whites by the California Supreme Court decision in *People v. Hall (Wikipedia,* 2007h).

People v. Hall not only protected whites from prosecution for committing crimes against Chinese-Americans, it also increased violence and discrimination against them. In Hells Canyon, Oregon, in 1887, 31 Chinese-American gold miners were murdered and their six killers were never convicted (Nokes, 2006).

After the attack on Pearl Harbor in 1941, Japanese-Americans were treated as members of a potential 5th column. Their civil rights were suspended and they were forcibly relocated to internment camps. In addition, although China was the U.S.'s ally during the war, Chinese-Americans were the subjects of harassment and intimidation by people who believed that all Asian Americans were a threat to the nation.

In recent decades, Asian Pacific Americans continue to be subjected to intimidation, including death threats and assaults. Anti-Japanese-American feelings persisted after World War II and were intensified by Americans' resentment over economic competition from Japan. The Korean Conflict and more recently, resentment against economic competition from South Korea worsened both anti-South Korean feelings and a general anti-Asian resentment. Vietnamese Americans were the targets of hate crimes as Americans experienced the trauma, shame, and humiliation of losing the Vietnam War.

Many individuals who evidence hostility toward minority groups seem to be unable to differentiate the ethnicity of one group from another. As a result, they lump all Asian Pacific Americans together, and are equally biased toward all. Their resentments have been exacerbated by the stereotypes of Asian Pacific Americans as harder working, better students, who are wealthier than most Americans. These stereotypes parallel those about Jewish Americans, which in turn may trigger hate crimes against the Jews. Others in the U.S. regard Asian Pacific Americans as foreigners and not as legitimate citizens, regardless of their birthplace or naturalization status (Wikipedia, 2007i).

Of the 4,831 racially motivated hate crimes reported to the FBI in 1995, 355 or 7.5% involved Asian Pacific American victims. The National Asian Pacific American Legal Consortium conducted an audit in 1995 and reported 458 hate crimes. They concluded that hate crimes against Asian Pacific Americans are underreported.

At times, single or small groups of young males will threaten and attack Asian Pacific Americans, while spewing ethnic epithets. In Coral Springs, Florida, in August, 1992, a group of young white people fatally assaulted a 19-year-old Vietnamese American pre-medicine student, calling him "chink" and "Vietcong."

In various incidents, people under the influence of alcohol or drugs have been involved in violent hate-based assaults against Asian Pacific Americans. In June, 1995, three intoxicated young white men taunted a 23-year-old Vietnamese-

American man, Thanh Mai, with an ethnic epithet: "What the f— are you looking at, gook." Mr. Mai tried to walk away, but one of the young men, Michael Hallman, hit him in the face with such force that he died five days later from severe head trauma.

Hate groups, such as "skin heads," have carried out death threats and assaults against Asian Pacific Americans. One such incident occurred in San Francisco, California, in October, 1995, when a white man, dressed in typical "skin head" attire, yelled: "Death to all minorities," and kicked a Filipino-American man in the leg, fracturing it.

Death Threats Against Individuals from the Middle East and South Asia

The total number of hate-crimes committed against Arab-Americans and South Asians is unknown, since the Justice Department does not recognize them as minority groups. Arab-Americans have been stereotyped as terrorists, religious fanatics, extremists, desert nomads, and belly dancers. Many Americans often resent small business owners of Middle-Eastern, Jewish and Asian Pacific descent. Nativism and anti-immigrant feelings trigger these animosities and lead to death threats and other forms of violence. These groups suffer the blame for problems caused by others. For example: in the three days following the 1995 Oklahoma City bombing of the federal office building, there were 227 incidents involving harassment of Muslims even though Muslims had no connection with this bombing.

During crises in the Middle East, such as wars, hostage-taking incidents, or terrorist attacks there and in the U.S., Arab-Americans and South Asian Americans face increasing intimidation and assaults, including death threats For example, following the Oklahoma City bombing, an Iraqi immigrant in her mid-20s was the target of anti-Muslim epithets and her house was attacked and vandalized (Minnesota Advisory Committee, 2002; Stephens, 2002).

Since the attacks of 9/11, Muslims, Arab-Americans, and South Asians have faced a backlash of harassment and violence, ranging from verbal harassment to physical assaults, death threats, and murder. Muslim women, who wear traditional Muslim covering, headscarves, and long dresses, have been targeted for death threats. One Muslim woman in Minnesota was inside her apartment when four men tried to break down her door. They were unsuccessful and told her that they would be back for her later (Minnesota Advisory Committee, 2002; Stephens, 2002).

The prevalence of these death threats and other hate crime incidents is not known. Persons of Muslim, Arab-American, and South Asian descent may be fearful of reprisals if they contact law enforcement agencies or the media about their hate crime attacks (Minnesota Advisory Committee, 2002; Stephens, 2002).

People of Middle Eastern and South Asian descent are faced with not only crimes against their person, but their houses of worship have been burned down or vandalized. Seven mosques were burned downed or vandalized in 1995 (Leadership Conference on Civil Rights, 2002; Stephens, 2002).

Death Threats and Native Americans and Alaskan Natives

The history of wars between Native Americans and Whites, especially in the nineteenth century, the genocide committed against Native Americans, the takeover of their lands, and their forced relocation to economically depressed reservations have led to animosities toward them. Negative stereotypes of Native Americans and Alaskan Natives such as their susceptibility to alcohol, their wide-spread poverty, different cultural attitudes and varying social problems have fostered harassment and intimidation. Of the 4,831 racially-based hate crimes reported to the FBI in 1995, 41 or about 1% targeted Native Americans and Alaskan Natives (Leadership Conference on Civil Rights, 2002).

Death Threats and Gay, Lesbian, Bisexual, and Transgender Hate Crimes

Herek (1989) notes that according to surveys, as many as 92% of lesbians and gay men report being the victim of anti-gay verbal abuse or threats. Surveys have shown that as many as 24% of gays and lesbians have reportedly been physically attacked because of their sexual orientation. According to the National Coalition of Anti-Violence Programs, there were 2,212 hate crimes against lesbians and male homosexuals in 1995. More recently, the NCVS data revealed that bias against the victim's sexual orientation was perceived to be the motivation for 17.9% of the victimizations (Harlow, 2005). Of the 1,019 incidents of hate crimes motivated by sexual orientation that were reported to the FBI in 1995, 735 involved male homosexuals and 146 were against lesbians.

Reverend Troy D. Perry, a human rights activist and delegate to the 1997 White House Conference on Hate Crimes, in 1968 had founded the Metropolitan Community Churches, a Christian denomination with more than 300 churches in 22 countries. He said that his churches, which have a primary, affirming ministry to gays, lesbian and transgender individuals, have been the targets of an unprecedented level of threats, hate calls and hate mail as well as arson, fire bombings, vandalism, graffiti, and desecration. Over the last three decades, Perry notes that seven percent of Metropolitan Community Churches have been the targets of arson or bombings. Moreover, Perry asserts that the media have basically ignored these hate crimes (Worldwide Faith News archives, 2002).

One example of a hate crime committed against a congregation of the Metropolitan Community Churches involved two telephone bomb threats against the Church of the Gentle Shepherd in Vancouver, Washington, and a death threat against the pastor of the church. In one of the telephone threats, the caller said that he was going to burn their (expletive deleted) church to the ground because they're gay and lesbian homosexuals. Earlier telephone calls to the church had been rambling and disoriented but a week later the calls became explicitly hostile and threatening. Casey Gene Peirsol, a 44-year-old man, was arrested on May 21, 2002, and charged with malicious harassment and making a bomb threat. The Vancouver Police, who traced the threatening phone calls to Peirsol, suspected that he was planning to blow up the church to murder Reverend Dianne Shaw, the senior pastor of the congregation (Worldwide Faith News archives, 2002).

Richmond and McKenna (1998) suggest that hatred of gays is a socially accepted and culturally based pattern of beliefs. Wilton (1999) explored various cultural roots of homophobia and found that in Great Britain and the U.S., anxiety about sexual differences, a fear of female sexuality, the sexualizing of lesbianism, and the inability to identify lesbians are some of the problems that underlie common cultural expressions of homophobia, thus contributing to a person's rational for making death threats and committing other hate crimes. Hatred of homosexuals may reflect a biased disgust of the homosexual lifestyle (Richmond and McKenna, 1998).

Cowan et al. (2005) evaluated heterosexuals' attitudes toward hate crimes and hate speech using a sample of 74 male and 95 female heterosexual college students. They discovered that traditional heterosexual beliefs were associated with homophobia and an acceptance of hate crimes.

Dunbar (2006) analyzed 1,538 hate crimes in Los Angeles County to assess the impact of the victims' race, gender, and sexual orientation on the severity of violence committed against them and found that hate crimes against gay and lesbian victims involved a greater level of violence compared to hate crimes that were motivated by other biases.

Moreover, attacks against gays and lesbians are becoming more violent. In 1995, almost 40% of the hate crimes against gays and lesbians consisted of assaults or attempted assaults with a weapon. Seven hundred and eleven victims sustained injuries from these attacks and 37% sustained serious injury or death. Thirty-eight percent of those who were injured received medical treatment, 10% were hospitalized, and 19% needed medical treatment but did not receive it. In 1995, there were 29 murders related to gay hate crimes and most of these murders involved mutilation or other serious injuries.

It is sometimes difficult to distinguish gays, lesbians, and bisexuals from heterosexuals in public settings. Although some may engage in a stereotypic behavior which seems to signal their sexual orientation, others do not. Consequently, there is a distinct possibility that some death threats are made based on erroneous perceptions of the targets' sexual orientation.

As in other race-and ethnic-based death threats, external factors also may influence the prevalence and nature of death threats against gays, lesbians, and bisexuals. Herek (1989) noted that assaults against gays and lesbians had increased in the mid 1980s and assailants had made reference to HIV during their attacks.

Gays, lesbians, and bisexuals may be more likely to become targets of death threats and other hate crimes when there are emotional and controversial media coverage of gay rights and their role in society. National debates over gay marriage, children raised by gays and lesbians, and gays in the military are some of the emotionally-charged issues that can trigger various forms of harassment and physical violence against this group. These issues, like the debates over immigration and affirmative action, can demonize minority groups who are already targeted for harassment and violence.

Threats and associated forms of violence against gays and lesbians in the military occur despite various directives, such as the Department of Defense Directive 1304.26, which prohibits harassment or violence against any service member, for any reason (SLDN, 2006).

Homosexuals, like other minority groups, frequently feel isolated and susceptible to attacks because of their precarious relationship with law enforcement agencies. Hate crimes against gays and lesbians are reported to the police at a lower rate (an estimated 36% in 1995) compared to 48% for all crimes. In many instances, when these hate crimes are reported to the police, the law enforcement officials list them under a general category such as "robbery" or "assault," instead of as a hate crime motivated by sexual discrimination. As a result, the prevalence of sexual orientation hate crimes is probably significantly under-reported on a regular basis.

Hate crimes against homosexuals involve sexually oriented epithets and slurs. In 1995, while a gay man was walking in a park in Washington, D.C., three men accosted him at gunpoint, and forced him to go underneath a bridge, where they beat him severely. Before he lost consciousness the victim heard one of the attackers say, "Were going to teach this f—— faggot a lesson!"

Hate crimes against homosexuals may involve a combination of epithets and hate-based symbols as well as written and verbal threats and harassment. Individuals who have multiple minority status, e.g., African-American and lesbian can be subjected to hate crimes that recognize these multiple statuses. For instance, an African-American lesbian discovered a note saying, "Hate Nigger Faggots" at her door, soon after moving to a new home in Minneapolis, Minnesota. The woman and her child were subjected to verbal epithets from their neighbors over the next several weeks. Her neighbors called her a "dyke," a "faggot," and a "nigger." The woman finally left the neighborhood after a burned cross was placed outside her home (Leadership Conference on Civil Rights, 2002).

Death Threats Based on Religion

In the NCVS study, hate-based death threats based on the victim's presumed religious background occurred in 12.4% of the victimizations (Harlow, 2005). A majority of hate crimes directed at individuals because of their religion have targeted Jews. Eighty-two percent of such crimes reported to the FBI for 1995 involved Jewish victims.

Death threats and other forms of hate crimes against Jews are an age-old problem. Jews have experienced centuries of assaults, from the pogroms in Eastern

Europe to the Nazi Holocaust to the cross-burnings of the Ku Klux Klan to the destruction of synagogues in the United States.

Anti-Semitism has been fueled by slanders and stereotypes that date back for centuries and seem to have originated in Europe. These slanders and stereotypes are based on various myths that over the years have become beliefs, such as the idea that the Jews killed Christ or are involved in a wide variety of conspiracies.

As in other minority groups, hate crimes against Jews reflect changing external conditions. During the 1950s and 1960s, civil rights activism in the U.S. led to burnings and bombings of Jewish synagogues and other places of worship whose members sympathized with racial integration.

Groups on both the extreme right and left have little in common except for their anti-Jewish rhetoric. As in previous centuries, these extremists have spread anti-Semitic conspiracy theories among African-Americans, which in turn has encouraged and exacerbated conflicts between African-Americans and Jews.

In different countries over time, Jews and other religious minority groups have been the victims of officially sanctioned discrimination in employment, education, and housing and have been targeted for death threats and other violence (U.S. DoS., 2006). For example, although Jews are a recognized religious minority in Iran, the Iranian government's anti-Israel policies create a hostile environment for the small Jewish community in that country. State-run Iranian television has been decidedly anti-Semitic. One show, Al-Shatat, which was previously shown on the Hezbollah's Al-Manar television channel, depicted Jews as being the cause of the problems of the world. One of the country's leading religious authorities, Ayatollah Hossein Nouri-Hamedani, told a group of clerics in April 2005 that the Jews should be fought and vanquished. He said that the death of the Jews would prepare the ground for the Hidden Imam to emerge.

In other countries, Jews have faced latent institutional anti-Semitism, creating fertile ground for death threats and other violence to be committed against this religious minority group. In the 1950s and 1960s, many Jewish professionals left Ireland because of institutional anti-Semitism (SRI, 2005). For example, Jewish physicians had difficulty obtaining hospital privileges in Catholic or state-run hospitals and faced obstacles in joining professional associations and clubs. The lord mayor of Cork, Gerald Goldberg, was the target of death threats. He attributed these death threats to the media's biased reporting on the Israeli army's invasion of Lebanon in 1982 and the death of two Irish peacekeeping soldiers in Lebanon. Also at about the same time, a synagogue in Cork was bombed. During the 1980s, Jewish community offices in Ireland reportedly received abusive and anti-Semitic telephone calls.

Of the 1,277 hate crimes in the U.S. motivated by religious hatred that were reported to the FBI in 1995, 1,058 or 82.9% involved Jewish victims.

A survey of anti-Semitic incidents reported to the Anti-Defamation League in 1995 indicated that there were 1,843 acts involving acts against persons or property. Included within these acts were 1,116 incidents involving harassment and 727 acts of vandalism.

Jews were threatened with death following a fatal traffic accident in Crown Heights, Brooklyn, which has a history of racial and religious conflicts among Hasidic Jews, African-Americans, and Caribbean Nationals. The driver of the car that killed Gavin Cato, a 7-year-old African-American and injured his cousin, Angela, was part of the motorcade of the Grand Rebbe of the Lubavitch Hasidic community, Menachem M. Schneerson. Following this accident, a riot erupted for 3 days in which crowds roamed the streets yelling such things as: "Get the Jews" and "Heil Hitler." The roaming groups attacked the Jewish-owned homes, automobiles and other property. One Jewish man, Yankel Rosenbaum, an Australian scholar, was assaulted by a gang of 20 youths and died from his injuries (Wikipedia, 2007j).

Setting fire to or vandalizing synagogues and other places of worship is a form of intimidation as well as a death threat against their congregations.

Members of religious minority groups are especially vulnerable to death threats. In a case that was decided by the 7th U.S. Circuit Court of Appeals, John Said Boctor, who belonged to the Coptic Orthodox Christian Church, testified that a fellow Copt, Hanna Mousa, and his wife began to receive death threats from Muslim extremists after the couple married and the wife converted from Islam to Christianity. Boctor, reported that he received death threats from individuals who said they would "cut his throat" unless he told them where the Mousa family was hiding. Boctor was accosted one night and beaten by three men who called him an infidel. The men threatened to kill him if he notified human rights organizations about the situation (Manson, 2007a).

Death threats frequently are made against those who violate deeply-held religious laws, customs, beliefs, and values. In Muslim countries, women who violate religious and cultural traditions may be subjected to death threats, honor killings and other forms of violence. The Muslim pop singer, Deeyah, reported receiving a string of death threats on her website from religious extremists after she tried to foster women's rights. In one of her videos, the pop singer dropped a burqa to show a bikini (Bharadwa, 2006).

Women and/or their relatives in Muslim communities face death threats and honor killings if: they refuse to participate in arranged marriage; have sexual relations outside of marriage; provide an inadequate dowry; or wear nontraditional clothes. In India, a Muslim woman living in a strict Muslim community was subjected to death threats from her cousin after he raped her, and as a result she was forced to marry him. The day after the wedding, he divorced her because her dowry was not to his liking. Again, he threatened to kill her and continued to harass her and her family. After her father filed a civil action against him, he threatened to kill her father. Later, her father was found dead under suspicious circumstances (International Campaign Against Honour Killings, 2005).

Employed women may also be the victims of death threats. For example, Feldman (2001) evaluated the increasing employment of women in the garment export industry in Bangladesh and discovered that the emergence of a fundamentalist Islamic party known as the Jamaat-i-Islami led to death threats against employed women.

Death Threats Based on Disability

Waxman (1991) suggested that cultural beliefs about disability can lead to violence, including sexual violence against disabled persons. According to the NCVS findings, 10.5% of the hate crime victimizations were attributable to the victim's disability (Harlow, 2005).

Studies indicate that women with disabilities are especially susceptible to domestic violence and sexual assault (Brownridge, 2006; Milberger et al., 2003; United Nations, 2006). Brownridge (2006), based on a representative sample of 7,027 women in Canada who were living in a marital or common-law union, found that, in the previous five years, women with disabilities had a 40% greater odds of partner violence than women without disabilities. Using a sample of 177 adult women with physical disabilities, Milberger et al. (2003) showed that 53% of the women reported a history of abuse.

In addition, Martin et al. (2006) discovered that women with disabilities were four times more likely to have been sexually assaulted in the previous year than women without disabilities. However, both women with disabilities and women without disabilities had the same risk of being physically assaulted.

Children with physical, psychosocial, and sensorial impairments are more susceptible to violence and maltreatment than "normal" children (Olivan Gonzalvo, 2005).

More research is needed to assess which factors increase the risks of death threats, harassment and physical violence against persons with disabilities.

Gender-Based Death Threats

Individuals may be threatened with death based on their gender. Many advocates for women's right and others believe that gender-associated violence should be viewed as a hate crime. However, in the U.S., the Hate Crime Statistics Act was passed and re-authorized without including gender in the hate crime victim category. Neither the NCVS nor the Uniform Crime Report publications include gender as a category for hate crimes (Harlow, 2005). It is possible that criminal justice officials in the U.S. may believe that violence against women is motivated more by a desire for power and control rather than due to gender bias (McPhail and Dinitto, 2005).

Chapter 11
Death Threats and Terrorism

There are many definitions of terrorism, but they all pretty much agree that it is a political tactic that involves the use of threats of violence, such as death threats or actual violence, often against civilians, to frighten members of the public or target group into accepting certain political demands.

Terrorism is generally used for political, not military objectives. Often groups employ terrorist strategies since they are when they are unable to initiate open attacks on governments. Terrorism is the weapon of choice of alienated persons and its psychological effects on the population have been exacerbated by the media's widespread and immediate coverage of terrorist events. Governments have great difficulty preventing terrorist activities, but increased monitoring of potential terrorists' planning and financial activities and international agreements to tighten border security and to deport terrorists back to their home countries for trial may help control terrorism, at least for a while.

Terrorism dates back to the time of ancient Greece and has existed since that time. The word, terror, was first employed to describe the state terrorism carried out by French revolutionaries between 1789 and 1795, especially during the so-called "Reign of Terror" between 1793 and 1794. The revolutionaries used kangaroo courts, executions by guillotine, and other forms of violence against individuals thought to be political opponents. Since that time, the term, terrorism, has broader meanings. It consists of a variety of actions, such as random executions, bombings, kidnappings, and hijackings designed to achieve political objectives and wreak terror in the population (Wikipedia, 2007o).

Individual terrorists and groups during the nineteenth century employed kidnappings, assassinations, and bombings to reduce popular support for what they considered to be tyrannical regimes. In the U.S., terrorist activities were first carried out on a wide scale in the latter part of the nineteenth century. An anarchist's bomb killed eight policemen during a demonstration in Chicago's Haymarket Square on May 4, 1886. Another anarchist's bomb killed 30 individuals and seriously injured

---

[1] Unless otherwise identified, the material in this chapter was obtained from the *Encyclopedia of American History*.

S.J. Morewitz, *Death Threats and Violence*, DOI: 10.1007/978-0-387-76663-8_11,
© Springer Science + Business Media, LLC, 2008

more than 200 people on Wall Street on September 16, 1920. Between 1850 and the 1960s, the "Ku Klux Klan" (KKK), a white supremacist hate group, was the most significant terrorist group in the U.S., although anarchists during this period received the most newspaper coverage. The KKK employed tactics such as lynching, beating, and marches to instill fear in African-Americans who wished to vote or participate in social and political activities (Wikipedia, 2007o).

Extreme-left terrorist groups, beginning in the late 1960s, used kidnappings and bomb attacks to protest the Vietnam War. Other groups like the "Symbionese Liberation Army" attacked civilians and the police in order to start a "people's revolution." These extreme left groups faded away in the 1970s and 1980s and were replaced by extreme-right terrorist groups. A truck bomb exploded outside the Alfred P. Murrah federal building in Oklahoma City, killing 168 people and destroying the building. At the time, this was the worst terrorist attack in the history of the U.S. In 1998, FBI Director Louis J. Freeh testified before the U.S. Senate, stating that extreme-right terrorist groups, including paramilitary (militia) groups, Puerto Rican terrorist groups, and special interest groups currently constitute the main domestic terrorist threat.

After the 1960s, there was an increase in international terrorist attacks on U.S. citizens in the Middle East and in Latin America. On November 4, 1979, Iranian terrorists kidnapped 66 diplomats at the U.S. Embassy in Tehran and did not release them until January 20, 1981. Between 1995 and 2000, 77 U.S. citizens were killed and 651 were injured abroad by international terrorists.

Beginning in the mid-1970s, international terrorists started to perpetrate terrorist attacks in the U.S. The Puerto Rican Armed National Liberation Front carried out a bomb attack on the Fraunces Tavern in New York City on January 24, 1975, killing four persons. On December 29, 1975, another bombing occurred at the TWA terminal at LaGuardia Airport, and eleven individuals were killed. No individual or group took responsibility for that bombing. Another major terrorist bombing attack took place in the basement of the World Trade Center in New York City on February 26, 1993. Terrorists exploded a truck bomb, killing six persons and injuring thousands. The mastermind of the bombing, Ramzi Yousef, stated at his trial that he supports terrorist attacks against the U.S. government and Israel (Wikipedia, 2007o).

Terrorist acts since the late 20th century have been perpetrated by a variety of groups, including the Italian Red Brigades, the Irish Republican Army, the Palestine Liberation Organization, the Shining Path in Peru, the Liberation Tigers of Tamil Ealam in Sri Lanka, and the militia organizations in the U.S. Religiously-inspired terrorists have also been prominent. Extremist Christian groups have attacked abortion clinics and providers in the U.S. Muslim extremists have participated in the terrorist activities of Hamas and Al Qaeda. Other examples of extremist religious groups are the extremist Sikhs in India and the Aum Shinrikyo in Japan, who launched a nerve gas attack in Tokyo's subway system in 1995. The U.N. Security Council in 1999 recommended more effective international cooperation against terrorism and requested that governments not offer assistance to terrorists.

The most deadly terrorist attack on U.S. soil took place on September 11, 2001, when 19 Middle-East terrorists hijacked four airplanes. Two planes destroyed the

World Trade Center in New York City, one crashed into the Pentagon, and one, which may have been flying to the White House, crashed in Pennsylvania, after passengers fought with the hijackers.

The September 11 attack appeared to be motivated by hatred of the U.S. and a desire to change U.S. policy in the Middle East. In response to this enormous terrorist attack on the U.S., political leaders in the U.S. called for a world war on terrorism. In his September 20, 2001, address to a joint session of Congress, President George W. Bush declared a "war on terror," which he predicted could last for years or decades. President Bush authorized the establishment of the Department of Homeland Security and other anti-terrorist measures. The Bush Administration initiated a preemptive-war model, in which the U.S. will attack terrorists around the world and will use all methods at its disposal. This preemptive-war model replaces the police-justice model, which consisted of law enforcement and intelligence agencies identifying and capturing terrorist suspects and then handing them over to the criminal justice system.

The adoption of the preemptive model laid the foundation for President Bush's January 2002 State of the Union address, in which he described Iran, Iraq, and North Korea as an "axis of evil." In this speech, President Bush threatened military conflict with Iraq. Some allies of the U.S. have felt uneasy about the Bush Administration's new war on terror since it represented a unilateral approach to U.S. foreign policy and disrupted international relations.

Terrorism is not a movement. It is a tactic employed by individuals and groups, many of which are viewed as "freedom fighters" in different countries or by different groups. The war on terrorism is particularly hampered by state-backed terrorism in which governments offer protection or support to terrorist groups that launch proxy attacks against other countries. To combat state-sponsored terrorism, the U.S. and other countries have placed financial sanctions on organizations that indirectly or directly provide assistance to terrorist organizations.

The U.S. government was initially successful in trying to destroy Al Qaeda and topple the Taliban government in Afghanistan that hosted the terrorist group. Robert S. Mueller III, Director of the Federal Bureau of Investigation, reported that in 2003, the U.S. and its allies had won a series of victories against Al Qaeda and its terrorist networks (Mueller, 2003).

The U.S. government has had successes in identifying and disrupting terrorist networks. In February 2003, the FBI director reported that his agency had charged 197 suspected terrorists with crimes and 99 of these individuals had been convicted. The FBI had also helped facilitate the deportation of 478 persons with suspected links to terrorist groups.

The FBI has disrupted a number of terrorist plots. Six suspects in Portland, Oregon, were arrested and charged with offering material support to terrorists. Seven Al Qaeda suspects were arrested in Buffalo, New York, and charged with providing material support to terrorist activities. Ernest James Ujaama (aka Bilal Ahmed) in Seattle, Washington, was charged with conspiracy to offer material support to terrorists and is suspected of launching a terrorist training facility in Bly, Oregon. Enaam Arnaout, Director of the Global Relief Foundation in Chicago,

Illinois, has been charged with funneling money to Al Qaeda terrorists. Three U.S. citizens in Florida were arrested and charged with obtaining weapons and explosives. They are suspected of plotting to bomb an Islamic Center in Pinellas County in retaliation for Palestinian bomb attacks in Israel.

The FBI director also reports that his agency has been successful in disrupting the financial sources of terrorist activities since the war on terrorism began. The FBI has frozen $113 million from 62 organizations. The agency has conducted 70 investigations, of which 23 have produced convictions.

According to U.S. intelligence officials and federal and state law enforcement experts, reports of terrorist threats in May, 2005, were at their lowest since 9/11 (Priest and Hsu, 2005). After 9/11, the U.S. intelligence community devised a daily terrorist threat assessment to inform political leaders informed. According to one counter-terrorism official, these threat assessments have revealed that there has been on average a 25 to 50% decrease in threats against targets in the U.S. between 2003 and 2005. Some intelligence experts believe that the decrease in terrorist threats may be a tactical strategy by Al Qaeda and related terrorists. A number of experts believe that Al Qaeda and similar terrorist groups, in part because of increased counter-terrorism measures in the U.S., have turned their efforts to carrying out terrorist attacks against Americans in Iraq, where they can operate with limited interference, and in Europe (Mueller, 2003).

Despite these successes, the U.S. continues to face terrorist threats both at home and abroad. Since its initial successes against Al Qaeda and the Taliban in Afghanistan, these groups have regained strength. In addition, there are many other terrorist groups in the U.S. and around the world. According to a National Defense Council Foundation report in 2003, there are about 60 terrorist groups working worldwide, and many of them are increasing their access to home made weapons of mass destruction (*Associated Press*, December 30, 2003). The report noted that terrorists are becoming more adept at financially supporting their activities through the drug trade and other crimes. According to Dale L. Watson, the FBI section chief on International Terrorism Operations, there is a growing presence of the Palestinian Hamas, Iranian-backed Hezbollah, and Egyptian-based Al-Gama at Al Islamiyya in the U.S. and their activities focus on fundraising and low-level intelligence activities (WorldWidestandard.com, 2006). For example, there is evidence that Hamas terrorists purchase automatic weapons, firearms, and ammunition with money that had been laundered through the Quranic Literacy Institute in Chicago, Illinois, a nonprofit, public charity. Stefan Leader indicates that nonprofit organizations in the U.S. raise millions of dollars or more for terrorists.

In addition, Al Qaeda and other terrorist groups are adept at eluding the law enforcement efforts of the U.S. and international agencies (U.S. Select Committee on Intelligence of the U.S. Senate, February 11, 2003; Micek, 2001). These terrorist groups learn from their mistakes, alter their tactics and are skillful in using technology to avoid detection. Terrorist groups rely on sports chat rooms, pornographic bulletin boards and other sites on the Internet to disguise their planning activities, and research target details such as maps and photographs of terrorist targets (Micek, 2001). Hezbollah, Hamas, and Al Qaeda rely on computer files, e-mail and encryption to facilitate their activities. For example, terrorists scramble messages using free encryption programs. According to one report, Palestinian hackers made 200 assaults on Israeli web sites, while Israeli hackers made only 40 assaults on Palestinian web sites.

Terrorists can use the Internet to launch attacks against critical information systems (Micek, 2001). The U.S. Critical Infrastructure Assurance Office found that many security experts believe that foreign governments, and/or terrorist groups could attack the Internet infrastructure that regulates transportation, telecommunication, and emergency services. However, other security experts believe that the possibility for this kind of information warfare is still years away.

Another concern of the U.S. and many other countries is that terrorists may try to use chemical, biological, and nuclear/radiological agents as weapons of mass destruction to influence the actions of governments or intimidate or coerce a civilian population (McKenzie et al., 2005). The Aum Shinrikyo cult in Matsumoto, Japan, released the chemical warfare agent, Sarin, in 1994, and in a subway in Tokyo in 1995 (*Encyclopedia of Public Health*, 2000). Chemical agents could be intentionally released into water and food supplies. There are biological agents, such as viruses, bacteria, their toxins, and other poisons that could be distributed by terrorists. An Oregon cult in 1984 allegedly contaminated salad bars with salmonella. Terrorist groups are benefiting from the proliferation of nuclear weapons and the possibility that these groups can make home made weapons of mass destruction.

The attacks on U.S. soil and the loss of life on 9/11 led to racial and ethnic-based death threats and other retaliation against persons presumed to be culturally similar to, involved with, or supportive of a terrorist organization. In the aftermath of 9/11, some individuals who might be mistaken for Middle-Easterners, modified their appearances and behaviors and changed their names to demonstrate their loyalty to the U.S. and to help them avoid death threats and other hate crime-related violence. For example, persons of Muslim and Hindu faiths dressed up in red-white-and-blue clothes and carried or wore flags to symbolize their allegiance to America. They engaged in other activities to "rally around the flag" such as attending pep rallies and memorials for the victims of 9/11.

Since 9/11, The U.S. Justice Department received hundreds of complaints of threats and violence against Arabs, Arab-Americans, Sikhs, and other persons of South-Asian descent who were living in the U.S. By May, 2002, the U.S. Attorneys' Offices, in collaboration with the FBI had conducted nearly 350 investigations of threats and violence against Arab-Americans, Sikhs, South-Asians, or Muslims. These incidents consisted of death threats, vandalism against residences, businesses, and places of worship, bomb attacks, shootings, and homicide. About 70 state and local criminal prosecutions had been launched against almost 80 persons who were suspects in these incidents. In 10 cases, federal charges were filed. One federal case involved a man who allegedly drove a truck through the door of the Islamic Center Mosque in Tallahassee, Florida. In Los Angeles, California, two individuals were charged with conspiracy, destruction of property, and explosives violations for allegedly carrying out a bombing of the Muslim Public Affairs Council.

To fight the ethnic and racial backlash following 9/11, the Justice Department established the National Origin Working Group, which receives complaints of discrimination in employment, housing, education, government, and law enforcement. The Group conducts community outreach efforts to inform individuals in vulnerable groups about the services available from the Justice Department (Stephens, 2002).

Death Threats Made by Terrorists

Terrorist groups, such as Islamic extremists and extremist-backed governments, make death threats and employ other forms of intimidation and terror to help them achieve their various ideological and strategic goals.

Insulting a person's religion has led to death threats, murders, and other forms of violence (Doughty and McDermott, 2006; Conger, 2006). Religious leaders, writers, and scholars who critically discuss and analyze religious and cultural ideologies have been targets of death threats. In addition, their organizations have been targeted for bombings, vandalism, and other acts of violence. On September 12, 2006, Pope Benedict XVI delivered a lecture at the University of Regensberg, in Germany. He quoted a comment made by Byzantine Emperor Manuel II Palaiologos made in 1391 in a comparison between Christian and Moslem views. In referring to the Islamic practice of forced conversion, "the Pope, (making clear that they were the Emperor's words, not his) quoted Manuel II Palaiologos as saying, *Show me just what Mohammad brought that was new and there you will find things only bad and inhuman, such as his command to spread by the sword the faith he preached*" (Wikipedia, 2007p). This comment was taken out of context, and repeated as though it were the Pope's own words. As a consequence the Pope became the target of various death threats. One group known as the Swords of Islamic Right threatened to blow up all churches and Christian organizations in the Gaza Strip to retaliate against the Pope's negative comments (Toameh, 2006). During this time period, the Swords of Islamic Right claimed responsibility for a shooting attack on the façade of a Greek Orthodox Church in Gaza City. They indicated that they would not accept an apology from the Pope. In Nablus, Palestinians carrying firearms, firebombs, and igniting fuel attacked four other Christian churches.

In retaliation these comments about Islam and jihad, the Mujahideen's Army movement in Iraq threatened to make a suicide attack against the Pope (Conger, 2006). On an Internet website, the Mujahideen's Army threatened that its members would "smash the crosses in the house of the dog from Rome." During a protest outside Westminster Cathedral in London, Anjem Choudary, a Muslim extremist and lawyer, told demonstrators that the Pope should be executed (Doughty and McDermott, 2006). In Somalia, a gunman reportedly shot and killed a nun in retaliation for the comment (thisislondon.co.uk).

Persons who portray other religions in a demeaning way also face the possibility of death threats. The manager and program director of an NBC affiliate in Indiana, KWBF-TV, received death threats after the station decided to run the NBC series,

"The Book of Daniel." In this television series, members of the church were portrayed in a variety of offensive situations. For example, two bishops committed adultery, a priest was shown to be corrupt, and the Savior was depicted in a joking manner. In response to the death threats, executives at KWBF-TV have been provided with security, and guards were placed at the station (Shapiro, 2006).

An outspoken critic of Islam and former member of the Dutch parliament, Ayaan Hirsi Ali, writes about what it is like to live under constant death threats because of her promotion of women's rights (Ali, 2007). Because of these death threats, Ali had to have bodyguards.

Entertainers and television producers who publicize the activities of terrorists may find themselves the targets of death threats from terrorists. Actors in the popular Saudi television serial, Tash Ma Tash, received death threats following the broadcast of "And Life Continues" (Ahmad, 2004). This episode reportedly exposed terrorist groups and showed their destructive qualities. The broadcast discussed the confessions of terrorists. This episode was considered realistic and emotional and was favorably received by many viewers. However, a terrorist group issued a threat over the Internet to kill the actors involved in the broadcast.

Persons who seek to promote women's rights in Islamic countries may be targeted for death threats. A group called Jaish Al Sahaba or Army of Sahaba (which is thought to have connections with Al Qaeda) reportedly emailed two death threats to Yanar Mohammed, who is the head of the Organization of Women's Freedom in Iraq (OWFI) and publisher of equalityiniraq.com, in 2004 (World Editors Forum, 2004).

The first death threat was specific in nature and was sent to Ms. Mohammed in January, 2004 (World Editors Forum, 2004). One month later, she was sent a second email death threat. In this second email, the sender threatened to blow her and her co-workers up unless they stopped their efforts to change the law to achieve gender equality. In response to these death threats, the International Federation of Journalists has requested that coalition forces in Iraq provide protection for Ms. Mohammed.

Extremists have threatened to kill newspaper professionals in Denmark and blow up their company's buildings and tourist attractions in that country for making disparaging cartoons about their religions. Anjem Choudary, a Muslim extremist who had called for the execution of Pope Benedict XVI, previously had organized demonstrations against the publication of cartoons in Denmark (Anon. Demark.dk, 2005). Protestors at one demonstration carried signs calling for the beheading of those who insult Islam. These threats increase the risk of terrorist attacks in Denmark. *Jyllands-Posten*, a Danish newspaper, received death threats and hate mail and was targeted as a possible terrorist target after printing twelve cartoons containing caricatures of Mohammed, the Muslim prophet.

Religious conversion under certain conditions can result in death threats and even death. For example, persons who convert from Islam may be targeted for death threats and assassination (U.S. DoJ., 2006). According to one report, unknown individuals in Iran killed a man who had converted from Islam to Christianity more than ten years earlier. The victim reportedly had received death threats over the past several years. After the man's death, other Christians in Iran were threatened and faced repression, and ten Christians were arrested.

Persons who try to broker peace initiatives may become targets of death threats from terrorists who seek to continue or even intensify the conflict between groups and governments. Sari Nusseibeh, the former president of Al-Quds University, in Jerusalem, and a major proponent of a two-state solution to the Israeli-Palestinian conflict, has been the target of death threats for trying to end the conflict (Matthews, 2007). Nusseibeh was asked by Arafat to be the Palestinian Liberation Organization's representative in Jerusalem. Nusseibeh has opposed the extremism of both sides of the conflict and as a consequence his life has been threatened. Palestinian thugs assaulted him and broke his arm. He was arrested and incarcerated by the Israelis for three years. Nusseibeh also discovered that he was next in line to be assassinated by the extremist group, Hamas.

With technological innovations, it is increasingly easy for terrorists to obtain phone numbers and addresses, for the purposes of making death threats against law enforcement, military, politicians, security personnel, and other individuals. According to one report in the United Kingdom, the wives and other family members of United Kingdom army personnel fighting in Iraq received telephone death threats possibly from terrorists in Iraq (Rayment, 2006). Apparently, insurgents in Iraq had obtained their home phone numbers from army personnel fighting in Iraq. The increased frequency of these death threats triggered an investigation by the Royal Military Police, who issued a warning to all soldiers to take precautions when calling home using their mobile telephones.

In North Carolina, in October, 1998, a former KKK member, E. H. Hennis, was arrested for carrying a fake bomb into a county commission meeting and threatening commissioners with the loss of body parts in automobile explosions (ADL, 1999). Hennis, a retired demolitions engineer, had been in a battle with local officials over zoning disputes for months. He had also discussed blowing up buildings with three tons of ammonium nitrate, which was stored at his farm near Greensboro. He was charged with making a bomb hoax and communicating threats.

Pro-life advocates have threatened to kill abortion providers and blow up their facilities. Dr. Warren Hern, former medical director of the Boulder (Colorado) Abortion Clinic, noted that every abortion provider in the U.S. "lives under death threats" (Hern, 1994).

Matt Daniel, the backer of Federal Marriage Amendment (FMA), which would alter the U.S. Constitution to define marriage as between one man and one woman, has been the target of many death threats because of his opposition to gays and lesbians. In addition, Daniel's family members have been threatened with death. The death threats began in 2001 when his organization, the Alliance for Marriage, announced their plans to introduce the constitutional amendment in the House of Representatives. Since that time, Daniel notes that he expects to receive additional death threats with each successful step of his organization's efforts to pass the FMA. To help minimize death threats and other violence, the location of the Alliance for Marriage is kept secret (Blunt, 2004).

Sport stars, entertainers and other celebrities have been the focus of death threats. Something about being in the public limelight seems to encourage unstable individuals to make threats. Perhaps they do it in an attempt to experience vicarious fame and glory. Celebrities who engage in controversies that violate widely held norms, values, and beliefs are also at risk.

The actor and producer, Mel Gibson, was targeted for death threats after making his acclaimed "The Passion of the Christ," because it was considered anti-Semitic. As a result, Gibson, James Cavizel, who portrayed Jesus in the movie, and his wife, Kerri, reportedly are protected by security personnel (Condit, 2004).

There have been rumors and allegations that the baseball star, Barry Bonds, has used illegal performance-enhancing steroids as he tries to surpass Hank Aaron's career record of 755 home runs. In March, 2007, Bonds reported that he had been the target of death threats. The San Francisco Giants' slugger declined to elaborate about the nature of these death threats. The exact reason for these death threats is unknown (Anonymous, 2005; Beacham, 2007).

Those celebrities who face jail or prison time are especially likely to be the targets of death threats and associated violence and may have to be separated from the general prison population for their own protection.

Chapter 12
Death Threats and the Legal System

Individuals complain about being threatened with death in a variety of court cases. Petitioners filing restraining orders in domestic courts may charge the respondent with threatening to kill them. In immigration cases, persons seeking asylum may present evidence that they have been threatened with death in their country of origin. In the U.S., the courts consider whether the asylum petitioner will face the threat of death, incarceration, or substantial harm or suffering if they are deported to back to their home land. For example, in *Arta Emini v. Alberto R. Gonzales* (2007), Arta Emini, a political activist in Albania, claimed that she was threatened with death, beaten, interrogated, and imprisoned by government officials who were trying to dissuade her from continuing her activities in the Albanian Democratic Party (*Arta Emini v. Alberto R. Gonzales*, 2007; Manson, 2007b).

Some immigration judges may not consider death threats and other violence severe enough to grant asylum to the petitioners. In the previously mentioned case, Judges William J. Bauer and Michael S. Kanne, serving on a 7th Circuit panel, noted that Immigration Judge O. John Brahos did not find the incidents that Arta Emini complained about were severe enough to constitute persecution (*Arta Emini v. Alberto R. Gonzales*, 2007; Manson, 2007b).

Many persons who make death threats are never arrested and prosecuted for doing so, partly because the laws controlling death threats vary by jurisdiction and the courts vary in how they regard and respond to death threats. For example, in Illinois, the police generally have probable cause to arrest an individual for assault if there is a gesture and threat that indicates imminent battery (Judge, 2004). In Illinois, individuals can be arrested for assault if they engage in "conduct which places another in reasonable apprehension of receiving a battery" (720 ILCS 5/12-i(a)).

For centuries, criminal or civil assault has consisted of: (1) a threatening gesture, or an innocent gesture that became threatening by accompanying words, that (2) produces in a person a reasonable apprehension of an imminent battery (*Merheb v. Illinois State Toll Highway Authority*, 2001; Restatement (Second) of Torts, section 29, 1979; Judge, 2004).

However, in Illinois, a verbal threat, which consists of a threat of indefinite action in the indefinite future does not constitute an assault (*People v. Floyd*, 1996;

S.J. Morewitz, *Death Threats and Violence*, DOI: 10.1007/978-0-387-76663-8_12,   137
© Springer Science+Business Media, LLC, 2008

Judge, 2004). This type of threat is missing the two essential elements: gesture and imminence. In *Kijonka v. Seitzinger* (2004), the former mayor, Henry Kijonka, one day saw Berle Shoulders, a former city dogcatcher, who had previously threatened and stalked him after Kijonka had fired Shoulders (*Kijonka*, 2004). Kijonka allegedly rolled down his automobile window, gave Shoulders a dirty look, and yelled: "You have a nice day, and your ass is mine you son of a bitch. And I will get you." Kijonka then drove away and a nearby police officer, Michael Seitzinger, did not hear what the former mayor had said.

The appeals court, noted that Kijonka's statements were not a threat because there was no threatening gesture or even a present threat (*Kijonka*, 2004; Judge, 2004). The court noted that a victim's fear, especially, when it is due to his or her own misbehaviors, cannot turn a remote threat into an assault. In this case, Kijonka offered no indication that he was about to assault Shoulders. The former mayor was inside his automobile and a police officer was nearby. Therefore, the police had no probable cause to arrest Kijonka.

In other instances, mere threats are criminalized under special circumstances. In Illinois and other states, mere threats are violations of criminal law if they involve intimidation, e.g., extortion (720 ILCS 5/12-6), threatening (or intimidating) a public official (720 ILCS 5/12-9; W. Va. Code 61-5-27), and making a terrorist threat (N.J.S.A. 2C12-3(a); 720 ILCS 5/29D-20).

In West Virginia, intimidation of a public official (and public employee, juror, or witness) occurs when "any person uses intimidation, physical force, harassment or fraudulent legal process or official proceeding, or threatens or attempts to use intimidation, physical force, harassment or fraudulent legal process or official proceeding with the intent to: impede or obstruct a public official or employee from performing his or her official duty; or impede or obstruct a juror or witness from performing his or her official duties in an official proceeding; or influence, delay or prevent testimony of any person in an official proceeding; or cause or induce a person to: (1) withhold testimony, or withhold a record, document or other object from an official proceeding (2) alter, destroy, mutilate or conceal a record, document or other object impairing its integrity or availability for use in official proceeding (3) evade an official proceeding summoning a person to appear as a witness or produce a record, document, or other object for an official proceeding; or (4) be absent from an official proceeding to which such person has been summoned" (W. Va. Code 61-5-27).

In New Jersey, in order to prove someone guilty of making a terrorist threat, the prosecution has to prove several elements beyond a reasonable doubt: (1) "the defendant made a threat, or threatened to commit a crime of violence against the victim (mentioned by name); (2) that the threat to commit a crime of violence was with the purpose to terrorize another or in reckless disregard of the risk of causing such terror or; (3) that the threat to commit a crime of violence was to cause evacuation of a building, place or assembly or facility of public transportation or otherwise to cause serious public inconvenience or in reckless disregard of the risk of causing such evacuation or inconvenience; (4) a person acts purposely with respect to the nature of (his/her) conduct or a result thereof if it (his/her) conscious object to engage in conduct of that nature or to cause such a result" (N.J.S.A. 2C12-3(a); 720 ILCS 5/29D-20). It is not necessary for the target to be terrorized or for the building, place of assembly, or facility of public transportation to be actually evacuated. However, the statute is not violated if a suspect merely makes a threat based on fleeting anger or if the suspect only intends to cause alarm.

In other countries, death threats also can be illegal. For example, in Canada, threatening death or bodily harm is a violation of the Criminal Code. According to the Criminal Code, a person cannot knowingly "utter or convey a threat to cause death or bodily harm to any person. It is also an offence to threaten to burn, destroy or damage property or threaten to kill, poison or injure an animal or bird that belongs to a person."

An accused person may face up to five years of incarceration if he elects a trial by jury and is convicted. The accused in a majority of cases has a trial before a lower court justice. In these instances, summary convictions can result in a maximum penalty of 18 months of incarceration.

To obtain a conviction at trial, the Crown must prove that the suspect knowingly made a threat. This means that the Crown must prove that the suspect was aware of the words that he used and the meaning of these words. Moreover, the Crown must prove that the suspect intended his threat to be taken seriously. In this context, it needs to shown that the suspect intended to intimidate or cause fear in the threat victim. It is not necessary to show that the suspect intended to carry out the threat or had the capacity to do so. It is also not necessary to determine the suspect's motive for making the threat. The victim does not need to know of a threat for it to be an offence.

The court uses objective criteria to determine if the words constitute a threat. The court evaluates the context and circumstances in which the threat was made. The court assesses the way in which the words were used and if a reasonable person would regard these words as a threat. A history of violence between the suspect and target may offer evidence that the words were used as a threat. In determining the suspect's intent, the court can assess whether he has the ability to carry out his threat, his use of gestures or other behaviors and differences in size between the suspect and the target.

The court has determined that a threat can be conditional. The Ontario Court of Appeal in 1986 held that it was a threat when a man telephoned the police and said that he would shoot a police officer if the officer did not leave his property. However, idle threats are not illegal. Idle threats or words spoken in the heat of anger, desperation, bitterness, or frustration are not regarded as a violation (Jourard, 1999–2007).

A threat made by the ex-Mayor of Toronto, Mel Lastman, illustrates this problem. During a city council meeting in May 1999, Lastman reportedly told a television reporter: "Leave my family alone. If you don't leave them alone, I'll kill you." The ex-mayor reportedly had been angry with the reporter who wrote a story in a satirical magazine that made reference to the ex-mayor's wife. Did Lastman mean his comments to be taken seriously or were they merely an angry outburst? The ex-mayor was never charged for making this death threat.

There are also lawful excuses for making a threat. For instance, individuals may be justified in making a threat as an act of self-defense if they are in imminent danger or distress when facing an aggressor.

Contacting the Police

Given the varying legal requirements in determining that a death threat is illegal and other barriers in seeking police assistance, it should not be surprising that many death threat (DT) victims never contact the police about being threatened with death (MacDonald, 1968). A study of workplace violence by Northwestern National Life Insurance revealed that about 25% of the workers experienced one episode of workplace violence between July 1992 and June 1993, although a substantial percentage of these individuals had not reported the violence (Eisele et al., 1998; Northwestern National Life Insurance, 1993). Victims of threats and other forms of violence may not believe that the threats are serious enough to warrant police action.

Findings from the Stalking and Violence Project (SVP) revealed that 37.3% of the DT victims were involved in police contacts (see Appendix B—Study Results, Table B.9). However, DT victims did not differ from non-DT victims (28.7%) in their involvement with the police. Similarly, DT victims did not differ from non-DT victims in the percentage of offenders who were arrested or who had gone to jail/prison.

In some instances, the targets of homicidal threats may not know that verbal death threats are illegal. The police and prosecutors themselves may not be familiar with the legality of death threats. For example, the appeals court held that the prosecutor's advice to the police in *Kijonka v. Seitzinger* was incorrect, ruling that there was no probable cause for arresting Kijonka for making a threat (*Kijonka*, 2004; Judge, 2004).

DT victims may have negative views of the police and the criminal justice system. Victims may believe that the police will not arrest the perpetrators for making a homicidal threat.

In fact, the police frequently do not arrest individuals for making death threats. For example, Randy and Judy Brown, the parents of a classmate of Eric Harris, one of the shooters in the Columbine massacre, had filed police reports indicating that their son was the target of a death threat on Harris' web site and their son had also received an anonymous email death threat (CNN, 1999e). The police did not charge Harris with a crime and, Lt. John Kiekbusch, of the Jefferson County Sheriff's Department at that time, said that it is not illegal to post threats on a web site.

In certain instances, death threats or plans to murder someone may be reported to officials, but not necessarily to the police. In Seattle, Washington, a parent notified a Seattle Public School district staff member that students on the Roosevelt High School football team planned to murder John Jasmer two days before the killing (Rosenberg, 2005). Reportedly, the school district employee left a voice mail with a Roosevelt High School vice principal. In addition, the parent who notified this school district employee also left a message for the vice principal. The vice principal stated that he did not receive either message. A new policy now requires that all death threats be reported promptly to the district security office.

Even if the perpetrators are arrested, the victims may feel that they will not be protected from the offenders since they will be quickly released (MacDonald, 1968). In addition, the victims may believe that the perpetrators will not be punished sufficiently. Given the variability in the laws dealing with death threats and the police's and courts' responses, targets of homicidal threats may have an accurate view of the deficits in the criminal justice system.

In domestic and partner violence incidents, the police traditionally have been reluctant to make arrests because society considered these disputes to be a private matter (Morewitz, 2003a,b; Morewitz, 2004; Hutchison et al., 1994). Law enforcement personnel may not take restraining orders seriously because of societal norms and values that foster a male-dominated view of women (Rigakos, 1995).

The police have been reluctant to intervene in partner abuse because restraining orders or orders of protection are often considered ineffective in handling the abusers (Pagelow, 1993). The police have also been frustrated that few domestic violence cases are prosecuted because the victims withdraw the charges. In recent decades, the police strategy of not arresting suspects has been criticized since it does not protect the victims of domestic abuse. With the enactment of anti-stalking laws, the initiation of no-option arrest policies (charges cannot be dropped by the victims), changes in police training, attitudes, and police organizational leadership, the police have new weapons in responding to death threats and other violence (Buzawa et al., 1992, 1998; Bell, 1984; Berk and Loseke, 1980–81; Bachman and Coker, 1995). Bell (1984) found that changes in the leadership of police departments, the type and amount of domestic violence training and community factors can influence arrest rates.

Mental health professionals often must assess their patients' propensity for violence. They must evaluate their patients' mental health problems and associated threatening behaviors, including death threats, to determine if they are a risk to themselves or others.

Many barriers remain in responding to death threats in different settings and contexts. In cases of intimate partner violence, the victims are frequently in an emotional bind when the violent incident has ended and the assailant offers the victim apologies and declarations of love (Tabak and Ehrenfeld, 1998). Seeking police involvement means that the victims will inevitably expose their intimate personal and family details to the police. The victims at this point may experience a wide range of intense, negative emotions, including guilt, shame and fear about contacting the authorities.

The victims may be especially fearful that their family will be broken up because of the criminal justice intervention and that their partners will be incarcerated. Fear of family break-up and other losses is common among domestic violence victims (Petersen et al., 2004).

Hart (1992) showed that 50% of the victims of domestic violence indicated that they were afraid that their partners would retaliate against them if they assisted in their prosecution. Their fears are justified. The National Crime Survey revealed that an estimated 32% of female victims of abuse were victimized again within six months of the original assault (Langan and Innes, 1986).

In other contexts, there have been a number of reports of individuals being tortured or threatened with death and physical or sexual violence for reporting criminal activity (Karmen, 2007). Wandita (1998) noted that potential witnesses to the rape of Chinese-Indonesian women in Jakarta, Indonesia, during the May 1998 student demonstrations faced intimidation and threats of sexual assaults. Public officials also denied that the rapes ever took place. In Nepal, the Asian Human Rights Commission reported that a police officer, who was reportedly detained and tortured by senior officials in his office, received death threats because he took legal action against his superiors (Asian Human Rights Commission, 2006).

The victims of death threats and other violence may be reluctant to contact the police since they themselves face possible arrest for defending themselves against their abusers (Gondolf, 1998).

For example, in SVP case B1, the police told Ms. E, who was in the third trimester of her pregnancy, that she could have been arrested for swinging a knife at her partner after he jumped on her.

In the context of partner violence, various factors may influence whether the police are contacted when death threats and other violence occur. For example, ethnic, cultural, family, and community factors may influence whether a woman decides to report partner violence (Yoshihama and Sorenson, 1994; U.S. DoJ., 2000; Bachman and Coker, 1995). The U.S. Department of Justice (2000) found that African-American women were 17% more likely to report partner abuse to the police than white women.

If death threat makers (DTMs) are threatening to kill their partners in a loud manner, other friends, family members, and neighbors may overhear the commotion and contact the police. In other instances, the victims themselves contact the police. In some situations, the DTMs who are acting in a violent, erratic, and controlling manner prevent their victims from contacting the police. The DTMs may actually make additional death threats and even kidnap or detain their victims to prevent them from contacting the police.

The characteristics of the police, themselves, may affect the frequency of arrests in cases involving death threats and other forms of violence (Buzawa et al., 1992; Waaland and Keeley, 1985; Homant and Kennedy, 1984). For example, the idiosyncrasies or demographic characteristics of the police may influence whether the police make an arrest.

The demographic and social characteristics of victims and DTMs also influence arrest rates (Bachman and Coker, 1995; Buzawa et al., 1992). The police have a lower probability of arresting assailants who are married and residing with their victims (Buzawa et al., 1992; Worden and Pollitz, 1984). In the 1980s, investigations revealed that White police officers, who held racial stereotypes were less likely to arrest domestic violence offenders in predominantly minority communities.

The victim's demeanor may influence whether the police will make an arrest (Buzawa et al., 1992; Skolnick, 1975). For instance, if the victim is belligerent and disrespectful to an officer, the officer will be less likely to arrest the DTM.

The demeanor of the DTMs also may affect whether an arrest is made. Not surprisingly, the police often will arrest assailants who are intoxicated or violent at the scene of the incident (Buzawa et al., 1992; Schuller and Stewart, 2000; Dolon et al., 1986).

The police may be more likely to make an arrest if witnesses are present (Buzawa et al., 1992). One investigation by Hutchison and Hirschel (2001) found that the presence of children at the scene of incidents increased the chance that the police would offer the victims information about domestic abuse and refer them to shelters.

Other conditions, such as pregnancy, may increase the likelihood that the victims of domestic violence will seek police assistance. In their survey of 329 pregnant Hispanic patients, Wiist and McFarlane (1998) discovered that the most heavily used domestic violence resource used during the previous year was the police.

Are DT victims in intimate partner incidents more likely to have police contacts than those who are not threatened with death? It is interesting to note that the victims of death threats may not have a higher rate of police involvement than victims of partner abuse who are not threatened with death. According to the Stalking and Violence (SVP) findings, those who made death threats were not more likely than those who did not make death threats to have police contacts (see Appendix B—Study Results, Table B.9). Likewise, there were no differences in offender arrest and jail/incarceration rates between DTMs and non-DTMs.

DT victims who have police contacts and are abused by an intimate partner are more likely than DT victims without police contacts to suffer different types of physical abuse and other forms of violence. In the SVP, DT victims who were involved in police contacts (18.9%) were more than two times likely to be raped than DT victims without police contacts (6.7%) (see Appendix B—Study Results, Table B.13). DT victims with police contacts were more likely to be hit (88.9%) than DT victims who did not have police contacts (58.4%).

DT Victims Who File Restraining Orders

In the U.S., about 1.5 million women are the victims of partner physical and/or sexual abuse annually, and about 20% of these women get restraining or protection orders against their assailants (Holt et al., 2002). These orders, whether they are temporary or permanent, prohibit perpetrators from making any kind of contact their victims. If the perpetrators violate the order, they can be arrested and charged with either a misdemeanor or a felony (NIJ, 1996).

The Violence Against Women Act (VAWA) of 1994 was enacted in the U.S. to ensure that restraining orders be more accessible to people and more enforceable (Violence Against Women Act (1994); Gist et al., 2001). The VAWA waives filing fees and service costs. The act has a provision that provides for the enforcement of restraining orders nation-wide, regardless of the state in which the order was issued. The act also has federal penalties for offenders who cross state lines so that they can continue to victimize another individual.

Despite the benefits of the VAWA, state legislators still have the ability to enact statutes that limit the qualifying criteria for obtaining a restraining order (Gist et al., 2001). For example, petitioners may be required to prove that they are partner violence victims or that there is probable reason that they will become a victim of violence in the future. Petitioners may also be required to show that they are in a former or current intimate relationship that included cohabiting or having a child in common with the alleged perpetrator (Texas Family Code, Title 4 (1995) Protection of the family, Chapter 71). The differences in qualification criteria for obtaining restraining orders reveal that there is a need for more standardized criteria throughout the entire country.

Social, Demographic, and Socioeconomic Status Characteristics of Individuals Who File Restraining Orders

Various researchers have assessed the social, demographic, and socioeconomic status attributes of persons who file restraining orders (Morewitz, 2004; McCabe, 2001; Gist et al., 2001). Based on a study of 876 protective orders filed in South Carolina, McCabe (2001) discovered that 83.1% of the protected persons were female, 66.9% white, and 66.9% in the 20–39 years age range. Females were more likely to obtain orders of protection against males than against other females. Males had a higher probability of getting protective orders against females than against other males.

In a study by Gist et al. (2001), the average age of women qualifying for orders of protective was 31.98 years and the racial and ethnic characteristics of the women were fairly evenly divided (34% African-American, 30.8% white, and 33.8% Hispanic).

Results from the SVP revealed that 83% of all victims of domestic violence who filed restraining orders were women and 17% male (Morewitz, 2004; see also Appendix B—Study Results, Table B.1). Fifty-six percent of all of the domestic violence (DV) victims were African-American, 21% white, 20%, Hispanic, and 3% Asian and others. Sixty-seven percent of the DV victims were married and 26% in a current or previous dating or engagement relationship.

In a study of abused pregnant women who filed restraining orders, Morewitz (2004) found only 28% were married and 12% were in a current or previous dating or engagement relationship. Fifty-three percent of all of the victims and 48% of the abused pregnant women were parents of at least one child.

Gist et al. (2001) discovered that 72.3% of the women who qualified for orders of protection had graduated high school and 66.2% had a job. In the SVP, 40% of the all of the DV victims resided in census tracts with an annual median household income of less than $20,000, and 50% in census tracts with annual median household incomes between $20,000 and $39,999 (Morewitz, 2004; see also Appendix B—Study Results, Table B.1).

How do DT victims who file restraining orders compare to other victims of partner violence? Among DV victims, certain social, demographic, and socioeconomic attributes may increase the likelihood that they are also threatened with death. However, findings from the SVP do not reveal any differences between DT victims and non-DT victims (see also Appendix B—Study Results, Table B.3). This is an area that requires further research.

Types of Court Protection Requested

DV victims in certain jurisdictions are able to request specific types of court protection (Morewitz, 2004). Petitioners may request protection from a range of behaviors, including protection from physical harm, harassment, stalking, harm to dependents, deprivation, loss of liberty, and neglect.

Researchers are beginning to evaluate which conditions may affect the specific type of court protection requested by DV victims (Morewitz, 2004). For example, pregnancy places special stresses for both mothers and their abusive partners. Therefore, abused pregnant women may differ from nonpregnant women in the kinds of court protection that they desire. Using data from the SVP, Morewitz (2004) showed that abused pregnant women had a greater likelihood than abused nonpregnant women of requesting court protection from child abuse of their dependent children.

To what extent do DT victims differ from non-DT victims in their request for court protection? Individuals who are threatened with death tend to face the most serious forms of violence, and therefore, may be more likely to seek different kinds of protection than those who are not threatened with death.

In fact, the severity of partner violence influences women's decision to seek police assistance, obtain orders of protection, or choose other strategies to cope with the abuse (Brookoff et al., 1997; Wiist and McFarlane, 1998; Dutton et al., 1999). Wiist and McFarlane (1998) found that Hispanic prenatal patients who had been frequently threatened and had suffered many acts of physical abuse were more likely to contact the police than those who had not.

Findings from the SVP revealed that although most of the partners filing protective orders asked for protection from harassment, DT victims were more likely than non-DT victims to request protection against harassment (97.5% vs. 92.5%) (see Appendix B—Study Results, Table B.8). DT victims also were more likely than non-DT victims to request protection of dependents (51.6% vs. 40.8%) (see Appendix B—Study Results, Table B.8). These results suggest that DT victims may have been more fearful of future harassment, including further death threats, and possible harm to their dependent children, when compared to non-DT victims.

However, DT victims were less likely than non-DT victims to seek protection against deprivation (12.0% vs. 13.8%) (see Appendix B—Study Results, Table B.8). These findings indicate that DT victims may have been less concerned than non-DT victims about future deprivation.

Court Responses to DT Victims Who File Restraining Orders

To what extent do the courts regard allegations of death threats as more serious, e.g., life-threatening than allegations of other forms of violence? In the SVP, there were no differences between how the courts responded to DT victims and non-DT victims with regard to their requests for specific types of protection, e.g., protection against physical harm, protection against harassment, and protection of dependents (see Appendix B—Study Results, Table B.8). With regard to protection against loss of liberty, the differences between the court's approval of protection for DT victims and non-DT victims (86.8% vs. 78.8%) approached statistical significance ($p < 0.051$).

The court tended to approve the requests of both the DT victims and non-DT victims and, in fact, there were sometimes a higher percentage of court approvals than victims' actual requests for certain types of requests (see Appendix B—Study Results, Table B.8). For example, among DT victims, 61.6% requested court protection from loss of liberty, while the court granted protection from loss of liberty for 86.8% of the DT victims. Similarly, 59.9% of the non-DT victims requested protection from loss of liberty, while the court granted this protection for 78.8% of the non-DT victims.

More research is needed to assess the ways in which the courts respond to DT victims' requests for protection and the effectiveness of such responses. In particular, researchers should focus on the possible impact of restraining orders and protection against specific offenses on the process of social control. Does court protection against specific offenses actually reduce the ability of DTMs to continue to dominate and control their victims and inflict further physical, sexual, and emotional abuse on them?

About the Author

Dr. Stephen J. Morewitz is President of the consulting firm, STEPHEN J. MOREWITZ, Ph.D., & ASSOCIATES, Buffalo Grove, Illinois, and San Francisco and Tarzana, California, which was founded in 1988. He is a Lecturer in the Department of Sociology, San Jose State University, and is a Lecturer in the Graduate Health Care Administration Program, Department of Public Affairs and Administration and the Department of Sociology, California State University, East Bay. Dr. Morewitz has been on the faculty or staffs of Michael Reese Hospital and Medical Center, University of Illinois at Chicago, College of Medicine and School of Public Health, DePaul University, and Argonne National Laboratory, Division of Biological and Medical Research, and the California School of Podiatric Medicine. Dr. Morewitz is the author of 100 publications, including the award-winning book *Domestic Violence and Maternal and Child Health* (New York: Kluwer Academic/ Plenum Publishers/Springer Science+Business Media, LLC, 2004), the award-winning book *Stalking and Violence: New Patterns of Trauma and Obsession* (New York: Kluwer Academic/Plenum Publishers/Springer Science+Business Media, LLC, 2003), and *Sexual Harassment and Social Change in American Society* (Bethesda, MD: Austin & Winfield, Rowman and Littlefield Publishing Group, 1996). He is past Chair of the Crime and Delinquency Division of the Society for the Study of Social Problems. He was elected to Sigma Xi, the Scientific Research Society, and to Pi Gamma Mu, the International Honor Society in Social Sciences. Dr. Morewitz earned his A.B. and M.A. from The College of William & Mary in Virginia and his Ph.D. from The University of Chicago.

Appendix A
Research Methods

Domestic violence victims in some domestic courts are now given an opportunity to formally complain about different types of partner abuse and request court protection against these forms of abuse. As part of the Stalking and Violence Project (SVP), a new interpersonal domestic violence and stalking protocol was constructed to code self-report data on different forms of domestic violence based on newly filed domestic orders of protection.

Sample

A random sample of 519 newly filed orders of protection (also known as restraining orders or protective orders) was drawn from new domestic court case listings that were published in legal newspapers in two cities (Midwest and West regions) between 1997 and 1999. The sample of orders of protection consisted of 519 self-reported victims and 519 accused persons.

Measures

An interpersonal stalking and domestic violence protocol was constructed to code self-report data obtained from a content analysis of the newly filed domestic orders of protection. The protocol was pretested using 25 randomly selected new domestic orders of protection. The final protocol consisted of 154 variables.

One section of the protocol consisted of 29 residential, demographic, and family variables and 20 census tract measures of socioeconomic status for both the self-reported victims and accused individuals. The self-reported victims are the persons who are filing orders of protection to bar the accused persons from contacting them. Socioeconomic status variables for both victims and accused persons could be coded directly from the orders of protection. Therefore, 20 census tract measures of socioeconomic status for both victims and accused individuals were obtained by matching known residential addresses of victims and accused persons with the 1990 U.S. Census Bureau Census Tract database.

Information about the incidents or problems that led the alleged victims to file orders of protection against the accused persons is contained in the second part of the protocol. This section contains 89 variables concerning the type of relationship between the victims and the accused individuals, the victims' self-report narrative of what reportedly transpired, and the victims' reasons for filing the orders of protection. Three to four research assistants coded the self-report narratives independently, and their findings were compared to each other in order to maximize inter-rater reliability.

One dichotomous death threat variable (Yes/No) was constructed from the victims' self-report narratives. If the victims reported that the respondents had threatened them with death, e.g., "I am going to kill you," the responses were coded: Yes.

Three stalking variables were constructed from the victims' self-report narratives. If the victims' narratives contained allegations that the accused individuals followed or stalked them, kept them under surveillance, or lay in wait for them, then these behaviors were coded as positive for the first stalking variable, "stalking." Before filing the orders of protection, victims were notified that stalking is illegal. The first stalking variable under-reports stalking since it may not include other behaviors such as receiving unwanted telephone calls and letters at home and at work that also are considered part of the stalking phenomenon. Thus, this variable only measures the victims' perception of stalking as a following or surveillance phenomenon.

The second stalking variable, "multiple stalking," was constructed to be as comprehensive as possible. If the victims' narratives contained allegations about any type of repeated and unwanted communication and intrusion, e.g., threatening the victims in their homes or at work and making threatening calls to the victims at work, then the data were coded on a scale from 1 (one form of stalking) to 7 (seven forms of stalking).

The third stalking variable, "stalking distance," was constructed based on data from the multiple stalking variable. The stalking distance variable measures the proximity of stalkers to the victims. Alleged perpetrators who stalked victims were ranked on a scale from 1 (sending a letter—least close) to 7 (being followed—most close). The stalking distance variable, like the multiple stalking variable, does not rely on the victims' perception of stalking.

The last section of the protocol consists of 16 variables related to the self-reported victims' request for domestic court protection and the courts' approval or disapproval of their requests. Victims indicated whether they sought court protection for a variety of complaints, including physical abuse, stalking, and intimidation of dependents. This section also contains information on whether the court approved the victims' request for court protection in these specific problem areas.

Appendix B
Study Results

Table B.1 Sample characteristics of the victims of domestic violence ($N=519$)

Variable	Classification	Percent	p value*
Gender	Female	83	
	Male	17	
			0.000
Racial/ethnic background	White	21	
	African-American	56	
	Hispanic	20	
	Asian and others	3	
			0.000
Age (unknown)			
Relational status	Married	67	0.000
	Dating/engaged	26	0.000
Parental status	Parents of at least one child	53	0.000
Income	Percent living in census tracts with a median income:		
	< $20,000	40	
	$20,000–$39,999	50	
	$40,000–$59,999	9	
	$60,000–$79,999	1	
			0.000

*Pearson chi-square tests of Significance.

Table B.2 Sample characteristics of the individuals accused of domestic violence ($N=519$)

Variable	Classification	Percent	p value*
Gender	Female	20	
	Male	80	
			0.000
Racial/ethnic background	White	22	
	African-American	54	
	Hispanic	21	
	Asian and others	3	
			N.S.
Age (years)	18–25	17	
	26–40	57	
	41–60	24	
	61 and older	2	
			N.S.
Relational status	Married	67	0.000
	dating/engaged	26	0.000
Income	Percent living in census tracts with a median income:		
	< $20,000	40	
	$20,000–$39,999	52	
	$40,000–$59,999	7	
	$60,000–$79,999	1	
			0.000

*Pearson chi-square tests of significance.
Abbreviation: N.S., not statistically significant.

Table B.3 Characteristics of the death threat victims ($N=147$) and non–death threat victims ($N=296$) (includes only current and former partners)

Variable/classification	Death threat victims (%)	Non–death threat victims (%)	p value*
Gender (female)	86.4	82.8	N.S.
Racial/ethnic background			
White	21.8	18.2	
African-American	50.4	59.7	
Hispanic	24.8	18.6	
Asian and others	3.0	2.3	
Age (unknown)			N.S
Marital/relation status			
Married	34.0	31.8	N.S.
Dating/engaged	28.6	31.8	N.S.
Parents of at least 1 child	67.4	62.0	N.S.
Percent living in census tracts with a median income:			
< $20,000	32.4	44.5	
$20,000–$39,999	59.0	45.6	
$40,000–$59,999	7.9	9.2	
$60,000–$79,999	.7	.7	
			N.S.

*Pearson chi-square tests of significance.
Abbreviation: N.S., not statistically significant.

Table B.4 Characteristics of the individuals accused of making death threats ($N=147$) and offenders not accused of making death threats ($N=296$) (includes only current and former partners)

Variable/classification	Individuals accused of making death threats (%)	Individuals not accused of making death threats (%)	p value*
Gender (male)	86.4	80.7	N.S.
Racial/ethnic background			
White	20.6	20.5	
African-American	51.4	56.6	
Hispanic	24.7	20.1	
Asian and others	3.4	1.7	
Age (years):			N.S
18–25	14.0	17.4	
26–40	56.6	58.0	
41–60	26.5	23.1	
61 and older	2.9	1.4	
Marital/relation status:			N.S
Married	34.0	31.8	N.S.
Dating/engaged	28.6	31.8	N.S.
Parents of at least 1 child	67.4	62.0	N.S.
Percent living in census tracts with a median income:			N.S
< $20,000	34.2	44.4	
$20,000–$39,999	57.5	48.0	
$40,000–$59,999	8.3	7.3	
$60,000–$79,999	.4	0	

*Pearson chi-square tests of significance.
Abbreviation: N.S., not statistically significant.

Table B.5 Types of abuse allegedly committed against death threat victims ($N=147$) and non–death threat victims ($N=296$) (includes only current and former partners)

Variable/classification	Death threat victims (%)	Non–death threat victims (%)	p value*
Types of abuse:			
Threatened with physical harm	60.5	42.2	0.000
Threatened with kidnapping self or victim's children	19.7	8.5	0.001
Accused person came to my job	10.9	11.2	N.S.
Victim stalked	36.7	29.4	N.S.
Victim hit by accused person	70.1	70.6	N.S.
Victim pushed by accused person	38.1	30.7	N.S.
Victim thrown down	21.8	14.9	N.S.
Victim choked	17.0	15.5	
Victim threatened with a weapon	19.1	5.1	0.000
Weapon used against victim	25.9	14.9	0.005
Objects thrown at victim	9.5	6.8	N.S.
Accused person raped victim	11.0	6.4	N.S.
Victim's property vandalized by offender	31.3	23.3	N.S.
Accused person stole victim's property	19.1	15.9	N.S.

*Pearson chi-square tests of significance.
Abbreviation: N.S., not statistically significant.

Table B.6 Causes for the partner violence committed against death threat victims ($N=108$) and non–death threat victims ($N=164$) (includes only current and former partners)

Variable/classification	Death threat victims (%)	Non–death threat victims (%)	p value*
Causes for the partner violence:			
Jealousy	13.9	7.9	N.S.
Relationship ended	31.5	25.5	N.S.
Alcohol/illicit drugs	25.9	26.8	N.S.
Child custody	25.0	18.3	N.S.
Divorce	3.7	3.0	N.S.

*Pearson chi-square tests of significance.
Abbreviation: N.S., not statistically significant.

Table B.7 Use of the emergency departments, shelters, counseling, and other responses of death threat victims ($N=144$) and non–death threat victims ($N=290$) (includes only current and former partners)

Variable/classification	Death threat victims (%)	Non–death threat victims (%)	p value*
Nonlegal responses and outcomes:			
Went to the ER	11.5	11.4	N.S.
Went to a shelter	7.6	4.5	N.S.
Went into counseling	8.5	5.6	N.S.
Told accused person to go away	4.9	5.5	N.S.
Took safety/security precautions	9.2	6.6	N.S.
Victim left home	8.5	8.5	N.S.
Remained in same residence with accused person	20.7	17.2	N.S.

*Pearson chi-square tests of significance.
Abbreviation: N.S., not statistically significant.

Table B.8 Request for protective order (P.O.) and court approval for type of P.O. for death threat victims ($N=159$) and non–death threat victims ($N=318$)

Variable/classification	Death threat victims (%)	Non–death threat victims (%)	p value*
Type of P.O. Requested/court approved P.O.:			
Requested protection against physical harm	85.5	78.8	N.S.
Court approved P.O. re: physical harm	94.6	88.7	N.S.
Requested protection against harassment	97.5	92.5	0.028
Court approved P.O. re: harassment	97.7	95.9	N.S.
Requested protection against loss of liberty	61.6	59.9	N.S.
Court approved P.O. re: loss of liberty	86.8	78.8	0.051
Requested protection of dependents	51.6	40.8	0.025
Court approved P.O. re: protection of dependents	52.3	42.5	N.S.
Requested protection against deprivation	12.0	13.8	0.030
Court approved P.O. re: deprivation	14.0	13.0	N.S.
Requested protection against neglect	10.1	14.7	N.S.
Court approved P.O. re: neglect	9.3	10.6	N.S.
Requested protection against exploitation	18.9	17.0	N.S.
Court approved P.O. re: exploitation	14.0	14.4	N.S.
Requested protection against stalking	64.8	65.1	N.S.
Court approved P.O. re: stalking	70.5	67.1	N.S.

*Pearson chi-square tests of significance.
Abbreviation: N.S., not statistically significant.

Table B.9 Other legal system responses and outcomes for individuals who allegedly made death threats ($N=142$) and individuals who did not make death threats ($N=272$) (includes only current and former partners)

Variable/classification	Individuals who allegedly made death threats (%)	Individuals who did not make death threats (%)	p value*
Other criminal justice responses and outcomes:			
Police contacted	37.3	28.7	N.S.
Accused person arrested	13.8	10.6	N.S.
Accused person went to jail/prison	9.8	7.9	N.S.

*Pearson chi-square tests of significance.
Abbreviation: N.S., not statistically significant.

Table B.10 Types of abuse allegedly committed against female death threat victims ($N=128$) and female non–death threat victims ($N=244$) (includes only current and former partners)

Variable/classification	Death threat victims (%)	Non–death threat victims (%)	p value*
Types of abuse:			
Threatened with physical harm	59.4	44.1	0.005
Threatened with a weapon	18.0	4.9	0.000
Weapon used against the victim	24.2	11.8	0.002
Threatened to kidnap victim or victim's children	21.1	8.6	0.001
Victim stalked	36.7	28.6	N.S.

*Pearson chi-square tests of significance.
Abbreviation: N.S., not statistically significant.

Table B.11 Types of abuse allegedly committed against death threat victims and non–death threat victims by offender age group (includes only current and former partners)

Variable/classification	Death threat victims(%)	Non–death threat victims (%)	p value*
Types of abuse allegedly committed by 18–25-year-old offender age group:			
Threatened victim with physical harm	79.0	30.6	0.000
Threatened victim with a weapon	21.1	0	0.001
Used a weapon against the victim	15.8	8.3	N.S.
Hit the victim	68.4	75.5	N.S.
Used alcohol/illicit drugs	15.8	8.3	N.S.
Types of abuse allegedly committed by 26–40-year-old offender age group:			
Threatened victim with physical harm	62.8	44.2	0.007
Threatened to kidnap victim or victim's children	28.2	9.8	0.000
Stalked the victim	39.7	29.5	0.029
Threatened the victim with a weapon	20.5	4.9	0.000
Used a weapon against the victim	28.2	16.0	0.026
Raped the victim	14.3	5.5	0.022
Vandalized the victim's property	39.7	23.3	0.008
Types of abuse allegedly committed by 41–60-year-old offender age group:			
Threw objects at the victim	8.3	1.5	N.S.
Stalked the victim	36.1	33.9	N.S.
Threatened the victim with physical harm	52.8	44.6	N.S.
Threatened to kidnap victim or victim's children	8.3	6.2	N.S.
Used alcohol or illicit drugs	19.4	26.2	N.S.
Hit the victim	69.4	73.9	N.S.
Vandalized the victim's property	19.4	18.5	N.S.

*Pearson chi-square tests of significance.
Abbreviation: N.S., not statistically significant.

Table B.12 Types of abuse associated with death threat victims' use or non-use of the emergency department for partner violence-related injuries ($N=131$) (includes only current and former partners)

Variable/classification	Death threat victims who used emergency department for partner violence-related injuries (%)	Death threat victims who did not use emergency department for partner violence-related injuries (%)	p value*
Types of abuse:			
Accused person hit the victim	93.3	66.4	0.033
Accused person used a weapon against the victim	73.3	21.6	0.000
Accused person choked the victim	26.7	17.2	N.S.
Accused person threw the victim down	33.3	20.7	N.S.
Accused person raped the victim	26.7	7.8	0.020
Accused person used alcohol/ illicit drugs	23.1	28.4	N.S.
Accused person threw objects at the victim	20.0	7.8	N.S.

*Pearson chi-square tests of significance.
Abbreviation: N.S., not statistically significant.

Table B.13 Types of abuse associated with death threat victims' contact and non-contact with the police ($N=143$) (includes only current and former partners)

Variable/classification	Death threat victims who had contact with the police (%)	Death threat victims who did not have contact with the police (%)	p value*
Types of abuse:			
Accused person hit the victim	88.9	58.4	0.000
Accused person used a weapon against the victim	33.3	20.2	N.S.
Accused person threatened victim with a weapon	20.4	18.0	N.S.
Accused person choked the victim	22.2	13.5	N.S.
Accused person threw the victim down	29.6	18.0	N.S.
Accused person raped the victim	18.9	6.7	0.027
Accused person vandalized the victim's property	38.9	24.7	N.S.
Accused person used alcohol/illicit drugs	24.1	15.7	N.S.

*Pearson Chi-Square tests of significance.
Abbreviation: N.S., not statistically significant.

Table B.14 Types of abuse allegedly committed against death threat victims and non–death threat victims by offenders' race/ethnicity (includes only current and former partners)

Variable/classification	Death threat victims (%)	Non–death threat victims (%)	p value*
Types of abuse committed by white offenders ($N=90$):			
Threatened to kidnap victim or victim's children	9.7	6.8	0.000
Threatened victim with a weapon	21.1	0	0.001
Used a weapon against the victim	22.6	1.7	0.001
Hit the victim	80.7	67.8	N.S.
Used alcohol/illicit drugs	12.9	28.8	N.S.
Accused person choked me	9.7	11.9	N.S.
Types of abuse committed by African–American offenders ($N=238$):			
Threatened victim with physical harm	44.8	55.2	0.000
Threatened to kidnap victim or victim's children	14.7	4.9	0.010
Came to the victim's home	52.0	38.0	0.043
Threatened the victim with a weapon	18.7	4.3	0.000
Types of abuse committed by Hispanic offenders ($N=94$):			
Threatened victim with a weapon	19.4	5.2	0.029
Raped the victim	25.0	6.9	0.013
Pushed the victim	52.8	29.3	0.023

*Pearson chi-square tests of significance.
Abbreviation: N.S., not statistically significant.

Bibliography

720 ILCS 5/12-i(a)

720 ILCS 5/12-6.

720 ILCS 5/12-9.

720 ILCS 5/29D-20.

ABCNEWS (2000). May 1, 2000, p. 1.

Aderibigbe, Y.A. (1997). Violence in America: A survey of suicide linked to homicides. J Forensic Sci, 42 (4): 662–665.

ADL (1999). Calendar of conspiracy. A chronology of anti-government extremist criminal activity, October to December 1998. A Militia Watchdog Special Report. The Militia Watchdog, 2 (4): 1–6, http://www.adl.org/mwd/cocv2n4.asp

ADL (2001). Hate crime laws. I. Introduction. http://www.adl.org/99hatecrime/intro.asp

Adler, L., Lehmann, K., Rader, K., et al. (1993). "Running amok"—content analytic study of 196 news presentations from industrialized countries. Fortschr Neurol Psychiatr, 61 (12): 424–433.

Adler, L., Marx, D., Apel, H., et al. (2006). Stability of the 'amok runner syndrome.' Fortschr Neurol Psychiatr, 74 (10): 582–590.

Ahmad, M. (2004). Tash Ma Tash actors receive death threats. Arab News, October, 27, 2004, http://www.arabnews.com/?page = 1&section = 0&article = 53524&d = 27&m = 10&y = 2004

Akhtar, S., Kramer, S., Parens, H. (1995). The Birth of Hatred. Northvale, NJ: Jason Aronson.

Ali, A.H. (2007). Living with death threats. The Globalist, http://www.theglobalist.com/StoryId.aspx?StoryId = 6060

Alikasifoglu, M., Erginoz, E., Ercan, O., et al. (2004). Violent behaviour among Turkish high school students and correlates of physical fighting. Eur J Public Health, 14 (2): 173–177.

Allen, C. (1962). A Textbook of Psychosexual Disorders. London: Oxford University Press.

Amnesty International (1998). Argentina, "Occupational hazards"? Attacks, threats and harassment against journalists. May 8, 1998, http://web.amnesty.org/library/Index/ENGAMR130051998?open&of = ENG-ARG

Amowitz, L.L., Kim, G., Reis, C., et al. (2004). Human rights abuses and concerns about women's health and human rights in southern Iraq. JAMA, 291 (12): 1471–1479.

Amowitz, L.L., Reis, C., Lyons, K.H., et al. (2002). Prevalence of war-related sexual violence and other human rights abuses among internally displaced persons in Sierra Leone. JAMA, 287 (4): 513–521.

Anderson, K.L. (1997). Gender, status, and domestic violence: An integration of feminist and family violence approaches. J Marriage Family, 59: 655–669.

Anderson, M., Kaufman, J., Simon, T.R., et al. (2001). School-associated violent deaths in the United States, 1994–1999. JAMA, 286 (21): 2695–2702.

Andreou, E. (2004). Bully/victim problems and their association with Machiavellianism and self-efficacy in Greek primary school children. Br J Educ Psychol, 74 (Pt 2): 297–309.

Anonymous (1993). Clamping down on clinic violence. Sun, Nov 16, p. 18A.

Anonymous (1996a). Violence against women in war: Rape, AIDS, sex slavery, International. AIDS Weekly Plus, pages 13–14, Nov. 25 – Dec. 2, 1996. http://www.ncbi.nlm.nih.gov/sites/entrez?cmd = Retrieve&db = PubMed&list_uids = 12347566&dopt = AbstractPlus

Anonymous (1996b). Bonds says he receives death threats. Examiner.com, March 1, 2007.

Anonymous (1997a). Conviction upheld despite prospect of death in prison. AIDS Policy Law, 12 (16): 11.

Anonymous (1997b). Sexual violence against women is a weapon of war. Special feature—Mothers as refugees. Safe Mother, 23: 8.

Anonymous (2005). Cartoons raise fears of terror attacks. http://www.Denmark.dk, October 21, 2005.

Apuzzo, M. (2007). Va. Tech gunman writings raise concerns. The Associated Press, Tuesday, April 17, 2007.

Archibold, R.C. (2007). Racial hate feeds a gang war's senseless killing. *New York Times*, January 17, p. A1, A15.

Armstrong, S. (1994). Rape in South Africa: An invisible part of apartheid's legacy. Focus Gend, 2 (2): 35–39.

Arta Emini v. Alberto R. Gonzales (2007) No. 06-3669 (7th Cir. 2007).

Asian Human Rights Commission (2006). Nepal: Torture victim faces continuous death threats due to his complaints to the court. February 28, 2006, http://www.ahrchk.net/ua/mainfile.php/2006/1557/

Asnis, G.M., Kaplan, M.L., Hunderfean, G., et al. (1997). Violence and homicidal behaviors in psychiatric disorders. Psychiatr Clin North Am, 20 (2): 405–425.

Aspy, C.B., Oman, R.F., Vesely, S.K., et al. (2004). Adolescent violence: The protective effects of youth assets. J Counsel Dev, 82: 269–277.

Associated Press (2003). 60 terrorist groups active worldwide, foundation reports. Arizona Daily Star, December 30, 2003, http://www.azstarnet.com/sn/printDS/3958.

Associated Press (2007). Suspect in journalist death makes threat. *New York Times*, nytimes.com, January 24, 2007.

Australian Broadcasting Corp. (2000). pp. 1–2.

Awit, J.G. (2005). Photojournalist's widow reports death threats. September 16, 2005, http://www.sunstar.com

Bachman, R., Coker, A.L. (1995). Police involvement in domestic violence: The interactive effects of victim injury, offender's history of violence, and race. Violence Vict, 10 (2): 91–106.

Bailey, D.N., Shaw, R.F. (1989). Cocaine- and methamphetamine-related deaths in San Diego County (1987): Homicides and accidental overdose. J Forensic Sci, 34 (2): 407–422.

Barnes, A., Ephross, P.H. (1994). The impact of hate violence on victims: Emotional and behavioral responses to attacks. Soc Work, 39 (3): 247–251.

Basile, K.C., Swahn, M.H., Chen, J., et al. (2006). Stalking in the United State: Recent national prevalence estimates. Am J Prev Med, 31 (2): 172–175.

Basoglu, M., Paker, M., Ozmen, E., et al. (1994). Factors related to long-term traumatic stress responses in survivors of torture in Turkey. JAMA, 272 (5): 357–363.

Beacham, G. (2007). Aaron, Bonds faced hatred on the way to historic homer marks. examiner.com, August 7, 2007.

Belfrage, H., Rying, M. (2004). Characteristics of spousal homicide perpetrators: A study of al cases of spousal homicide in Sweden 1990–1999. Crim Behav Ment Health, 14 (2): 121–133.

Bell, D. (1984). The police responses to domestic violence: A replication study. Police Studies, 7: 136–143.

Berk, S.F., Loseke, D.R. (1980–81). Handling family violence: Situational determinant of police arrests in domestic disturbances. Law Soc Rev, 15 (2): 317–346.

Bharadwa, W. (2006). Islam: Islamic fanatics tell Muslim singer: We'll kill you. The Independent, U.K, Feb. 19, 2006, http://www.religionnewsblog.com/13692/islamic-fanatics-tell-muslim-singer-well-kill-you.

Bjerregaard, B. (2000). An empirical study of stalking victimization. Violence Vict, 15 (4): 389–406.

Black, D. (1980). The manners and customs of the police. New York: Academic Press.

Blunt, S.H. (2004). The man behind the Marriage Amendment. Alternative News Network, August 24, 2004.

Boeringer, S.B. (1996). Influences of fraternity membership, athletics, and male living arrangements on sexual aggression. Violence Against Women, 2 (2): 134–147.

Borowsky, I.W., Ireland, M., Resnick, M.D. (2002). Violence risk and protective factors among youth held back in school. Ambul Pediatr, 2 (6): 475–484.

Boulton, M.J., Underwood, K. (1992). Bully/victim problems among middle school children. Br J Educ Psychol, 62 (Pt 1): 73–87.

Bradley Center Inc. v. Wessner (1982) 161 Ga. App. 576, 287 S.E. 2d 716, 723 (1982).

Brady v. Hopper (1983). 570 F. Supp. 1333, 1338 (D. Colo. 1983).

Bragason, O.O. (no date). Assaults against police officers: A self-report study among Icelandic police officers. Skulagata 21, 101 Reykjavik, Iceland: The Office of the National Police Commissioner.

Brener, N.D., Simon, T.R., Anderson, M., et al. (2002). Effect of the incident at Columbine on students' violence- and suicide-related behaviors. Am J Prev Med, 22 (3): 146–150.

Brewster, M.P. (2000). Stalking by former intimates. Verbal threats and other predictors of physical violence. Violence Vict, 15 (1): 41–54.

Britannica, Terrorism, http://www.answers.com/topic/terrorism

Bronski, M. (1999). Littleton, movies, and gay guys. zmag.org, July 1999. http://www.zmag.org/ZMag/articles/july99bronski.htm

Brookoff, D., O'Brien, K.K., Cook, C.S., Thompson, T.D., Williams, C. (1997). Characteristics of participants in domestic violence. JAMA, 277 (17): 1369–1373.

Brown, B. (1994). Assaults on police officers: An examination of the circumstances in which such incidents occur. Police Research Series Paper 10. London: Home Office Police Department.

Brown, L., Thurman, T., Bloem, J., et al. (2006). Sexual violence in Lesotho. Stud Fam Plann, 37 (4): 269–280.

Browne, A. (1984). Assault and homicide at home: When battered women kill. Paper presented at the Second National Conference for Family Violence Researchers, Durham, N.H.

Browne, A. (1987). When Battered Women Kill. New York: Free Press.

Brownridge, D.A. (2006). Partner violence against women with disabilities: Prevalence, risk, and explanations. Violence Against Women, 12 (9): 805–822.

Buda, M.A., Butler, T.L. (1985). The battered wife syndrome: A backdoor assault on domestic violence. Social Act Law, 10: 63–70.

Bullock, L., Bloom, T., Davis, J., et al. (2006). Abuse disclosure in privately and Medicaid-funded pregnant women. J Midwifery Womens Health, 51 (5): 361–369.

Buzawa, E., Austin, T.L., Bannon, J., et al. (1992). Role of victim preference in determining police response to victims of domestic violence. (pp. 255–269). In E.S. Buzawa, C.G. Buzawa (Eds.), Domestic Violence—The Changing Criminal Justice Response. Westport, CT: Auburn House.

Buzawa, E., Hotaling, G., Klein, A. (1998). The response to domestic violence in a model court: Some initial findings and implications. Behav Sci Law, 16 (2): 185–206.

Campbell, J.C. (1986). Nursing assessment for risk of homicide with battered women. Adv Nurs Sci, 8: 36–51.

Campbell, J.C. (1995). Assessing Dangerousness. Newbury Park, CA: Sage.

Campbell, J.C., Oliver, C., Bullock, L. (1993). Why battering during pregnancy? AWHONN, 4: 343.

Campbell, J.C., Webster, D., Koziol-McLain, J., et al. (2003). Risk factors for femicide in abusive relationships: Results from a multisite case control study. Am J Public Health, 93 (7): 1089–1097.

CDC (1991). Current trends homicide followed by suicide—Kentucky, 1985—1990. MMWR Morb Mortal Wkly Rep, 40 (38): 652–653, 659.

CDC (1996a). Violence in the workplace. Homicide in the workplace. Centers for Disease Control and Prevention, http://www.cdc.gov/niosh/violhomi.html

CDC (1996b). Violence in the Workplace. Risk factors and prevention strategies. Centers for Disease Control and Prevention, http://www.cdc.gov/niosh/violrisk.html

CDC (2001). Temporal variations in school-associated student homicide and suicide events—United States, 1992–1999. MMWR Morb Mortal Wkly Rep, 50 (31): 657–660.

CDC (2003). Source of firearms used by students in school-associated violent deaths—United States, 1992–1999. MMWR Morb Mortal Wkly Rep, 52 (9): 169–172.

CDC (2004). Youth risk behavior surveillance—United States, 2003. MMWR Morb Mortal Wkly Rep, 53 (SS02): 1–96.

CDC (2006). Web-Based Injury Statistics Query and Reporting (WISQARS) System {online}. Centers for Disease Control and Prevention (2006). National Center for Injury Prevention and Control {cited 2006 Feb 8}. www.cdc.gov/ncipc/wisqars

CDC (2007). Youth violence: Fact sheet. Centers for Disease Control and Prevention, National Center for injury Prevention and Control http://www.cdc.gov/ncipc/factsheets/yvfacts.htm

Chapell, M.S., Hasselman, S.L., Kitchin, T., et al. (2006). Bullying in elementary school, high school, and college. Adolescence, 41 (164): 633–648.

Chescheir, N.C. (1997). Domestic violence-A clinician's strategy. N C Med J, 58 (5): 316–318.

Chinadaily.com.cn (2005). Paris Hilton receives death threats. CNN, April 17, 2007. http://www.chinadaily.com.cn/english/doc/2005–12/26/content_506700.htm

CNN (1999a). Poll: More parents worried about school safety. CNN.com, April 22nd, 1999. http://www.cnn.com/ALLPOLITICS/stories/1999/04/22/school.violence.poll/

CNN (1999b). Fatalities at Columbine High. CNN.com, April 23rd, 1999. http://www.cnn.com/US/9904/23/victims.list/index.html

CNN (1999c). Columbine shooter was prescribed anti-depressant. CNN.com, April 29th, 1999. http://www.cnn.com/HEALTH/9904/29/luvox.explainer/index.html

CNN (1999d). 5 middle school students charged with conspiracy to blow up Brooklyn school. CNN.com, April 29th, 1999. http://www.cnn.com/US/9904/29/brooklyn.bomb.threat/index.html

CNN (1999e). Littleton authorities warned about Harris' death threats. CNN.com, April 30th, 1999. http://www.cnn.com/US/9904/30/school.shooting.03/

CNN (1999f). Town meeting looks at lessons from Littleton. Parental involvement focus of discussion. CNN.com, April 29th, 1999. http://www.cnn.com/US/9904/29/listening.after.littleton/index.html

CNN (2007a). In morbid plays, Cho's characters dreamed of killing. CNN.com, April 18th, 2007. http://www.cnn.com/2007/US/04/17/vatech.writings/index.html

CNN (2007b). Killer's manifesto: "You forced me into a corner". CNN.com, April 18th, 1999. http://www.cnn.com/2007/US/04/18/vtech.shooting/index.html

CNN (2007c). Virginia Tech killer a self-described "question mark." CNN.com, April 18th, 2007. http://www.cnn.com/2007/US/04/18/cho.profile/index.html

CNN (2007d). Cho's high school classmates recall "kid who never spoke." CNN.com, April 20, 2007. http://www.cnn.com/2007/US/04/20/shooter.childhood/index.html?iref = newssearch

CNN (2007e). Those who knew gunman return to classes. CNN.com, April 22nd, 2007.

Coleman, D.H., Straus, M.A. (1983). Alcohol abuse and family violence. In E. Gottheil, K.A. Druley, et al. (Eds.), Alcohol, Drug Abuse and Aggression. Springfield, IL: Thomas.

Condit, J., Jr. (2004). The physical safety of Mel Gibson. February 23, 2004. http://www.adlagainstmel.com/adl-d-openletter.html - safety; see also: http://www.adlagainstmel.com/frontpage.html & http://www.adlagainstmel.com/news-04–0309-wnd.html

Conger, G. (2006). Mujahideen's Army threatens Pope with suicide attack. The Jerusalem Post, September 16, 2006. http://www.jpost.com/servlet/Satellite?cid = 1157913641658&pagename = JPost%2FJPArticle%2FShowFull

Cowan, G., Heiple, B., Marquez, C., et al. (2005). Heterosexuals' attitudes toward hate crimes and hate speech against gays and lesbians: Old-fashioned and modern heterosexism. J Homosex, 49 (2): 67–82.

Cowan, P., Morewitz, S. (1995). Encouraging discussion of psychosocial issues at student health visits. J Am College Health, 43: 197–200.

Criminal Justice Commission (1967). Criminal homicides in Baltimore, Maryland, 1960–1964. Baltimore, MD.

Criminal Statistics England and Wales, 1986. (1987). Home Office. London: Cm. 233 HMSO.

CSUEB (2007). The California State University, East Bay, From the Office of University Communications, July 16, 2007.

Cunradi, C.B., Caetano, R., Schafer, J. (2002). Alcohol-related problems, drug use, and male intimate partner violence severity among US. Couples. Alcohol Clin Exp Res, 26 (4): 493–500.

Cupach, W.R., Spitzberg, B.H. (1998). Obsessive relational intrusion and stalking. (pp. 233–263). In B.H. Spitzberg, W.R. Cupach (Eds.), The Dark Side of Close Relationships. Mahwah, NJ: L. Erlbaum.

D'Augelli, A.R. (1989). Lesbians' and gay men's experiences of discrimination and harassment in a university community. Am J Community Psychol, 17 (3): 317–321.

Daly, M. (2007). Domestic violence victims pressure Congress. Chicago Daily Law Bulletin, April 18, 2007, p. 1.

Dannenberg, A.L., Carter, D.M., Lawson, H.W., Ashton, D.M., Dorfman, S.F., Graham, E.H. (1995). Homicide and other injuries as causes of maternal deaths in New York City, 1987 through 1991. Am J Obstet Gynecol, 172 (5): 1557–1564.

Davis, K.E., Frieze, I.H. (2000). Research on stalking: What do we know and where do we go? Violence Vict, 15 (4): 473–487.

Davis, K.E., Coker, A.L., Sanderson, M. (2002). Physical and mental health effects of being stalked for men and women. Violence Vict, 17 (4): 429–443.

de Clerambault, C.G. (1921). Les psychoses passionelles. (pp. 315–322). In: Oeuvres Psychiatriques. Paris: Universitaires de France, 1942.

De Silva, H., Hobbs, C., Hanks, H. (2001). Conscription of children in armed conflict—A form of child abuse. A study of 19 former child soldiers. Child Abuse Rev, 10 (2): 125–134.

Deirmenjian, J.M. (2000). Hate crimes on the internet. J Forensic Sci, 45 (5): 1020–1022.

Delos, R.C. (2002). Tolerance in the news. Arab, Muslim students targeted for racial harassment. Tolerance.org, A Web Project of the Southern Poverty Law Center, http://www.tolerance.org/news/article_tol.jsp?id = 573.

DHHS (2001). Youth violence: A report of the Surgeon General. Department of Health and Human Services http://www.surgeongeneral.gov/library/youthviolence/toc.html

Dewan, S., Santora, M. (2007). Killer showed troubled state in fall of 2005. The New York Times, Thursday, April 19, 2007, pp. A1–A18.

Dietz, N.A., Martin, P.Y. (2007). Women who are stalked: Questioning the fear standard. Viol Against Women, 13 (7): 750–776.

Dietz, P.E., Matthews, D., Van Duyne, C., et al. (1991a). Threatening and otherwise inappropriate letters to Hollywood celebrities. J Forensic Sci, 36: 185–209.

Dietz, P.E., Matthews, D., Martell, D., et al. (1991b). Threatening and otherwise inappropriate letters to members of the United States Congress. J Forensic Sci, 36: 1445–1468.

Dobnik, V. (2007). 2 NY teens charged with school plot. USATODAY.com

Dolon, R., Hendricks, J., Meagher, M.S. (1986). Police practices and attitudes toward domestic violence. J Police Sci Admin, 14 (3): 187–192.

Doughty, S., McDermott, N. (2006). The Pope must die, says Muslim. Daily Mail, September 18, 2006. http://www.dailymail.co.uk/pages/live/articles/news/news.html?in_article_id = 405622&in_page_id = 1770

Dressing, H., Kuehner, C., Gass, P. (2005). Lifetime prevalence and impact of stalking in a European population: Epidemiological data from a middle-sized German city. Br J Psychiatry, 187: 168–172.

Dressing, H., Gass, P., Kuehner, C. (2007). What can we learn from the first community-based epidemiological study on stalking in Germany? Int J Law Psychiatry, 30 (1): 10–17.

Dunbar, E. (2006). Race, gender, and sexual orientation in hate crime victimization: Identity politics or identity risk? Violence Vict, 21 (3): 323–337.

Duncan, S.M., Hyndman, K., Estabrooks, C.A., et al. (2001). Nurses' experience of violence in Alberta and British Columbia hospitals. Can J Nurs Res, 32 (4): 57–78.

DuRant, R.H., Kahn, J., Beckford, P.H., et al. (1997). The association of weapon carrying and fighting on school property and other health risk and problem behaviors among high school students. Arch Pediatr Adolesc Med, 151 (4): 360–366.

DuRant, R.H., Krowchuk, D.P., Kreiter, S., et al. (1999). Weapon carrying on school property among middle school students. Arch Pediatr Adolesc Med, 153 (1): 21–26.

DuRant, R.H., Krowchuk, D.P., Sinal, S.H. (1998). Victimization, use of violence, and drug use at school among adolescents who engage in same-sex sexual behavior. Pediatric, 133 (1): 113–118.

Dutton, M.A., Goodman, L.A., Bennett, L. (1999). Court-involved battered women's responses to violence: The role of psychological, physical, and sexual abuse. Violence Vict, 14 (1): 89–104.

Dutton, M.A., Hohnecker, L.C., Halle, P.M., et al. (1994). Traumatic responses among battered women who kill. J Traumatic Stress, 7 (4): 549–564.

Eaton, L., Luo, M. (2007). Shootings rekindle debate over gun rights. Chicago Daily Law Bulletin, April 18, 2007, p. 2.

Eckhardt, v.Kirts. (1989). 179 Ill. App. 3d 863, 534 N.E. 2d 1339 (2nd Dist. 1989).

Eisele, G.R., Watkins, J.P., Matthews, K.O. (1998). Workplace violence at government sites. Am J Ind Med, 33 (5): 485–492.

Encyclopedia of American History, http://www.digitalhistory.uh.edu/encyclopedia/encyclopedia.cfm

Encyclopedia of Public Health (2000). Terrorism, The Gale Group Inc. http://www.answers.com/topic/terrorism?cat=biz-finEncyclopedia,Terrorism,http://www.amswers.com/topic/terrorism

Erickson, M.J., Hill, T.D., Siegel, R.M. (2001). Barriers to domestic violence screening in the pediatric setting. Pediatrics, 108 (1): 98–102.

Esquirol, J.E.D. (1838). Mental maladies: A treatise on insanity. Trans. E.K. Hunt. New York: Hafner, 1965.

Everett, E. (1997). Women's rights, the family, and organizational culture: A Lesotho case study. Gend Dev, 5 (1): 54–59.

Ewing, C.P. (1987). Battered Women Who Kill: Psychological Self-Defense as Legal Justification. Lexington, MA: D.C. Heath.

Farr, K.A. (2002). Battered women who were "being killed and survived it": Straight talk from survivors. Violence Vict, 17 (3): 267–281.

Favaro, A., Degortes, D., Colombo, G., et al. (2000). The effects of trauma among kidnap victims in Sardinia, Italy. Psychol Med, 30 (4): 975–980.

Federal Bureau of Investigation, U.S. Department of Justice (1967). Uniform crime reports, 1966. Washington, DC: Government Printing Office.

Feldman, S. (2001). Exploring theories of patriarchy: A perspective from contemporary Bangaladesh. Signs, 26 (4): 1097–1127.

Figueredo, A.J., McCloskey, L.A. (1993). Sex, money, and paternity: The evolutionary psychology of domestic violence. Ethology Sociobiol, 14: 353–379.

Fildes, J., Reed, L., Jones, N., et al. (1992). Trauma: The leading cause of maternal death. J Trauma, 32 (5): 643–645.

Fisher, K., Kettle, P. (2003). Teachers' perceptions of school violence. J Pediatr Health Care, 17 (2): 79–83.

Fog, L. (2006). Death threats against Colombian researchers. Science and Development Network, July 27, 2006. http://www.scidev.net/news/index.cfm?fuseaction = printarticle&itemid = 3009&language = 1

Follain, J. (2005). A life in the day: Somaly Mam. Timesonline. December 4, 2005. http://www.timesonline.co.uk/tol/life_and_style/article596932.ece?print = yes

Foster, L.A., Veale, C.M., Fogel, C.I. (1989). Factors present when battered women kill. Issues Ment Health Nurs, 10: 273–284.

Fremouw, W.J., Westrup, D., Pennypacker, J. (1997). Stalking on campus: The prevalence and strategies for coping with stalking. J Forensic Sci, 42: 664–667.

Freud, A. (1966). The Ego and the Mechanisms of Defense. (Rev. Ed.). New York: International Universities Press.

Fund (2002). Reports and curricula. Cause for concern: Hate crimes in America. http://www.civilrights.org/publications/reports/cause_for_concern/p8.html.

Garmisa, S.P. (2007). Court sees "transferred negligence" in case of murdered spouse. Chicago Daily Law Bull, 153 (135): 1–4.

Gist, J.H., McFarlane, J., Malecha, A. (2001). Women in danger: Intimate partner violence experienced by women who qualify and do not qualify for a protective order. Behav Sci Law, 19: 637–647.

Glew, G.M., Fan, M.Y., Katon, W., et al. (2005). Bullying, psychosocial adjustment, and academic performance in elementary school. Arch Pediatr Adolesc Med, 159 (11): 1026–1031.

Godfroid, I.O. (2001). Violence, desire and death. Reflections on 3 taboos in psychiatry. Encephale, 27 (1): 22–27.

Godwin, M. (2007). Cyberstalking. pp. 1–2. ++ www.investigativepsych.com/stalk.htm

Goetting, A. (1988). Patterns of homicide among women. J Interpersonal Viol, 3 (1): 3–19.

Golomb, B.A., Kane, T., Dimsdale, J.E. (2004). Severe irritability associated with statin cholesterol-lowering drugs. QJM, 97 (4): 229–235.

Gondolf, E.W. (1998). The victims of court-ordered batterers. Their victimization, helpseeking, and perceptions. Violence Against Women, 4 (6): 659–676.

Grant, C.A. (1995). Women who kill: Impact of abuse. Issues Mental Health Nurs, 16: 315–326.

Green, D.P., Glaser, J., Rich, A. (1998). From lynching to gay bashing: The elusive connection between economic conditions and hate crime. J Pers Soc Psychol, 75 (1): 82–92.

Grimes, D.A., Forrest, J.D., Kirkman, A.L., et al. (1991). An epidemic of antiabortion violence in the United States. Am J Obstet Gynecol, 165 (5 Pt 1): 1263–1268.

Grunbaum, J.A., Kann, L., Kinchen, S.A., et al. (2000). Youth risk behavior surveillance. National Alternative High School Youth Risk Behavior Survey, United States, 1998. J Sch Health, 70 (1): 5–17.

Gunnarsdottir, H.K., Sveinsdottir, H., Bernburg, J.G., et al. (2006). Lifestyle harassment at work and self-assessed health of female flight attendants, nurses and teachers. Work, 27 (2): 165–172.

Guth, A.A., Pachter, L. (2000). Domestic violence and the trauma surgeon. Am J Surg, 179 (2): 134–140.

Hanson, G.R., Venturelli, P.J., Fleckenstein, A.E. (2006). Drugs and society. (9th Edit.). Sudbury, MA: Jones and Bartlett Publishers.

Hanzlick, R., Koponen, M. (1994). Murder-suicide in Fulton County, Georgia, 1988–1991. Comparison with a recent report and proposed typology. Am J Forensic Med Pathol, 15 (2): 168–173.

Harlow, C.W. (2005). Hate crime reported by victims and police. Bureau of Justice Statistics Special Report. U.S. Department of Justice, Office of Justice Programs, NCJ 209911.

Harmon, R., Rosner, R., Owens, H. (1995). Obsessional harassment and erotomania in a criminal court population. J Forensic Sci, 40: 188–196.

Harris, M.H., Weber, M. (2002). Providing crisis counselors on-site to victims of domestic violence in the emergency department: A report of a local pilot project. S Dakota J Med, 55 (4): 147–149.

Harruff, R.C., Francisco, J.T., Elkins, S.K., et al. (1988). Cocaine and homicide in Memphis and Shelby County: An epidemic of violence. J Forensic Sci, 33 (5): 1231–1237.

Hart, B. (1992). Battered women and the criminal justice system. In E. Buzawa, C. Buzawa (Eds.), Do Arrests and Restraining Orders Work? Newbury Park, CA: Sage Publications.

Harvey, B. (2007). Suspect in journalist death makes threat. CBS News, January 24, 2007. http://www.cbsnews.com/stories/2007/01/24/ap/world/mainD8MRRE0O0.shtml

Hedlund v. Superior Court of Orange County (1983). 34 Cal. 3d 695, 669 P.2d 41, 45 (1983).

Henshaw, S.K. (1995). Factors hindering access to abortion services. Fam Plann Perspect, 27 (2): 54–59.

Herek, G.M. (1989). Hate crimes against lesbians and gay men. Issues for research and policy. Am Psychol, 44 (6): 948–955.

Hern, W.M. (1994). Life on the front lines. Womens Health Issues, 4 (1): 48–54.

Hill, H.M., Jones, L.P. (1997). Children's and parents' perceptions of children's exposure to violence in urban neighborhoods. J Natl Med Assoc, 89 (4): 270–276.

Holt, V.L., Kernic, M.A., Lumley, T., et al. (2002). Civil protection orders and risk of subsequent police-reported violence. JAMA, 288 (5): 589–594.

Homant, J.R., Kennedy, D.B. (1984). Content analysis of statements and police-women's handling of domestic violence. Am J Police, 3 (2): 265–283.

Horon, I.L., Cheng, D. (2001). Enhanced surveillance for pregnancy-related mortality—Maryland, 1993–1998. JAMA, 285 (11): 1455–1459.

Hospital Security and Safety Management (1999). Dealing with school shooting violence: How Jonesboro and Denver hospitals met this new challenge to emergency preparedness. Hosp Secur Saf Manage, 20 (4): 5–10.

Hough, M. (1990). Threats: Findings from the British Crime Survey. Int Rev Victimology, 1: 169–180.

Hough, M., Mayhew, P. (1983). The British crime survey: First report. Home Office Research Study No. 76. London: HMSO.

Hough, M., Mayhew, P. (1985). Taking account of crime: Key findings from the 1984 British Crime Survey. London: Home Office Research Study No. 85. HMSO. http://www.adlagainst-mel.com/frontpage.html http://www.adlagainstmel.com/news-04-0309-wnd.html http://www.itstime.com/apr97.htm, Online newsletter, p. 1–13.

Hudson, W., McIntosh, S. (1981). The assessment of spousal abuse: Two quantifiable dimensions. J Marriage Fam, 43: 873–888.

Husni, M.E., Linden, J.A., Tibbles, C. (2000). Domestic violence and out-of-hospital providers: A potential resource to protect battered women. Acad Emerg Med, 7 (3): 243–248.

Hutchison, I.W., Hirschel, J.D. (2001). The effects of children's presence on woman abuse. Violence Vict, 16 (1): 3–17.

Hutchison, I.W., Hirschel, J.D., Pesackis, C.E. (1994). Family violence and police utilization. Violence Vict, 9 (4): 299–313.

ILO, ICN, WHO and PSI (2002). Framework guidelines for addressing workplace violence in the health sector. Geneva: International Labour Organization, International Council of Nurses, World Health Organization and Public Services International.

IME (1997). Institute for Management Excellence, Newsletter. April 1997. (http://www.itstime.com/apr97.htm).

Immelman, A. (1999). Indirect evaluation of Eric Harris. Prepared for *U.S. News & World Report* Unit for the Study of Personality in Politics, April 30, 1999, http://www.csbsju.edu/uspp/Research/Harris.html

infoplease.com, (2007a). A time line of recent worldwide school shootings. http://www.info-please.com/ipa/A0777958.html

infoplease.com, (2007b). Use of guns responsible for increased homicides by juveniles. http://www.infoplease.com/ipa/A0862712.html

International Campaign Against Honour Killings (2005). Campaign for European asylum for victims of honour crime. http://www.stophonourkillings.com/index.php.

International Federation of Journalists (2005). World journalists condemn death threats against three media directors in Colombia. http://www.ifj.org/default.asp?index = 3144&Language = EN).

Jonassen, J.A., Pugnaire, M.P., Mazor, K. (1999). The effect of domestic violence interclerkship on the knowledge, attitudes, and skills of third-year medical students. Acad Med, 74 (7): 821–828.

Jourard, R. (1999–2007). Website of Ron Jourard, criminal lawyer specializing in defence of drinking and driving charges. Toronto, Ontario, Canada.

Judge, J. (2004). Verbal threat not enough to justify man's arrest. Chicago Daily Law Bulletin, May 25, 2004, p. 5.

Kachur, S.P., Stennies, G.M., Powell, K.E., et al. (1996). School-associated violent deaths in the United States, 1992 to 1994. JAMA 275 (22): 1729–1733.

Kamphuis, J.H., Emmelkamp, P.M. (2001). Traumatic distress among support-seeking female victims of stalking. Am J Psychiatry, 158 (5): 795–798.

Kantor, G.K., Straus, M.A. (1989). Substance abuse as a precipitant of wife abuse victimizations. Am J Drug Alcohol Abuse, 15 (2): 173–189.

Karmen, A. (2007). Crime Victims—An Introduction to Victimology, 6th Edition. Belmont, CA: Thomson Wadsworth.

Kaye, J., Donald, C.G., Merker, S. (1994). Sexual harassment of critical care nurses: A costly workplace issue. Am J Crit Care, 3 (6): 409–415.

Keller, A., Lhewa, D., Rosenfeld, B., et al. (2006). Traumatic experiences and psychological distress in an urban refugee population seeking treatment services. J Nerv Ment Dis, 194 (3): 188–194.

Khoury-Kassabri, M., Benbenishty, R., Astor, R.A., et al. (2004). The contributions of community, family, and school variables to student victimization. Am J Community Psychol, 34 (3–4): 187–204.

Kienlen, K.K. (1998). Developmental and social antecedents of stalking. In J.R. Meloy (Ed.), The Psychology of Stalking: Clinical and Forensic Perspectives. San Diego: Academic Press.

Kienlen, K.K., Birmingham, D.L., Solberg, K.B., et al. (1997). A comparative study of psychotic and non-psychotic stalking. J Am Acad Psychiatry Law, 25 (3): 317–334.

Kijonka v. Seitzinger (2004), 363 F.3d 645 (7th Cir. 2004).

Kim, Y.S., Koh, Y.J., Leventhal, B.L. (2004). Prevalence of school bullying in Korean middle school students. Arch Pediatr Adolesc Med, 158 (8): 737–741.

Kim, Y.S., Leventhal, B.L., Koh, Y.J., et al. (2006). School bullying and youth violence: Causes or consequences of psychopathologic behavior? Arch Gen Psychiatry, 63 (9): 1035–1041.

Kimmel, M.S., Mahler, M. (2003). Adolescent masculinity, homophobia, and violence. Am Behav Sci, 46 (10): 1439–1458.

Kitzmiller, E. (2002). Wait...don't open that letter: The changing face of violence in the workplace. Presented at the Mid-Year Convention of the Utah State Bar, St. George, Utah, March 23, 2002. http://www.utahbar.org/sites/midyear/html/violence_in_the_workplace.html

Klein, J. (2006). Sexuality and school shootings: What role does teasing play in school massacres? J Homosex, 51 (4): 39–62.

Kolbe, A.R., Hutson, R.A. (2006). Human rights abuse and other criminal violations in Port-au-Prince, Haiti: A random survey of households. Lancet, 368 (9538): 864–873.

Kostinsky, S., Bixler, E.O., Kettl, P.A. (2001). Threats of school violence in Pennsylvania after media coverage of the Columbine High School massacre: Examining the role of imitation. Arch Pediatr Adolesc Med, 155 (9): 994–1001.

Kowalenko, T., Walters, B.L., Khare, R.K., et al. (2005). Workplace violence: A survey of emergency physicians in the state of Michigan. Ann Emerg Med, 46 (2): 142–147.

Koziol-McLain, J., Webster, D., McFarlane, J., et al. (2006). Risk factors for femicide-suicide in abusive relationships: Results from a multistate case control study. Violence Vict, 21 (1): 3–21.

Kuehner, C., Gass, P., Dressing, H. (2006). Mental health impact of stalking in men and women. Psychother Psychosom Med Psychol, 56 (8): 336–341.

Kulbarsh, P. (2006). Homicide followed by suicide. Preventing further tragedy. Officer.com, September 12, 2006.

Kumari, R. (1995). Rural female adolescence: Indian scenario. Soc Change, 25 (2–3): 177–188.

Kurt, J.L. (1995). Stalking as a variant of domestic violence. Bull Am Acad Psychiatry Law, 23 (2): 219–230.

Langan, P.A., Innes, C.A. (1986). Preventing domestic violence against women: Discussion paper. Washington, D.C.: U.S. Bureau of Justice Statistics.

Langstrom, N., Grann, M. (2000). Risk for criminal recidivism among young sex offenders. J Interpers Psychiatry, 15 (8): 855–871.

Leadership Conference on Civil Rights (2002) Leadership Conference on Civil Rights Education.

Lecomte, D., Fornes, P. (1998). Homicide followed by suicide: Paris and its suburbs, 1991–1996. J Forensic Sci, 43 (4): 760–764.

Lee, R. (2005). "Boy-code" a factor in fatal school shootings? (Gay) Experts say masculinity standards overlooked in search for answers. washingtonblade.com, http://www.washblade. com/2005/4-15/news/national/boycode.cfm

Leong, G.B., Silva, J.A., Garza-Trevino, E.S., et al. (1994). The dangerousness of persons with the Othello syndrome. J Forensic Sci, 39 (6): 1445–1454.

Lipsey, M.W., Derzon, J.H. (1998). Predictors of violent and serious delinquency in adolescence and early adulthood: A synthesis of longitudinal research. In R. Loeber, D.P. Farrington (Eds.), Serious and Violent Juvenile Offenders: Risk Factors and Successful Interventions. Thousand Oaks, CA: Sage Publications, pp. 86–105.

Lobe, J. (2004). Bush failing women of Afghanistan, charge group. OneWorld US, Sept 23, 2004. http://us.oneworld.net/article/view/94647/1/339?

Lom, P. (2004). The Story: The Synopsis of "The Kidnapped Bride". March 2004. http://www. pbs.org/frontlineworld/stories/kyrgyzstan/thestory.html

Lund, L.E., Smorodinsky, S. (2001). Violent death among intimate partners: A comparison of homicide and homicide followed by suicide in California. Suicide Life Threat Behav, 31 (4): 451–459.

MacDonald, J. (1961). The Murderer and his Victim. Springfield, IL: Charles C. Thomas.

MacDonald, J. (1968). Homicidal Threats. Springfield, IL: Charles C. Thomas.

Magin, P., Adams, J., Ireland, M., et al. (2006). The response of general practitioners to the threat of violence in their practices: Results from a qualitative study. Fam Pract, 23 (3): 273–278, Epub 2006 Feb. 3.

Magin, P.J., Adams, J., Sibbritt, D.W., et al. (2005). Experiences of occupational violence in Australian urban general practice: A cross-sectional study of GPs. Med J Aust, 183 (7): 352–356.

Manson, P. (2007a). Court: Man's religion, not his relationship, reason for attack. Chicago Daily Law Bulletin, January 25, pp. 3, 24.

Manson, P. (2007b). 7th Circuit panel split over review of persecution in asylum appeal. Chicago Daily Law Bulletin, September 11, pp. 3, 24.

Marshall, L.L. (1992). Development of the severity of violence against women scales. J Fam Violence, 7 (2): 103–121.

Martin, S.L., Ray, N., Sotres-Alvarez, D., et al. (2006). Physical and sexual assault of women with disabilities. Violence Against Women, 12 (9): 823–837.

Matthews, C. (2007). A risk-taker for peace. Palestinian intellectual braves death threats to end conflict with Israel as PLO representative. San Francisco Chronicle, Book Review, Section, pp. M1, M4, April 8, 2007.

May, D.D., Grubbs, L.M. (2002). The extent, nature, and precipitating factors of nurse assault among three groups of registered nurses in a regional medical center. J Emerg Nurs, 28 (1): 11–7.

Mayer, L., Liebschutz, J. (1998). Domestic violence in the pregnant patient. Obstet Gynecol Surv, 53 (10): 627–635.

McCabe, K.A. (2001). Protective orders in South Carolina: An examination of variables for 1997–1999. South Carolina Department of Public Safety.

McClellan, A.C., Killeen, M.R. (2000). Attachment theory and violence toward women by male intimate partners. J Nurs Sch, 32 (4): 353–360.

McFarlane, J., Parker, B., Soeken, K., et al. (1992). Assessing for abuse during pregnancy: Severity and frequency of injuries and associated entry into prenatal care. JAMA, 267 (23): 3176–3178.

McFarlane, J., Parker, B., Soeken, K. (1995). Abuse during pregnancy: Frequency, severity, perpetrator, and risk factors of homicide. Public Health Nurs, 12 (5): 284–289.

McFarlane, J., Soeken, K., Reel, S., et al. (1997). Resource use by abused women following an intervention program. Associated severity of abuse and reports of abuse ending. Public Health Nurs, 14 (4): 244–250.

McFarlane, J., Campbell, J.C., Watson, K. (2002a). Intimate partner stalking and femicide: Urgent implications for women's safety. Behav Sci Law, 29 (1–2): 51–68.

McFarlane, J., Campbell, J., Sharps, P., et al. (2002b). Abuse during pregnancy and femicide: Urgent implications for women's health. Obstet Gynecol, 100(1): 27–36.

McKay, D.R. (2007). Preventing violence in Long Island schools. About.com, Long Island, NY (July 18, 2007). http://longisland.about.com/b/a/257315.htm

McKenna, B.G., Poole, S.J., Smith, N.A., et al. (2003). A survey of threats and violent behaviour by patients against registered nurses in their first year of practice. Int J Ment Health Nurs, 12 (1): 56–63.

McKenzie, J.F., Pinger, R.R., Kotecki, J.E. (2005). An Introduction to Public Health. (5th Edit.). Sudburg, MA: Jones and Bartlett Publishers.

McKnight, C.K., et al. (1966). Mental illness and homicide. Canad Med Assoc J, 11: 91–98.

McPhail, B.A., Dinitto, D.M. (2005). Prosecutorial perspective on gender-bias hate crimes. Violence Against Women, 11 (9): 1162–1185.

Mears, B. (2006). Justice Ginsburg details death threat. Cnn.com, March 15, 2006, http://www.cnn.com/2006/LAW/03/15/scotus.threat/index.html?iref = newssearch

Meloy, J.R. (1989). Unrequited love and the wish to kill: The diagnosis and treatment of borderline erotomania. Bull Menninger Clin, 53: 477–492.

Meloy, J.R. (1992). Violent Attachments. Northvale, NJ: Jason Aronson.

Meloy, J.R. (1996). Stalking (obsessional following): A review of some preliminary studies. Aggress Violent Behav, 1 (2): 147–162.

Meloy, J.R. (1998). The Psychology of Stalking: Clinical and Forensic Perspectives. San Diego: Academic Press.

Meloy, J.R. (1999). Stalking—An old behavior, a new crime. Psychiatry Clin N Am, 22 (1): 85–99.

Meloy, J.R., Boyd, C. (2003). Female stalkers and their victims. J Am Acad Psychiatry Law, 31 (2): 211–219.

Meloy, J.R., Gothard, S. (1995). Demographic and clinical comparison of obsessional followers and offenders with mental disorders. Am J Psychiatry, 152: 258–263.

Mercy, J., Butchart, A., Farrington, D., et al. (2002). Youth violence. In E. Krug, et al. (Eds.), The World Report on Violence and Health. Geneva, Switzerland: World Health Organization, pp. 25–56.

Merecz, D., Rymaszewska, J., Moscicka, A., et al. (2006). Violence at the workplace—A questionnaire survey of nurses. Eur Psychiatry, 21 (7): 442–450.

Merheb v. Illinois State Toll Highway Authority (2001). 267 F.3d 710 (7th Cir. 2001).

Micek, J.L. (2001). Terrorists hide out in plain sight on the net. February 6, 2001. http://www.newsfactor.com/perl/story/7274.html

Milberger, S., Israel, N., LeRoy, B., et al. (2003). Violence against women with physical disabilities. Violence Vict, 18 (5): 581–591.

Miller, G., Maharaj, D. (1999). Infowar.com, Jan. 27, 1999, pp. 1–3.

Miller, M., Azrael, D., Hemenway, D. (2002a). Firearm availability and unintentional firearm deaths, suicide, and homicide among 5–14 year olds. J Trauma, 52 (2): 267–274; discussion 274–275.

Miller, M., Hemenway, D., Wechsler, H. (2002b). Guns and gun threats at college. J Am Coll Health, 51 (2): 57–65.

Minnesota Advisory Committee (2002), Minnesota Advisory Committee to the U.S. Commission on Civil Rights. Briefing on civil rights issues facing Muslims and Arab Americans in Minnesota post September 11. Proceedings on February 12, 2002.

Mohammed, N.A., Eapen, V., Bener, A. (2001). Prevalence and correlates of childhood fears in Al-Ain, United Arab Emirates. East Mediterr, 7 (23): 422–427.

Morewitz, S. (1996). Sexual Harassment and Social Change in American Society. Lanham, MD: University Press of America (Austin & Winfield, Publishers) (Rowman and Littlefield Publishing Group).

Morewitz, S. (2003a). Racial/ethnic differences in threatening to murder a partner and parental child abductions. (abstract) Proceedings of the 15th Meeting of the International Association of Forensic Sciences (IAFS 2003), September 2003.

Morewitz, S.J. (2003b). Stalking and Violence: New Patterns of Trauma and Obsession. New York: Kluwer Academic/Plenum Publishers (Springer Science + Business Media, Inc.).

Morewitz, S.J. (2004). Domestic Violence and Maternal and Child Health: New Patterns of Trauma, Treatment, and Criminal Justice Responses. New York: Kluwer Academic/Plenum Publishers (Springer Science + Business Media, LLC).

Morewitz, S. (2005). Gender differences in partners who receive death threats and are threatened with parental child kidnapping. (abstract) Proceedings of the 17th Meeting of the International Association of Forensic Sciences (IAFS 2005), August 21–26, 2005.

Morrison, K.A. (2001). Predicting violent behavior in stalkers: A preliminary investigation of Canadian cases in criminal harassment. J Forensic Sci, 46 (6): 1403–1410.

Muelleman, R.L., Feighny, K.M. (1999). Effects of an emergency department-based advocacy program for battered women on community resource utilization. Ann Emerg Med, 33 (1): 62–66.

Mueller, R.S. (2003). U.S. Select Committee on Intelligence of the U.S. Senate (2003). Statement for the Record of Robert S. Mueller, III, Director. Washington, DC: Federal Bureau of Investigation. February 11, 2003.

Muleta, M., Williams, G. (1999). Postcoital injuries treated at the Addis Ababa Fistula Hospital, 1991–97. Lancet, 354 (9195): 2051–2052.

Mullen, P., Pathe, M. (1994). Stalking and the pathologies of love. Aust N Z J Psychiatry, 28: 469–477.

Mushinski, M. (1996). Teenagers' view of violence and social tension in U.S public schools. Stat Bull Metropol Life Insur Co, 77 (3): 2–10.

Myrdal, G. (1944). An American Dilemma: The Negro Problem and Modern Democracy. New York: Harper Brothers Publishers.

Nansel, T.R., Overpeck, M.D., Pilla, R.S., et al. (2001). Bullying behaviors among US youth: Prevalence and association with psychosocial adjustment. JAMA, 285 (16): 2094–2100.

Nansel, T.R., Overpeck, M.D., Haynie, D.L., et al. (2003). Relationships between bullying and violence among U.S. youth. Arch Pediatr Adolesc Med, 157 (4): 348–353.

National Center for Education Statistics (2006a). Indicator 13: Students carrying weapons on school property and anywhere. Indicators of school crime and safety: 2006. http://nces.ed.gov/programs/crimeindicators/ind_04.asp

National Center for Education Statistics (2006b). Indicator 4: Threats and injuries with weapons on chool property. Indicators of school crime and safety: 2006. http://nces.ed.gov/programs/crimeindicators/ind_04.asp

NIJ (1996). Domestic violence, stalking, and anti-stalking legislation-An annual report to Congress under the Violence Against Women Act. Rockville, MD: National Institute of Justice, National Criminal Justice Reference Service.

NIJ (1998a). Stalking and domestic violence: A new challenge for law enforcement and industry—A report from the Attorney General to the Vice President. Rockville, MD: National Institute of Justice, National Criminal Justice Reference Service.

NIJ (1998b). Stalking and domestic violence: The Third Annual Report to Congress under the Violence Against Women Act. Rockville, MD: National Institute of Justice, National Criminal Justice Reference Service.

NIJ (1999). Cyberstalking: A new challenge for law enforcement and industry—A report from the Attorney General to the Vice President. Rockville, MD: National Institute of Justice, National Criminal Justice Reference Service.

Navia, C.E., Ossa, M. (2003). Family functioning, coping, and psychological adjustment in victims and their families following kidnapping. J Trauma Stress, 16 (1): 107–112.

Netcu (2007). National Extremism Tactical Coordination Unit.

Nguyen, M.H., Annest, J.L., Mercy, J.A., et al. (2002). Trends in BB/pellet gun injuries in children and teenagers in the United States, 1985–99. Inj Prev, 8 (3): 185–191.

N.J.S.A. 2C12–3(a).

Nokes, R.G. (2006). "A most daring outrage": Murders at Chinese Massacre Cove, 1887. (case overview). *Oregon Historical Quarterly*, September 22, 2006. http://www.accessmylibrary. com/coms2/summary_0286–27754672_ITM

Northwestern National Life Insurance (1993). Fear and violence in the workplace. Minneapolis, MN: Peggy Lawless, Research Project Director.

Ogletree, C.J., Jr. (2002). Black man's burden: Race and the death penalty in America. Oregon Law Rev, 81 (1): 1–21.

O'Keefe, M. (1998). Posttraumatic stress disorder among incarcerated battered women: A comparison of battered women who killed their abusers and those incarcerated for other offenses. J Trauma Stress, 11 (1): 71–85.

Olivan Gonzalvo, G. (2005). What can be done to prevent violence and abuse of children with disabilities? An Pediatr (Barc), 62 (2): 153–157.

Olsen, D.R., Montgomery, E., Carlsson, J., et al. (2006). Prevalent pain and pain level among torture survivors: A follow-up study. Dan Med Bull, 53 (2): 210–214.

Ouattara, M., Sen, P., Thomson, M. (1998). Forced marriage, forced sex: The perils of childhood for girls. Gend Dev, 6 (3): 27–33.

Pagelow, M.D. (1993). Justice for victims of spouse abuse in divorce and child custody cases. Violence Vict, 8 (1): 69–83.

Pakieser, R.A., Lenaghan, P., Muelleman, R.L. (1998). Battered women: Where they go for help. J Emerg Nurs, 24: 16–9.

Palarea, R.E., Zona, M.A., Lane, J.C., et al. (1999). The dangerous nature of intimate relationship stalking: Threats, violence, and associated risk factors. Behav Sci Law, 17 (3): 269–283.

Palinkas, L.A., Prussing, E., Reznik, V.M., et al. (2004). The San Diego East County school shootings: A qualitative study of community-level post-traumatic stress. Prehospital Disaster Med, 19 (1): 113–121.

pamspaulding.com, Death threats to TV station manager over "Daniel." January 10, 2006. http:// www.pamspaulding.com/weblog/2006/01/death-threats-to-tv-station-manager.html

Parsons, L.H., Harper, M.A. (1999). Violent maternal deaths in North Carolina. Obstet Gynecol, 94 (6): 990–993.

Partridge, J. (2007). Knut death threat. Reuters April 19, 2007. http://www.reuters.com/news/ video/videoStory?videoId = 49198

Pathe, M., Mullen, P.E. (1997). The impact of stalkers on their victims. Br J Psychiatry, 170: 12–17.

Paulson, A., Jonsson, P. (2005). How judges cope with everyday threats on the job. CS Monitor, March 04, 2005, http://www.csmonitor.com/2005/0304/p01s04-usju.html

PBS (2006). African American lives, profiles: Bishop T.D. Jakes. http://www.pbs.org/wnet/ aalives/profile_jakes2.html

Pennington, A., Darby, M., Bauman, D., et al. (2000). Sexual harassment in dentistry: Experiences of Virginia dental hygienists. J Dent Hyg, 74 (4): 288–295.

People v. Floyd (1996). 278 Ill.App.3d 568, 663 N.E.2d 74 (1996).

People v. Joseph Cuevas (2007). No.2–05–0385, Chicago Daily Law Bulletin, Case summaries. Criminal law & procedure – orders of protection. February 9, 2007, p. 1, 4.

Petersen, R., Moracco, K.E., Goldstein, K.M. (2004). Moving beyond disclosure: Women's perspectives on barriers and motivators to seeking assistance for intimate partner violence. Women Health, 40 (3): 63–76.

Pharoah, R. (2005). An unknown quantity. Kidnapping for ransom in South Africa. SA Crime Q, 14: 1–36, http://www.iss.co.za/static/templates/tmpl_html.php?node_id = 673&link_id = 24

Planansky, K., Johnston, R. (1977). Homicidal aggression in schizophrenic men. Acta Psychiatry Scand, 55 (1): 65–73.

Potter, S. (2007). Thin security at Daley Center fuels concern. Chicago Daily Law Bulletin, February 1, 2007, pp. 1, 24.

Powers, R.J., Kutash, I.L. (1982). Alcohol, drugs, and partner abuse. In M. Roy (Ed.), The Abusive Partner: An Analysis of Domestic Battering. New York: Van Nostrand Reinhold.

Presley, C.A., Meilman, P.W., Cashin, J.R. (1997). Weapon carrying and substance abuse among college students. J Am Coll Health, 46 (1): 3–8.

Priest, D., Hsu, S. (2005). U.S. sees drop in terrorist threats. washingtonpost.com, May 1, 2005; A01,http://www.washingtonpost.com/wp-dyn/content/article/2005/04/30/AR2005043000704.html

Purcell, R., Pathe, M., Mullen, P.E. (2001). A study of women who stalk. Am J Psychiatry, 158 (12): 2056–2060.

Purcell, R., Pathe, M., Mullen, P.E. (2002). The prevalence and nature of stalking in the Australian community. Aust N Z J Psychiatry, 36 (1): 114–120.

Purcell, R., Pathe, M., Mullen, P.E. (2005). Association between stalking victimization and psychiatric morbidity in a random community sample. Br J Psychiatry, 187: 416–420.

Rasekh, Z., Bauer, H.M., Manos, M.M., et al. (1998). Women's health and human rights in Afghanistan. JAMA, 280 (5): 449–455.

Rayment, S. (2006). Army wives get phone death threats from Iraq. Telegraph.co.uk, June 25, 2006, http://www.telegraph.co.uk/news/main.jhtml?xml = /news/2006/06/25/wirq25.xml&sSheet = /

Renaud, S. (2004). Crisis interventions with patients with borderline personality disorder. Part 1: Preventive and resolving approaches in individual psychodynamic therapy. Sante Ment Que, 29 (2): 241–252.

Report of the Committee on the Elimination of Discrimination Against Women (2004), January 12–30, 2004.

Resnick, M.D., Ireland, M., Borowsky, I. (2004). Youth violence perpetration: What protects? What predicts? Findings from the National Longitudinal Study of Adolescent Health. J Adolesc Health, 35: 424.e1–424.e10.

Restatement (Second) of Torts, section 29 (1979).

Richmond, J.P., McKenna, H. (1998). Homophobia: An evolutionary analysis of the concept as applied to nursing. J Adv Nurs, 28 (2): 362–369.

Riedel, M., Zahn, M.A., Mock, L.F. (1985). The Nature and Patterns of American Homicide. Washington, D.C.: Government Printing Office.

Rigakos, G.S. (1995). Constructing the symbolic complainant: Police subculture and the non-enforcement of protection orders for battered women. Violence Vict, 10 (3): 227–247.

Risk Control Strategies. (2003). Workplace Violence Survey Results. http://www.riskcontrolstrategies.com/workplace_violence_survey.htm

Roberts, A.E. (1996a). Battered women who kill. A comparative study of incarcerated participants with a community sample of battered women. J Fam Viol, 11 (3): 291–304.

Roberts, A.R. (1996b). Helping Battered Women: New Perspectives and Remedies. A.R. Roberts (Ed.). New York: Oxford University Press.

Rosenbaum, M. (1981). Women on Heroin. New Brunswick, NJ: Rutgers University Press.

Rosenberg, M. (2005). Seattle schools ignored death threat: Price tag = $250K. Soundpolitics.com March 26, 2005 http://www.soundpolitics.com/archives/004059.html

Rosenberg, T. (2007). Where covering a wedding can bring death threats. The New York Times, January 12, 2007. http://select.nytimes.com/search/restricted/article?res= F10A16FC38540 C718DDDA80894DF404482

Rothman, E.F., Hemenway, D., Miller, M., et al. (2005). Batterers' use of guns to threaten intimate partners. J Am Med Womens Assoc, 60 (1): 62–68.

Rothstein, D.A. (1964). Presidential assassination syndrome. Arch Gen Psychiat (Chicago), 11: 245–254.

Rougé-Maillart, C., Jousset, N., Gaudin, A., Bouju, B., Penneau, M. (2005). Women who kill their children. Am J Forensic Med Pathol, 26 (4): 320–326.

Ruff, J.M., Gerding, G., Hong, O. (2004). Workplace violence against K-12 teachers: Implementation of prevention programs. AAOHN, 52 (5): 204–209.

Russo, S. (2001). Gay student commits hate crime against self. Accuracy in Academia, http://www.academia.org/campus_reports/2001/oct_2001_5.html

Ryan, K.M. (1995). Do courtship-violent men have characteristics associated with a "battering personality"? J Family Viol, 10 (1): 99–120.

Samms-Vaughan, M.E., Jackson, M.A., Ashley, D.E. (2005). Urban Jamaican children's exposure to community violence. West Indian Med J, 54 (1): 14–21.

Sanchez, J. (1999). IDG News Service/London Bureau, June 13, 1999, p. 1.

Sandmaier, M. (1980). The Invisible Alcoholics: Women and Alcohol Abuse in America. New York: McGraw-Hill.

Schubert, B., Seiring, W. (2000). Weapons in school—experiences and approaches in Berlin. Prax Kinderpsychol Kinderpsychiatr, 49 (1): 53–69.

Schuller, R.A., Stewart, A. (2000). Police responses to sexual assault complaints: The role of perpetrator/complainant intoxication. Law Hum Behav, 24 (5): 535–551.

Seals, D., Young, J. (2003). Bullying and victimization: Prevalence and relationship to gender, grade level, ethnicity, self-esteem, and depression. Adolescence, 38 (152): 735–747.

SLDN (2006). Survival guide. Harassment/death threats/hate crimes. Servicemembers Legal Defense Network (2006). http://www.sldn.org/templates/legalhelp/record.html?section = 19&record = 51

Shapiro, B. (2006). TV station threatened over series with gay character. 365Gay.Com, January 10, 2006 http://www.365gay.com/Newscon06/01/010906daniel.htm

Sharps, P.W., Campbell, J., Campbell, D., Gary, F., Webster, D. (2001a). The role of alcohol use in intimate partner femicide. Am J Addict, 10 (2): 122–135.

Sharps, P.W., Koziol-McLain, J., Campbell, J., et al. (2001b). Health care providers' missed opportunities for preventing femicide. Prev Med, 33 (5): 373–380.

Shenon, P., Weiser, B. (2007). A Washington outsider with many sides. Chicago Daily Law Bulletin, September 18, 2007, pp. 2, 24.

Sheridan, L.P., Blaauw, E., Davies, G.M. (2003). Stalking: Knowns and unknowns. Trauma Violence Abuse, 4 (2): 148–162.

Sherman, M. (2006). Threats against judges are on the rise. Boston.com news, July 27, 2006. http://www.boston.com/news/nation/washington/articles/2006/07/27/threats_against_judges_are_on_the_rise/?rss_id = Boston.com + %2F + News

Silva, J.A., Leong, G.B., Garza-Trevino, E.S., et al. (1994). A cognitive model of dangerous delusional misidentification syndromes. J Forensic Sci, 39 (6): 1455–1467.

Silverman, J.G., Decker, M.R., Gupta, J., et al. (2007). Experiences of sex trafficking victims in Mumbai, India. Int J Gynaecol Obstet, 97 (3): 221–226.

Sinclair, H.C., Frieze, I.H. (2000). Initial courtship behavior and stalking: How should we draw the line? Violence Vict, 15 (1): 23–30.

Skolnick, J.H. (1975). Justice Without Trial. New York: John Wiley.

Smith, C.S. (2005). The bridal "grab and run." International Herald Tribune, April 29, 2005 http://www.iht.com/articles/2005/04/29/news/bride.php

Smith, P.H., Gittelman, D.K. (1994). Psychological consequences of battering. Implications for women's health and medical practice. N C Med J, 55 (9): 434–439.

Smith, R.C. (1972). Speed and violence: Compulsive methamphetamine abuse and criminality in the Haight-Ashbury District. In C.J.D. Zarafonetis (Ed.), Drug Abuse: Proceedings of the International Conference. Philadelphia: Lea & Febiger.

Smith-Khuri, E., Iachan, R., Scheidt, P.C., et al. (2004). A cross-national study of violence-related behaviors in adolescents. Arch Pediatr Adolesc Med, 158 (6): 539–544.

Snyder, H., Sickmund, M. (1999). Juvenile offenders and victims, 1999. National report. Washington, D.C.: Office of Juvenile and Delinquency Prevention.

Sorenson, S.B., Wiebe, D.J. (2004). Weapons in the lives of battered women. Am J Public Health, 94 (8): 1412–1417.

Spector, N.D., Kelly, S.F. (2006). Pediatrician's role in screening and treatment: Bullying, prediabetes, oral health. Curr Opin Pediatr, 18 (6): 661–670.

SRI (2005). Antisemitism and racism: Republic of Ireland, 2003–2004. Stephen Roth Institute Annual Reports http://www.tau.ac.il/Anti-Semitism/asw2003–4/ireland.htm

Stark, E., Flitcraft, A., Zuckerman, D., et al. (1981). Wife Abuse in the Medical Setting: An introduction to Health Personnel. (Monograph Series, 7). Washington, D.C.: National Clearinghouse on Domestic Violence.

Starks, C. (2007). Essay writer back in school. Chicago Tribune, May 05, 2007 http://www.topix. net/content/trb/0469851718142595123029199735994016952706

Steinberg, A., Brooks, J., Remtulla, T. (2003). Youth hate crimes: Identification, prevention, and intervention. Am J Psychiatry, 160 (5): 979–989.

Stephens, J. (2002). Remarks by Jay Stephens. National Association of Attorneys General Civil Rights Seminar, Washington, D.C., May 8, 2002. http://www.usdoj.gov/aag/speeches/2002/naagcrtspeech_jbs.htm

Stewart, D.E., Cecutti, A. (1993). Physical abuse in pregnancy. Can Med Assoc J, 149: 1257.

Stockdale, M.S., Hangaduambo, S., Duys, D., et al. (2002). Rural elementary students', parents', and teachers' perception of bullying. Am J Health Behav, 26 (4): 266–277.

Stoddard, E. (2007). Texas-based pizza chain accepts pesos. Reuters.com, January 9, 2007. http://www.reuters.com/article/oddlyEnoughNews/idUSN1830363820070109 Stop Violence Against Women.

Straus, M.A. (1979). Measuring intrafamily conflict and violence. The conflict tactics (CT) scales. J Marriage Fam, 41: 75–88.

Stueve, A., Dash, K., O'Donnell, L., et al. (2006). Rethinking the bystander role in school violence prevention. Health Promot Pract, 7 (1): 117–124.

Suhr, J. (2007). Student Accused of Terrorist Threat. The Associated Press, July 25, 2007.

Sun, K. (2006). The legal definition of hate crime and the hate offender's distorted cognitions. Issues Ment Health Nurs, 27 (6): 597–604.

Svalastoga, K. (1956). Homicide and social contact in Denmark. Am J Sociol, 62: 37–41.

Tabak, N., Ehrenfeld, M. (1998). Battered women: Dilemmas and care. Med Law, 17 (4): 611–618.

TamilNet (2006). IFJ condemns death threats against a Shakthi TV journalist. November 21, 2006, http://www.tamilnet.com/art.html?catid = 13&artid = 20351

Tarasoff v. Regents of the University of California (1976). 17 Cal. 3d 425, 131 Cal Rptr. 14, 551 P.2d 334 (1976).

Tardiff, K., Marzuk, P.M., Leon, A.C., et al. (1994). Homicide in New York City. Cocaine use and firearms. JAMA, 272 (1): 43–46.

Tardiff, K., Marzuk, P.M., Leon, A.C., et al. (1995a). Cocaine, opiates, and ethanol in homicides in New York City: 1990 and 1991. J Forensic Sci, 40 (3): 387–390.

Tardiff, K., Marzuk, P.M., Leon, A.C., et al. (1995b). A profile of homicides on the streets and in the homes of New York City. Public Health Rep, 110 (1): 13–17.

Taub, R.P., Wilson, W.J. (2006). There goes the neighborhood: Racial, ethnic and class tensions in four Chicago neighborhoods and their meaning for America. New York: Alfred A. Knopf.

Tedrick v. Community Resource Center Inc. (2007). WL 1487421 (5th Dist., May 17).

Teplin, L.A., McClelland, G.M., Abram, K.M., et al. (2005). Early violent death among delinquent youths: A prospective longitudinal study. Pediatrics, 115 (6): 1586–1593. http://www.thisislondon.co.uk/news/article-23367232-details/The + Pope + must + die%2C + says + Muslim/article.do

Texas Family Code, Title 4 (1995). Protection of the family, Chapter 71.

The Jerusalem Post (2006). Death threats sent to journalists in PA. mideast.jpost.com, January 8, 2006, 21: 47.

The Jerusalem Post (2007). PA Minister Suboh says multiple press offices had received mailed death threats. May 12, 2007. http://www.jpost.com/servlet/Satellite?cid=1136361038491&pagename = JPost%2FJPArticle%2FShowFull thisislondon.co.uk (2006). The Pope must die, says Muslim. September 18, 2006,

Thompson v. County of Alameda (1980). 27 Cal. 3d 741, 167 Cal. Rptr. 70, 614 P.2d 728 (1980).

Tinklenberg, J. (1973). Drugs and crime 1. Literature review. In National Commission on Marihuana and Drug Abuse. Drug Use in America: Problem in Perspective. Vol. 1, Pt. 2. Washington, D.C.: U.S. Government Printing Office.

Tjaden, P., Thoennes, N. (2000). The role of stalking in domestic violence crime reports generated by the Colorado Springs Police Department. Violence Vict, 15 (4): 427–41.

Tjaden, P., Thoennes, N., Allison, C.J. (2000). Comparing stalking victimization from legal and victim perspectives. Violence Vict, 15 (1): 7–22.

Toameh, K.A. (2006). Churches attacked in Gaza, W. Bank. The Jerusalem Post, September 15, 2006, http://www.jpost.com/servlet/Satellite?c = JPArticle&cid = 1157913638028&pagename = JPost%2FJPArticle%2FShowFull

Tolhurst, H., Baker, L., Murray, G., et al. (2003). Rural general practitioner experience of work-related violence in Australia. Aust J Rural Health, 11 (5): 231–236.

Turmanis, S.A., Brown, R.I. (2006). The Stalking and Harassment Behaviour Scale: Measuring the incidence, nature, and severity of stalking and relational harassment and their psychological effects. Psychol Psychother, 79 (Pt 2): 183–198.

Twemlow, S.W., Fonagy, P. (2005). The prevalence of teachers who bully students in schools with differing levels of behavioral problems. Am J Psychiatry, 162 (12): 2387–2389.

Twemlow, S.W., Fonagy, P., Sacco, F.C., et al. (2006). Teachers who bully students: A hidden trauma. Int J Soc Psychiatry, 52 (3): 187–198.

Tyler, J. (2007). Paris Hilton getting death threats. May 9, 2007, http://www.cinemablend.com/celebrity/Paris-Hilton-Getting-Prisoner-Death-Threats-4147.html

UNESCO (2004). Director-General condemns assassination of Philippines journalist Allan Dizon (no date). Portal1.org, http://portal.unesco.org/en/ev.php-URL_ID = 23937&URL_DO = DO_TOPIC&URL_SECTION = 201.html

United Nations (2006). Convention on the rights of persons with disabilities. Some facts about persons with disabilities. http://www.un.org/disabilities/convention/facts.shtml

U.S. DoA. (2000). U.S. Department of Agriculture, Report of Recommendations: Workplace Violence Prevention Taskforce 2000. http://www.fsis.usda.gov/OA/topics/violence.pdf

U.S. DoJ. (1982, 1984). U.S. Department of Justice, Federal Bureau of Investigation. (1982, 1984). Uniform Crime Reports. Unpublished data.

U.S. DoJ. (1998). U.S. Department of Justice, Office of Justice Programs, Bureau of Justice Statistics. Workplace Violence, 1992–96, July 26, 1998, NCJ-168634.

U.S. DoJ. (2000). U.S. Department of Justice, Office of Justice Programs, Bureau of Justice Statistics. Intimate partner violence. Washington, D.C.: U.S. Government Printing Office.

U.S. DoJ. (2005a). U.S. Department of Justice, Office of Justice Programs, Bureau of Justice Statistics. Homicide trends in the U.S. intimate homicide. Revised July 11, 2007 http://www.ojp.usdoj.gov/bjs/homicide/intimates.htm

U.S. DoJ. (2005b). U.S. Department of Justice, Office of Justice Programs, Bureau of Justice Statistics. Homicide trends in the U.S. Trends by gender. http://www.ojp.usdoj.gov/bjs/homicide/gender.htm Revised July 11, 2007

U.S. DoJ. (2006). International Religious Freedom Report, 2006, Iran. Released by the U.S. Department of State, Bureau of Democracy, Human Rights, and Labor, September 15, 2006, http://www.state.gov/g/drl/rls/irf/2006/71421.htm

U.S. History Encyclopedia http://www.answers.com/library/US + History + Encyclopedia-letter-1A

U.S. Select Committee on Intelligence of the U.S. Senate, February 11, 2003.

Vaillant, G. (1993). The Wisdom of the Ego. Cambridge, MA: Harvard University Press.

Valevski, A., Averbuch, I., Radwan, M., et al. (1999). Homicide by schizophrenic patients in Israel. Eur Psychiatry, 14 (2): 89–92.

Van Ommeren, M., de Jong, J.T., Sharma, B., et al. (2001). Psychiatric disorders among tortured Bhutanese refugees in Nepal. Arch Gen Psychiatry, 58 (5): 475–482.

Vinas, A. (1997). Mexico not another Colombia: News analysis. Summary of news analysis originally published in *Diario de Juarez*. http://www.nmsu.edu/ frontera/old_1997/dec97/1297comx.htm

Violence Against Women Act (1994) 40701, 108 stat. 1953 (1994) (Codified at 8USCA 1154 (a)(1), 1154(a)(2), 1254(g (West Supp 1995).

W. Va. Code 61-5-27.

Waaland, P., Keeley, S. (1985). Police decision making in wife abuse: The impact of legal and extralegal factors. Law Human Behav, 9 (4): 355–366.

Waddington, P., Badger, D., Bull, R. (2006).The Violent Workplace. Devon, UK: Willan Publishing.

Wadman, M.C., Muelleman, R.L. (1999). Domestic violence homicides: ED use before victimization. Am J Emerg Med, 17 (7): 689–691.

Walker, L.E. (1984). The Battered Woman Syndrome. New York: Springer.

Wandita, G. (1998). The tears have not stopped, the violence has not ended: Political upheaval, ethnicity, and violence against women in Indonesia. Gend Dev, 6 (3): 34–41.

Waxman, B.F. (1991). Hatred: The unacknowledged dimension in violence against disabled people. Sex Disabil, 9 (3): 185–199.

Weiss, R.S. (1976). The emotional impact of marital separation. J Soc Issues, 32 (1): 135–145.

Westrup, D., Fremouw, W.J., Thompson, R.N., et al. (1999). The psychological impact of stalking on female undergraduates. J Forensic Sc, 44 (3): 554–557.

Whitted, Cleary & Takiff (2007). Breaking confidentiality: Duty to warn. http://www.whitted-clearylaw.com/CM/Publications/publications13.asp

Wiist, W.H., McFarlane, J. (1998). Utilization of police by abused pregnant Hispanic women. Viol Against Women, 4 (6): 677–93.

Wikipedia (2007a). Joan Lefkow. http://en.wikipedia.org/wiki/Joan_Lefkow

Wikipedia (2007b). Jonesboro massacre. http://en.wikipedia.org/wiki/Jonesboro_massacre

Wikipedia (2007c). Martin Luther King, Jr. http://en.wikipedia.org/wiki/Martin_Luther_King,_Jr

Wikipedia (2007d). Timeline of school shootings. http://en.wikipedia.org/wiki/School_shootings - Bibliography

Wikipedia (2007e). Animal Liberation Front. http://en.wikipedia.org/wiki/Animal_Liberation_Front

Wikipedia (2007f). Going postal. http://en.wikipedia.org/wiki/Going_postal

Wikipedia (2007g). Hate crime. http://en.wikipedia.org/wiki/Hate_crime

Wikipedia (2007h). People v. Hall. http://en.wikipedia.org/wiki/People_v._Hall

Wikipedia (2007i). Sinophobia. http://en.wikipedia.org/wiki/Sinophobia

Wikipedia (2007j). Crown Heights riot. http://en.wikipedia.org/wiki/Crown_Heights_Riot

Wikipedia (2007k). Somaly Mam. http://en.wikipedia.org/wiki/Somaly_Mam

Wikipedia 2007l). Heath High School shooting. http://en.wikipedia.org/wiki/Heath_High_School_shooting

Wikipedia (2007m). Daniel Pearl. http://en.wikipedia.org/wiki/Daniel_Pearl

Wikipedia (2007n). Nick Berg. http://en.wikipedia.org/wiki/Nick_Berg

Wikipedia (2007o). http://en.wikipedia.org/wiki/History_of_terrorism#Definition

Wikipedia (2007p). http://en.wikipedia.org/wiki/Pope_Benedict_XVI_Islam_controversy

Williams, J. (2006). Schwarzenegger says immigration debate has prompted threats. Associated Press, http://sfgate.com/cgi-bin/article.cgi?file = /n/a/2006/04/24/state/n162303D54.DTL&type = printable

Williams, M.F. (1996). Violence and sexual harassment: Impact on registered nurses in the workplace. AAOHN J, 44 (2): 73–77.

Willis, D.G. (2004). Hate crimes against gay males: An overview. Issues Ment Health Nurs, 25 (2): 115–132.

Wilton, T. (1999). Towards an understanding of the cultural roots of homophobia in order to provide a better midwifery service for lesbian clients. Midwifery, 15 (3): 154–164.

Wing, C.I., Richter, M. (1999). Little River students arrested. Race hate, rape threats, death threats; Sent from computers in Little River High School. http://www.iwchildren.org/studentarrests.htm

Wisconsin v. Mitchell (1993). 508 U.S. 476 (1993).

Wolfgang, M.E. (1958). Patterns of Criminal Homicide. Philadelphia: University of Pennsylvania Press.

World Editors Forum (2004). Iraqi publisher faces down death threats. The Editors Weblog – Print Journalism, March 4, 2004. http://www.editorsweblog.org/print_newspapers/2004/03/iraqi_publisher_faces_down_death_threats.php - more

Worden, R.E., Pollitz, A.A. (1984). Police arrests in domestic disturbances: A further look. Law Soc Rev, 18: 105–119.

Worldwide Faith News archives (2002). Predominantly gay church in Vancouver, WA receives bomb death threat. May 30, 2002, http://www.wfn.org/2002/05/msg00335.html

WorldwideStandard.com (2006). Bankrolling Terror: Hamas Fundraising in the U.S., M. Goldfare (Ed.). http://www.weeklystandard.com/weblogs/TWSFP/2006/01/bankrolling_terror_hamas_fundr.html

Wyatt, K. (2007). Law prof finds scars from Eastern Shore lynchings. Chicago Daily Law Bulletin, 153 (112): 1, 24.

Yang, S.J., Kim, J.M., Kim, S.W., et al. (2006). Bullying and victimization behaviors in boys and girls at South Korean primary schools. J Am Acad Child Adolesc Psychiatry, 5 (1): 69–77.

Yoshihama, M., Sorenson, S. (1994). Physical, sexual, and emotional abuse by male intimates: Experiences of women in Japan. Violence Vict, 9 (1): 63–77.

Young, D.M., Beier, E.G., Beier, P., et al. (1975). Is chivalry dead? J Commun, 28: 57–64.

Zhu, B.L., Oritani, S., Shimotouge, K., et al. (2000). Methamphetamine-related fatalities in forensic autopsy during 5 years in the southern half of Osaka city and surrounding areas. Forensic Sci Int, 113 (1): 443–447.

Zinberg, N.E. (1980). The social setting as a control mechanism in intoxicant use. In D. J. Lettieri, et al. (Eds.), Theories on Drug Abuse: Selected Contemporary Perspectives. Rockville, MD: U.S. Department of Health and Human Services.

Zona, M., Lane, J., Palarea, R. (1997). The psychodynamics of stalking. Presented at the Seventh Annual Threat Management Conference, Los Angeles, CA, August, 1997.

Zona, M., Sharma, K., Lane, J. (1993). A comparative study of erotomanic and obsessional subjects in a forensic sample. J Forensic Sci, 38: 894–903.

Index

Lightning Source UK Ltd.
Milton Keynes UK
UKHW020100221118
332646UK00004B/202/P